T0328525

THE
REDISCOVERED
BENJAMIN GRAHAM

THE
REDISCOVERED
BENJAMIN GRAHAM

Selected Writings
of the Wall Street Legend

JANET LOWE

JOHN WILEY & SONS, INC.
New York • Chichester • Weinheim • Brisbane • Singapore • Toronto

Published by John Wiley & Sons, Inc.
Published simultaneously in Canada

This publication is designed to provide accurate and authoritative information in regard to the subject matter covered. It is sold with the understanding that the publisher is not engaged in rendering professional services. If professional advice or other expert assistance is required, the services of a competent professional person should be sought.

Library of Congress Cataloging-in-Publication Data:

ISBN 978-0-471-24472-1 (hardcover) ISBN 978-1-119-08705-2 (paperback)

10 9 8 7 6 5 4 3 2 1

To the Johnsons:
Art, Risé, Laurel Ann, and A. J.

Preface

When Warren Buffett, the world's most successful investor, had the opportunity to give Microsoft founder Bill Gates some investment advice, what nugget did the fortunate Bill receive?

The same message that Buffett has been delivering for years to whomever would listen. Read Benjamin Graham. Buffett is the first to admit that he has moved on from Graham, discarded some of his teachings, expanded on others, and added ideas of his own. But Buffett continues to insist that Ben Graham, the father of value investing, is the place to begin. Graham's 1949 classic *The Intelligent Investor* remains the *Dick and Jane* of any investor's library.

Graham was a prolific and popular writer on investment and economic subjects, starting in the 1920s until his death in 1976. In addition to five books, starting with *Security Analysis* in 1934, Graham wrote articles for learned journals, the popular press, and magazines.

Twice, once after the crash of 1929 and again after a long bear market in the 1970s, he triggered massive stock market rallies by his articles. Graham's lectures guided and inspired a half century of Wall Street professionals. Some of his work appeared in the respected *Financial Analysts Journal* under the pseudonym The Cogitator. Graham's thoughts on the national and international economies led to responses from such great thinkers as John Maynard Keynes.

Because he was so respected, Graham was called to testify before the prestigious Fulbright Committee in the U.S. Senate regarding new developments in the securities industry. In every case, his words were marked with intelligence, wit, and original ideas. Always, he sought a fair deal for shareholders.

Graham's magazine pieces, speeches, and lectures are widely quoted even today, but until now those who wished to read Graham's early writings were in for a lot of leg work. The material has not been easy to find.

After so many readers had asked for copies of the Graham material that I keep in my own files, it seemed like a good idea to produce the collected, not-exactly-lost-nonetheless-difficult-to-find Graham material in a single book.

It is not practical to put all of Graham's lectures and essays in a single volume, and, frankly, some of Ben's writings would be of limited interest to today's readers. We've chosen the very best he had to offer, most of it with no editing at all. When value judgements were involved, every effort was made to remain true to Graham's own principles.

The New York Institute of Finance lectures have been edited, partly because of length, and partly because they were transcribed verbatim from his class, and they included a certain amount of extraneous material—classroom business and commentary on minor events of the time. Over the course of a semester, Graham may have talked several times about a single subject. In that case, less complete and less compelling versions were cut. In the editing, care has been taken to make certain that all the major philosophies and methods presented in the lectures were retained. Those who wish to read the unabridged New York Institute of Finance lectures will find them posted on the John Wiley & Sons website, www.wiley.com/bgraham.

The Rediscovered Benjamin Graham is like a time machine to the investment world of the past. Graham talked about the railroad industry as it waned, the aircraft manufacturing industry as it emerged, and the anticipation of a housing boom following World War II. He often warned that it is dangerous to try to predict the future, and Graham never fully anticipated the postwar technological changes and the economic surge that followed. As always, the past has a lot to teach us.

Nevertheless, Graham still has one of the largest and most loyal followings of any investment philosopher of this century. The more readers study Graham's value-investing principles, the more loyal they are likely to become. Warren Buffett's words in the preface to the fourth edition to *The Intelligent Investor* surely apply to the remainder of Graham's work: "The sillier the market's behavior, the greater the opportunity for the business-like investor. Follow Graham and you will profit from folly rather than participate in it."

So many people have made this book possible, and over such a long period of time; I apologize now if I've omitted anyone. My special thanks to Warren Buffett, Walter Schloss, Irving Kahn, and all the other wonderful students of Benjamin Graham at Columbia University. They've done so much to preserve documents and to keep Graham's memory alive. Dr. Benjamin Graham Jr. has been generous with his encouragement and permission to print certain material from his father's personal collection. Myles Thompson, Jennifer Pincott, and Mary Daniello at John Wiley & Sons contributed enormously to this book, as did Bernice Pettinato of Beehive Production Services. Austin Lynas did an excellent job compiling the index. I would also like to express appreciation to my professional support team, Alice Fried Martell, Jolene Crowell, and Phyllis Kenney.

I hope you enjoy reading this book as much as I enjoyed compiling and editing the material.

JANET LOWE

Del Mar, California
March 1999

Contents

THE
REDISCOVERED
BENJAMIN GRAHAM

Benjamin Graham
and *Security Analysis*:
A Reminiscence

Walter J. Schloss

B en Graham was an original thinker as well as a clear thinker. He had high ethical standards and was modest and unassuming. He was one of a kind. I worked for him for nearly 10 years as a security analyst.

In re-reading the preface to the first edition of *Security Analysis*, I am impressed all over again with Ben's views. I quote . . . "[W]e are concerned chiefly with concepts, methods, standards, principles, and above all with logical reasoning. We have stressed theory not for itself alone but for its value in practice. We have tried to avoid prescribing standards which are too stringent to follow or technical methods which are more trouble than they are worth."

Security Analysis says it all. It is up to analysts and investors to put Ben's ideas into practice.

Back in 1935 while working at Loeb Rhodes (then called Carl M. Loeb & Co.), one of the partners, Armand Erpf, gave a good piece of advice when I asked him how I could get into the "statistical department." In those days and perhaps today to some extent, the best way to advance was by bringing in business. If you had a wealthy family or friends, you brought in commissions. Security analysis was in its infancy and who you knew was much more important than what you knew. If you didn't have connections, it was difficult to get ahead. In any case Mr. Erpf told me that there was a new book called *Security Analysis* that had just been written by a man called Ben Graham.

Reproduced by permission from the private writings (1976) of Walter J. Schloss.

"Read the book and when you know everything in it, you won't have to read anything else."

I took Ben's course in Advanced Security Analysis at the New York Stock Exchange Institute (New York Institute of Finance).

Ben was a good speaker, enthusiastic and logical. Ben did something that I haven't seen done often. He would take an undervalued situation at that time, such as the bankrupt bonds of Baldwin Locomotive, and show how much the new securities would be worth based on their projected earning power and assets and relate this to the price of the bonds. Many bright Wall Streeters such as Gus Levy of Goldman Sachs, who later became the top arbitrageur in the country, used to take his course. I often wondered how much money people made on Ben's ideas by transforming them into investments.

Ben was very generous with his thoughts and his time, particularly with young people. By offering me a job as his security analyst as I was about to leave the Army at the end of 1945, he changed my life. I know he helped others in our field too.

At Ben's memorial service, Dave Dodd, Ben's co-author, told how he had got involved in the book.

It seems that Ben was asked to teach a course at Columbia University on investments and he agreed to do it with the stipulation that he would only do so if someone would take notes. Dave Dodd, a young instructor, volunteered and took copious notes at each of Ben's lectures. Ben, using the notes, then went ahead and wrote *Security Analysis*. As Dave said, Ben did the work but he insisted that Dave get credit by being co-author.

Professor Dodd went on to become a very successful investor and a director of Graham-Newman Corporation, an investment trust that Ben had founded in 1936 with his partner, Jerome Newman.

The ability to think clearly in the investment field without the emotions that are attached to it, is not an easy undertaking. Fear and greed tend to affect one's judgment. Because Ben was not really very aggressive about making money, he was less affected by these emotions than were many others.

Ben had been hurt by the Depression, so he wanted to invest in things that would protect him on the downside. The best way to do this was to lay out rules which, if followed, would reduce his chance of loss.

A good example of this was the day I happened to be in his office at Graham-Newman when he received a telephone call that they had bought 50 percent of Government Employees Insurance Co. (now GEICO). He turned to me and said, "Walter, if this purchase doesn't work out, we can always liquidate it and get our money back."

The fact that GEICO worked out better than his wildest dreams wasn't what he was looking for. As the saying goes, a stock well bought is half sold. I think Ben was an expert in that area.

Graham-Newman followed the precepts set down by Ben and the fund prospered. Compared to today's investment company, it was tiny. Its total net assets on January 31, 1946, were $3,300,000.

Ben's emphasis was on protecting his expectation of profit with minimum risk. If one wants to get hold of Moody's Investment Manuals for the 1947–1956 period, it is interesting to see Graham-Newman's holdings. Many of them were small, practically unknown companies but they were cheap on the numbers. It is instructive to read their annual report for the year ended January 1946. It states that their general investment policies were twofold.

1. To purchase securities at prices less than their intrinsic value as determined by careful analysis with particular emphasis on the purchase of securities at less than their liquidating value.
2. To engage in arbitrage and hedging operations.

I helped Ben with the third edition of *Security Analysis*, published in 1951. In the appendix is an article on special situations that first appeared in *The Analysts Journal* in 1946. In the article, he had worked out an algebraic formula for risk-reward results that could be applied today, 37 years later.

In 1949, *The Intelligent Investor* was published. This was a book for the layman but it focused on security analysis and gave prestige to the field. Its fourth revised edition is still in print.

One day, I came across a very cheap stock based on its price at the time, Lukens Steel. We bought some but expected to buy more.

At this point, Ben went out to lunch with a man who kept telling Ben about one blue chip after another. At the end of the meal he asked Ben if he liked anything and Ben said we were buying some Lukens Steel.

I doubt if it took a day before the man went out and bought a great deal of Lukens and pushed the stock out of our buying range. I had the impression after Ben told me the story that he didn't want to be rude and hadn't realized how important his comments were.

He tried to keep things simple. He wrote that he didn't believe security analysts should use more than arithmetic and possibly a little algebra for any investment decision.

Because Ben was a cultured, many-faceted man, he didn't spend as much time on investments as did others in the field. He liked to try new ideas. In the late 1930s he became involved in promoting his ever-normal granary theory and wrote a book on it called *Storage and Stability* in which some commodities and metals would be used as a backing for our currency. His ideas made sense and with cotton at six cents a pound and other raw materials at low prices, it was an interesting proposal. He never had the clout to sell it to the Congress, although Bernard Baruch, a friend of his, supported the idea and it could have been a useful way to help the farmers and reduce the threat of inflation.

Of all the things that Ben accomplished in his lifetime, *Security Analysis* was, to me, his greatest achievement.

Ben Graham was the leader in giving status to security analysts. It was a privilege to know him.

PART ONE

THE BUSINESS AND ETHICS OF FINANCE

He had integrity that wouldn't quit.

Rhoda Sarnat, Ben Graham's niece

When Ben Graham's three-part series, "Is American Business Worth More Dead Than Alive?" was published in *Forbes* magazine, America, and indeed the world, had gone through the punishing stock market crashes of 1929 and 1930 and was in the depths of the Great Depression. Though the Depression continued until nearly the end of the decade, Graham's articles signaled to investors that it was now safe to return to the stock market. At that time, Graham pointed out, more than 30 percent of the companies listed on the New York Stock Exchange were selling at less than what they would be worth if they were broken up and sold. In this series of articles, Graham took corporate management to task for taking advantage of investors and putting their own welfare ahead of that of the shareholders.

Additionally, Graham's articles sounded the call for investors to return to the stock market. It took courage for Graham to write these articles. The fund that he managed with his partner, Jerome Newman, had lost 50 percent of its value in the crashes of 1929 and 1930. Though at 38 years old, Graham was a relatively young man when he wrote these articles, he already was a well-respected investment thinker and writer. Through these articles, he provided the desperately needed leadership that the financial community needed to get back into business.

The last piece in this part is excerpted from a speech Graham delivered in California shortly after he retired from professional investing. As it illustrates, Graham never lost his passion for business ethics.

Is American Business Worth More Dead Than Alive?

A Three-Part Series of Articles by
Benjamin Graham in *Forbes*

Inflated Treasuries and Deflated Stockholders: Are Corporations Milking Their Owners?

With this article The Editors introduce a series on one of the most amazing, far-reaching, and important situations which business and financial America has ever witnessed, a situation whose solution affects the interests of every investor.

Read the points mentioned under the caption below, and you will quickly discover why this series is one of the timeliest and most significant which could be proposed.

The author, a lecturer at Columbia University, and with many years of practical experience and study in business, finance, and stock markets will lead you through an amazing consideration of facts, to equally amazing conclusions regarding your rights and duties as a stockholder.

Most of these facts, while logical and apparent, have received scant attention in public print. *Forbes* takes pleasure in offering this exposé of injustice and maladjustment in the stock and corporation world, presented in a fearless, frank, and interesting series, of which this is the first article.

From *Forbes*, June 1, 1932. Reprinted by permission of FORBES Magazine © Forbes Inc., 1932.

SELLING AMERICA FOR 50 CENTS
ON THE DOLLAR

More than one-third of all industrial stocks are selling in the open market for less than the companies' net quick assets.

Scores of common stocks are selling for less than their pro rata of cash in the company's treasury.

Corporations who are good risks for commercial loans do not need to borrow. They still have large unused cash balances furnished by their stockholders in the New Era days.

Corporation treasurers sleep soundly while stockholders walk the floor.

Banks no longer lend directly to big corporations. They lend to stockholders who have over-financed the companies through rights to buy stock at inflated prices.

What are the responsibilities of the corporation, its directors, its stockholders? What is the proper way out? Are stockholders part-owners of their companies, or just suckers?

Shall companies reverse the 1929 method—give the stockholder rights to sell back the stock he bought, reduce capitalization, and equalize the burden between the corporations and the stockholder?

If market quotations discount huge cash reserves due to probable long-continued future losses then should not the stockholder demand liquidation before his money is thus dissipated?

Are corporations playing fair with their stockholders?

Suppose you were the owner of a large manufacturing business. Like many others, you lost money in 1931; the immediate prospects are not encouraging; you feel pessimistic and willing to sell out—*cheap*. A prospective purchaser asks you for your statement. You show him a very healthy balance sheet, indeed. It shapes up something like this:

Cash and U.S. Gov. Bonds	$ 8,500,000
Receivables and Merchandise	15,000,000
Factories, Real Estate, etc.	14,000,000
	$37,500,000
Less owing for current accounts	1,300,000
Net Worth	$36,200,000

The purchaser looks it over casually, and then makes you a bid of $5 million for your business—the cash, Liberty Bonds, and everything else included. Would you sell? The question seems like a joke, we admit. No one in his right mind would exchange $8.5 million in cash for $5 million, to say nothing of the $28 million more in other assets. But preposterous as such a transaction sounds, the many owners of White Motors stock who sold out between $7 and $8 per share did that very thing—or as close to it as they could come.

The figures given above represent White Motors condition on December 31st last. At $7.37 per share, the low price, the company's 650,000 shares were selling for $4.8 million—about 60 percent of the cash and equivalent alone, and only *one-fifth of the net quick assets*. There were no capital obligations ahead of the common stock, and the only liabilities were those shown above for current accounts payable.

The spectacle of a large and old established company selling in the market for such a small fraction of its quick assets is undoubtedly a startling one.

But the picture becomes more impressive when we observe that there are literally dozens of other companies which also have a quoted value less than their cash in bank. And more significant still is the fact that an amazingly large percentage of *all* industrial companies are selling for less than their *quick* assets alone—leaving out their plants and other fixed assets entirely.

This means that a great number of American businesses are quoted in the market for much less than their liquidating value; that, in the best judgment of Wall Street, these *businesses are worth more dead than alive.*

For most industrial companies should bring, in *orderly* liquidations, at least as much as their quick assets alone. Admitting that the factories, real estate, etc., could not fetch anywhere near their carrying price, they should still realize enough to make up the shrinkage in the proceeds of the receivables and merchandise below book figures. If this is not a reasonable assumption, there must be something radically wrong about the accounting methods of our large corporations.

A study made at the Columbia University School of Business under the writer's direction, covering some 600 industrial companies listed on the New York Stock Exchange, disclosed that over 200 of them—or nearly one out of three—have been selling at less than their net quick assets.

Over 50 of them have sold at less than their cash and marketable securities alone. In the appended table [Table 1] is given a partial list, comprising the more representative companies in the latter category.

What is the meaning of this situation? The experienced financier is surely to answer that stocks always sell at unduly low prices after a boom collapses. As the president of the New York Stock Exchange testified, "times like these frightened people of this United States of ours away."

Stated differently, it happens because those with enterprise haven't the money, and those with money haven't the enterprise, to buy stocks when they are cheap. Should we not have had the same phenomenon existing in previous bear markets—for example, 1921?

The facts are quite otherwise, however. Stocks sold at low prices in the severe post-war depression, but very few of them could be bought on the stock exchange for less than quick assets, and not one for less than the company's available cash.

The comparative figures for both periods, covering representative companies, are little short of astounding especially when it is noted that they showed no materially poorer operating results in 1931 than in 1921. Why these companies are selling in the aggregate for half their working capital; 10 years ago working capital was only half the bottom prices. With respect to cash assets the present prices are relatively *six* times lower than in 1921.

We must recognize, therefore, that the situation existing today is *not* typical of all bear markets. Broadly speaking, it is new and unprecedented. It is a strange, ironical aftermath of the New Era madness of 1928–1929. It reflects the extraordinary results of profound but little understood changes in the financial attitude of the people and the financial fabric of the country.

Two plausible and seemingly innocent ideas—the first, that good stocks are good investments; the second, that values depend on earning power—were distorted and exploited into a frenzied financial gospel which ended by converting all our investors into speculators, by making our corporations rich and their stockholders poor, by reversing the relative importance of commercial loans and Wall Street loans,

TABLE 1
Some Stocks Which Are Selling for Less Than Their Cash Assets

Company	1932 Market Low	Market Value of Company at Low Price	Cash and Marketable Securities	Current Assets Less All Liabilities	Cash Assets per Share	Net Quick Assets per Share
			(000 omitted)			
*Am. Car & Fdry	20¼	$ 9,225	$14,950	$32,341	$ 50	$108
*Am. Locomotive	30¼	14,709	14,829	22,630	41	63
*Am. Steel Foun.	60	8,021	8,046	11,720	128	186
*Am. Woolen	15¼	8,354	14,603	40,769	30½	85
Congoleum	7	10,078	10,802	16,288	7	12
Howe Sound	6	2,886	4,910	5,254	10	11
Hudson Motors	4⅛	6,377	8,462	10,712	5½	7
Hupp Motors	2	2,664	7,236	10,000	5½	7½
Lima Locomotive	8½	1,581	3,620	6,772	19	36
Magma Copper	4½	1,836	3,771	4,825	9	12
Marlin Rockwell	7½	2,520	3,834	4,310	11½	13
Motor Products	13	2,457	2,950	3,615	15½	19
Munsingwear	10⅞	1,805	2,888	5,769	17	34
Nash Motors	10	27,000	36,560	37,076	13½	14
N.Y. Air Brake	4½	1,170	1,474	2,367	5	9
Opp'hm Collins	5	1,050	2,016	3,150	9½	15
Reo Motors	1½	2,716	5,321	10,332	3	5½
S. O. of Kansas	7	2,240	2,760	4,477	8½	14
Stewart Warner	2⅜	3,023	4,648	8,303	3½	7
White Motors	7¾	4,938	8,620	22,167	13	34

*Preferred stock.

11

by producing topsy-turvy accounting policies and wholly irrational standards of value—and in no small measure was responsible for the paradoxical depression in which we find ourselves submerged.

Behind the simple fact that a great many stocks are selling for much less than their working capital lies a complex of causes, results, and implications. The remainder of this article will deal with the causes of the present unique situation, while other ramified aspects will be developed in succeeding articles.

The current contrast between market prices and liquid assets is accounted for in large measure by the huge flood of new cash which stockholders in recent years have poured into the treasuries of their corporations by the exercise of subscription rights. This phenomenon, which was one of the distinguishing features of the 1928–1929 bull market, had two quite opposite consequences. On the one hand the additional funds received greatly improved the companies' cash and working capital position; on the other hand the additional shares issued greatly increased the supply of stocks, weakened their technical position, and intensified their market decline. The same circumstance, therefore, served both to improve the *values* behind stock and to depress the *price*.

It is doubtful, however, that the declines would have gone to the current extraordinary lengths if during the last decade investors had not lost the habit of looking at balance sheets. Much of the past year's selling of stocks has been due to fear rather than necessity. If these timid holders were thoroughly aware that they were selling out at only a fraction of the liquid assets behind their share, many of them might have acted differently.

But since value has come to be associated exclusively with earning power, the stockholder no longer pays any attention to what his company owns—not even its money in bank.

It is undoubtedly true that the old-time investor laid too much stress upon book values and too little upon what the property could earn. It was a salutary step to ignore the figures at which the plants were carried on the books, unless they showed a commensurate earning power.

But like most sound ideas in Wall Street, this one was carried too far. It resulted in excessive emphasis being laid on the reported earnings—which might only be temporary or even deceptive—and in a complete eclipse of what had always been regarded as a vital factor in security values, namely, the company's working capital position.

Businesses have come to be valued in Wall Street on an entirely different basis from that applied to private enterprise. In good times the prices paid on the stock exchange were fantastically high, judged by ordinary business standards; and now, by the law of compensation, the assets of these same companies are suffering an equally fantastic undervaluation.

A third reason that stocks now sell below their liquid asset value is the fear of future operating losses. Many readers will assert that this is the overshadowing cause of the present low market level. These quotations reflect not only the absence of earning power, but the existence of "losing power" which threatens to dissipate the working capital behind the shares to-day.

Is it true that one out of three American businesses is destined to continue losing money until the stockholders have no equity remaining? This is what the stock market says in no uncertain tones.

In all probability it is wrong, as it always has been wrong in its major judgments of the future. The logic of Wall Street is proverbially weak. It is hardly consistent, for example, to despair of the railroads because the trucks are going to take most of their business, and at the same time to be so despondent over the truck industry as to give away shares in its largest units for a small fraction of their liquid capital alone.

But since even in prosperous times many undertakings fall by the wayside, it is certain that the number of such ill-starred ventures must now be greatly increased. The weakly situated business will find it difficult, perhaps impossible, to survive. Hence in a number of individual cases the market's prophecy of extinction will be borne out. Nevertheless, there must still be a basic error in this wholesale dumping of shares at a small fraction of liquidating value.

If a business is doomed to lose money, why continue it? If its future is so hopeless that it is worth much less as a going concern than if it were wound up, why not wind it up?

Surely the owners of a business have a better alternative than to give its present cash away, for fear that it is later going to be dissipated. We are back to the contract between the White Motors stockholder and the individual factory owner, with which we started our article.

The issue is merely one of simple logic. Either White Motors is worth more as a going concern than its cash in bank, or it is not. If it is worth more, the stockholder is foolish to sell out for much less than this cash, unless he is compelled to do so. If it isn't, the business should be liquidated and each stockholder paid out his share of the cash plus whatever the other assets will bring.

Evidently stockholders have forgotten more than to look at balance sheets. They have forgotten also that they are *owners of a business* and not merely owners of a quotation on the stock ticker. It is time, and high time, that the millions of American shareholders turned their eyes from the daily market reports long enough to give some attention to the enterprises themselves of which they are the proprietors, and which exist for their benefit and at their pleasure.

The supervision of these businesses must, of course, be delegated to directors and their operation to paid officials. But whether the owners' money should be dissipated by operating losses, and whether it should be tied up unproductively in excessive cash balances while they themselves are in dire need of funds, are questions of major policy which each stockholder must ponder and decide for himself.

These are not management problems; these are *ownership problems*. On these questions the management's opinion may be weighty but it is not controlling.

What stockholders need today is not alone to become *balance sheet conscious*, but more than that, to become *ownership conscious*. If they realized their rights as business owners, we would not have before us the insane spectacle of treasuries bloated with cash and their proprietors in a wild scramble to give away their interest on any terms they can get. Perhaps the corporation itself buys back the shares they throw on the market, and by a final touch of irony, we see the stockholders' pitifully inadequate payment made to them with their own cash.

The waggish barber of the legend painted on his sign:

What, do you think—
We shave you for nothing and give you a drink!

That, without the saving comma, might as well be blazoned as the motto of the stock seller of today, who hands over his share in inventories and receivables for less than nothing, and throws in real estate, buildings, machinery, and what-not as a lagniappe or trading stamp.

The humor of the situation could be exploited further, but the need is not for witticism but for a straightforward presentation of the vitally important issues that face stockholders, managements, and bankers. These will be dealt with in succeeding articles.

Should Rich Corporations Return Stockholders' Cash?

In our first article, the present disparity between the cash asset position of many companies and the price of their stocks was ascribed in part to the huge issues of additional shares which transferred money from stockholders' pockets into corporate treasuries. According to the New York Stock Exchange's compilation, the funds so absorbed by listed companies alone, between 1926 and 1930, amounted to no less than $5 billion.

The total sale of corporate securities to the public in this period exceeded $29 billion, of which a small part perhaps was turned over to private individuals, but the major portion was paid into the businesses, and either expended in plant additions or added to working capital.

It must not be forgotten that other enormous sums have also been accumulated in the form of undistributed earnings. After this tremendous influx of cash it is no wonder that corporate treasuries are still bulging, despite all the money that has been spent, or lost, or paid in dividends.

But what of the people who supplied the bulk of this money; the investor who bought new offerings; the stockholder who subscribed to additional shares? They are not rolling in wealth today, nor burdened with a plethora of idle funds. They stripped themselves of cash to enrich their corporations' treasuries; they borrowed heavily in order that these corporations might be able to pay off their debts.

The grotesque result is that the people who own these rich American businesses are themselves poor, that the typical stockholder is weighed down by financial problems while his corporation wallows in cash. Treasurers are sleeping soundly these nights, while their stockholders walk the floor in worried desperation.

True, the public has more stock certificates to represent the new shares which it paid for, and each certificate carries ownership in the cash held by the company. But somehow this doesn't help the stockholder very much. He can't borrow from the bank, or margin his existing loans, on the basis of the cash behind his shares. If he wants to sell, he must accept the verdict of the ticker. If he should appeal to the officers of the company for a little of his own cash, they would probably wave him away with a pitying smile. Or perhaps they may be charitable enough to buy his stock back at the current market price—which means a small fraction of its fair value.

Meanwhile, the prodigal transfer of cash by the public to corporations in the new-era days has not only made infinite trouble for the security holder, but it has seriously demoralized our banking structure. Commercial loans have always been the heart and the bulwark of our credit system. Loans on securities have been secondary in volume and drastically subordinated in their standing.

But what have the corporations and the public done between them in recent years? They have paid off the cream of the country's commercial borrowings and substituted security loans in their place. Instead of lending directly to big business, the banks have been forced to lend to their stockholders against pledges of their shares, or to purchase securities on their own account.

Some idea of the extent of this shift of banking accommodation can be gleaned from the comparative figures of the reporting member banks of the Federal Reserve System [see Table 2].

The whole development has proved most disastrous to stockholders and most embarrassing to the banks. The best form of borrowing has been replaced by the worst. The safety of the loans, and to some extent

TABLE 2

Change in the Composition of Banking Resources, 1920–1932
(in millions)

	Commercial Loans	Loans on Securities	Total
Oct. 1920	$9,741	$ 7,451	$17,192
May 1932	6,779	12,498	19,277

the solvency of the banks making them, has been placed at the mercy of stock market fluctuations, instead of resting on the financial strength of our large corporations.

Thousands of stockholders—the owners of their company's business—find themselves today in an absurd position. The market value of their stock may be, for instance, only $10 million, its borrowing value at best $8 million. Yet not only may the company have $15 million in the treasury, but it could borrow large additional amounts against its many millions of other quick assets. If the owners of the business really controlled such a company, they could draw out not only the $15 million in cash but another $5 million from bank loans, and still have a business in sound condition with substantial equities.

The very banks which hesitate to lend $10 per share on a stock would probably be glad to lend the company itself enough to enable it to pay out $15 per share to the stockholders.

Consider on the one hand a typical standard business with its enormous cash and credit resources; and then consider the people who own this business and who poured millions into its treasury, unable to realize or borrow more than a miserable fraction of the cash value of their own property.

This is the result of undue generosity by stockholders towards their corporations in good times—and of undue parsimony by the corporations towards their stockholders today.

The banks may seem like co-villains in such a situation, but in fact they, too, are victims of circumstance—handicapped by a soundly conceived system which is out of harmony with the actualities of the present situation. They have been educated and they are directed to give first consideration to commercial loans.

But who now are the commercial borrowers? Strong corporations with good past (if not recent) records, requiring money for seasonal requirements? Not at all. Such corporations don't need the banks; they raised all the money they could use from the stockholders when the raising was good.

There are left three classes of bank borrowers: (a) Small or privately owned enterprises—maybe good, maybe not; (b) Large industrial corporations with poor records even in the late prosperity; (c) Railroads and utilities needing temporary (cash) accommodation, to be paid off by permanent financing—a fruitful source of trouble for all concerned.

It must be recognized, therefore, that the replacement of good commercial loans on stock collateral has been harmful alike to our banking system and to the vast army of stockholders. Is there a remedy for this condition? There certainly is, and a very simple one:

Let corporations return to their stockholders the surplus cash holdings not needed for the normal conduct of their business.

The immediate result of such a movement would be to benefit the individual stockholder, by placing funds in his hands to meet his urgent needs or to use as he sees fit. The secondary result would be to improve the price of the shares affected and the stock market generally, as the public is made aware in this forceful fashion of the enormous cash values behind American business today. The third result would be to improve the balance of our banking structure, making for a larger proportion of sound commercial loans (especially when business again expands) and permitting the repayment of a certain quantity of frozen security loans.

How should this return of cash be accomplished? Preferably by the direct retracing of the financial steps which have led to the present predicament. Instead of rights to buy stocks, let companies offer their stockholders the right to sell stock in a fixed proportion and at a stated price. This price should be above the current market but in most cases below the net quick assets per share and therefore far below the book value. From the corporation's point of view the result of such repurchases at a discount will be an increase both in the surplus and in the net current assets per share of stock remaining.

A few corporations have followed this procedure, one of the earliest being Simms Petroleum. Recently Hamilton Woolen has offered to buy one-sixth of the outstanding shares pro rata $65, which is about equal to the net quick assets and considerably above the previous market price. This represents the return of a large portion of the new money paid in by stockholders in 1929.

Other companies have returned surplus cash to stockholders in the form of special distributions without cancellation of stock. Peerless Motors is a case in point, and another is Eureka Vacuum Cleaner, which accompanied its action by a statement recommending a similar move to other corporations as an aid in relieving the depression. A few companies, notably the Standard Oil pipe lines and some New England mills, have returned surplus cash capital to shareholders by reducing the par value of the stock.

All these methods accomplish the same purpose and the differences between them are largely technical. The repurchase of shares pro rata, which we recommend, is more practical in most cases than a reduction in par value, and it has certain bookkeeping advantages over a straight special dividend. Furthermore, as a direct reversal of the process of taking money from stockholders by issuing subscription rights, this method undoubtedly has a strong logical appeal.

A sizable number of enterprises have been employing surplus funds to acquire stock by purchase in the open market. This also represents a transfer of corporate funds to stockholders. It is undoubtedly helpful to the market price and hence to those constrained to sell, and the repurchase of shares at bargain prices presumably benefits the surviving stockholders. Certainly, corporations using excess cash in this manner are acting more liberally than those who hold on like grim death to every dollar in bank.

But this form of procedure is open to objections of various kinds. If the price paid turns out to have been too high, the directors are subject to criticism from those whom they still represent, while those they have benefitted are no longer interested in them or in the company. If to avoid this danger, they buy only when the price is exceedingly low, they cannot avoid the appearance of having taken unfair advantage of the necessities of their stockholders. Furthermore, such undisclosed market operations may afford opportunities for questionable profit by directors and insiders.

The Bendix Aviation Company recently passed its dividend and concurrently announced its intention of purchasing a large block of shares in the open market. Other companies rich in cash have followed the same policy, though generally without even this saving grace of revealing their plan to buy in stock. Such a procedure contains possibilities of grave injustice to the shareholders. When there is an accumulated surplus and excess cash on hand, the directors' first duty is to use the free cash to maintain a reasonable dividend.

The prime reason for accumulating the surplus in good years was to make possible the continuance of dividends in bad years. Hence the absence of earnings is in itself no justification for stopping all payments to shareholders. To withhold the owners' money from them by suspending dividends, and then to use this same money to buy back their stock at the abnormally low price thus created, comes perilously close to sharp practice.

Such considerations should make it clear why the writer does not regard open-market purchases as the best method of returning corporate cash to stockholders. Retirement of stock pro rata involves no conflict of interest between those selling out and those staying in; and it provides no opportunity for errors in judgment of unfair tactics on the part of the management.

Examination of the partial list of companies selling in the current market for less than their net current assets, as well as reference to the table [Table 1] offered in our first article last issue, will disclose many instances in which the cash holdings are clearly excessive. If stockholders will bring sufficiently strong pressure upon their managements, they can secure the return of a good part of such surplus cash, with great benefit to their own position, to stock market sentiment, and to the general banking situation.

In order to obtain these desirable results, stockholders must first be aware that surplus cash exists; and therefore they must direct at least a fleeting glance to their company's balance sheet. In recent years financial writers have been unanimous in pointing out how unimportant are asset values as compared with earning power; but no one seems to have realized that both the ignoring of assets and the emphasis on earnings can be—and have been—carried too far, with results of the most disastrous kind.

The whole New Era and blue chip madness is derived from this exclusive preoccupation with the earnings trend. A mere $1 increase in profits, from $4 to $5 per share, raised the value of a stock from $40 to $75, on the joyous assumption that an upward trend had been established which justified a multiple of 15 instead of 10. The basis of calculating values thus became arbitrary and mainly psychological, with the result that everyone felt free to gamble unrestrainedly under the respectable title of "investment."

It was this enticement of investors into rampant speculation which made possible the unexampled duration and extent of the 1928–1929 advance, which also made the ensuing collapse correspondingly disastrous, and which—as later appeared—carried the business structure down into ruin with the stock market.

A peculiar offshoot of the obsession with earnings is the new practice of writing fixed assets down to $1, in order to eliminate depreciation charges and thus report larger profits. The theory is that by destroying asset values we can increase earning power and therefore enhance the market value. Since no one pays any attention to assets, why carry any assets on the books? This is another example of Alice in Wonderland financial logic.

It is in amusing contrast with the much berated stock watering practice of a generation ago. In those days fixed assets were arbitrarily written up, in order to enlarge the book values, and thus facilitate a fictitious market price. In place of watering of assets, we now have watering of earnings. The procedures are directly opposite, but the object and the underlying deception are exactly the same.

Because of the superstitious reverence now accorded the earnings statement by both investors and speculators, wide variations in market prices can be occasioned by purely arbitrary differences in accounting methods. The opportunities for downright crookedness are legion, nor are they ignored.

One company, listed on the New York Stock Exchange, recently turned an operating loss into a profit by the simple expedient of marking up its goodwill and adding the difference to earnings, without bothering to mention this little detail. The management apparently relied, and not unreasonably, on the fact that stockholders would not examine the balance sheets closely enough to detect their charming artifice.

The disregard of assets has also introduced some new wrinkles into reorganizations and mergers. Creditors are no longer permitted to receive the cash directly available to pay off their claims; stockholders are forced into consolidations which give other securities a prior claim on cash which formerly was theirs.

The Fisk Rubber Co., for example, showed around $400 in cash on hand for each $1,000 of overdue debt, and nearly $900 in net quick assets, excluding the extensive factories, etc. Yet the proposed reorganization plan offers these creditors no cash at all, but only stock in a new company.

Similarly, while Prairie Pipe Line stockholders were taking comfort from the fact that there had lately appeared to be $12 per share in cash equivalent behind their stock, they suddenly found themselves owners of shares in another company which had no cash at all directly applicable to their holdings, this new stock, moreover, having a total market value equal to less than half the cash equivalent alone which they formerly owned.

In the writer's view, all these strange happenings flow from the failure of the stockholder to realize that he occupies the same fundamental position and enjoys the same legal rights as the part-owner in a private business. The panoply and pyrotechnics of Wall Street have obscured this simple fact. If it only could be brought home to the millions of investors the country over, a long step would be taken in the direction of sounder corporate practices and a sane attitude towards stock values.

Should Rich by Losing Corporations Be Liquidated?

Which Is Right—the Stock Market or Corporation Management?

Another aspect of the current maladjustment between corporations and their stockholders is the question of possible liquidation. Many

From *Forbes*, July 1, 1932. Reprinted by permission of FORBES Magazine © Forbes Inc., 1932.

stocks sell for less than their cash value because the market judges that future operating losses will dissipate this cash.

If that is the case, then should not the stockholder demand liquidation before his cash is used up? The management says "No,"—naturally, but the stock market says "Yes,"—emphatically. Which is right? What are the salient factors on both sides of the question? *Forbes* presents herewith the third, and last, article in this series by Mr. Graham, which reaches down to the very roots of the present (troublesome) situation.

The unprecedented spectacle confronts us of more than one industrial company in three selling for less than its net current assets, with a large number quoted at less than their unencumbered cash. For this situation we have pointed out, in our previous articles, three possible causes: (a) Ignorance of the facts; (b) Compulsion to sell and inability to buy; and (c) Unwillingness to buy from fear that the present liquid assets will be dissipated.

In the preceding articles we discussed the first two causes and their numerous implications. But neither the ignorance nor the financial straits of the public could fully account for the current market levels.

If *gold dollars without any strings attached* could actually be purchased for 50 cents, plenty of publicity and plenty of buying power would quickly be marshaled to take advantage of the bargain. Corporate gold dollars are now available in quantity at 50 cents and less—but they *do* have strings attached. Although they belong to the stockholder, he doesn't control them. He may have to sit back and watch them dwindle and disappear as operating losses take their toll. For that reason the public refuses to accept even the cash holdings of corporations at their face value.

In fact, the hardheaded reader may well ask impatiently: "Why all this talk about liquidating values, *when companies are not going to liquidate?* As far as the stockholders are concerned, their interest in the corporation's cash account is just as theoretical as their interest in the plant account. *If* the business were wound up, the stockholders would [get] the cash; *if* the enterprise were profitable, the plants would be worth their book value. "*If* we had some cash, etc., etc."

This criticism has force, but there is an answer to it. The stockholders don't have it in their power to make business profitable but they do have it in their power to liquidate. At bottom it is not a theoretical question at all; the issue is both very practical and very pressing.

It is also a highly controversial issue. It includes an undoubted conflict of *judgment* between corporate managements and the stock market, and a probable conflict of *interest* between corporate managements and their stockholders.

In its simplest terms the question comes down to this: Are these managements wrong or is the market wrong? Are these low prices merely the product of unreasoning fear, or do they convey a stern warning to liquidate while there is yet time?

Today stockholders are leaving the answer to this problem, as to all other corporate problems, in the hands of their management. But when the latter's judgment is violently challenged by the verdict of the open market, it seems childish to let the management decide whether itself or the market is right. This is especially true when the issue involves a strong conflict of interest between the officials who draw salaries from the business and the owners whose capital is at stake. If you owned a grocery store that was doing badly, you wouldn't leave it to the paid manager to decide whether to keep it going or to shut up shop.

The innate helplessness of the public in the face of this critical problem is aggravated by its acceptance of two pernicious doctrines in the field of corporate administration. The first is that directors have no responsibility for, or interest in, the market price of their securities. The second is that outside stockholders know nothing about the business, and hence their views deserve no consideration unless sponsored by the management.

By virtue of dictum number one, directors succeed in evading all issues based upon the market price of their stock. Principle number two is invoked to excellent advantage in order to squelch any stockholder (not in control) who has the temerity to suggest that those in charge may not be proceeding wisely or in the best interest of their employers. The two together afford managements perfect protection against the necessity of justifying to their stockholders the continuance of the business when the weight of sound opinion points to better results for the owners through liquidation.

The accepted notion that directors have no concern with the market price of their stock is as fallacious as it is hypocritical. Needless to say, managements are not responsible for market fluctuations, but they should take cognizance of excessively high or unduly low price levels for the shares. They have a duty to protect their stockholders against avoidable depreciation in market value—as far as is reasonably in their power—equal to the duty to protect them against avoidable losses of earnings or assets.

If this duty were admitted and insisted upon, the present absurd relationship between quoted prices and liquidating values would never have come into existence. Directors and stockholders both would recognize that the true value of their stock should under no circumstances be less than the realizable value of the business, which amount in turn would ordinarily be not less than the net quick assets.

They would recognize further that *if the business is not worth its realizable value as a going concern it should be wound up*. Finally, directors would acknowledge their responsibility to conserve the realizable value of the business against shrinkage and to prevent, as far as is reasonably possible, the establishment of a price level continuously and substantially below the realizable value.

Hence, instead of viewing with philosophic indifference the collapse of their stock to abysmally low levels, directors would take these declines as a challenge to constructive action. In the first place, they would make every effort to maintain a dividend at least commensurate with the minimum real value of the stock. For this purpose they would draw freely on accumulated surplus, provided the company's financial position remained unimpaired. Secondly, they would not hesitate to direct the stockholders' attention to the existence of minimum liquidating values in excess of the market, and to assert their confidence in the reality of these values. In the third place, wherever possible, they would aid the stockholders by returning to them surplus cash capital through retirement or share pro rata at a fair price, as advocated in our previous article.

Finally, they would study carefully the company's situation and outlook, to make sure that the realizable value of the shares is not likely to suffer a substantial shrinkage. If they find there is danger of serious future loss, they would give earnest and fair-minded consideration to the question whether the stockholders' interests might not best be served by sale or liquidation.

However forcibly the stock market may be asserting the desirability of liquidation, there are no signs that managements are giving serious consideration to the issue. In fact, the infrequency of voluntary dissolution by companies with diversified ownership may well be a subject of wonder, or of cynicism. In the case of privately owned enterprises, withdrawing from business is an everyday occurrence. But with companies whose stock is widely held, it is the rarest of corporate developments.

Liquidation *after* insolvency is, of course, more frequent, but the idea of shutting up shop *before* the sheriff steps in seems repugnant to the canons of Wall Street. One thing can be said for our corporate managements—they are not quitters. Like Josh Billings, who in patriotic zeal stood ready to sacrifice all his wife's relations on the altar of his country, officials are willing to sacrifice their stockholders' last dollar to keep the business going.

But is it not true that the paid officials are subject to the decisions of the board of directors, who represent the stockholders, and whose duty it is to champion the owners' interests—if necessary, against the interests of the operating management? In theory this cannot be gain-said, but it doesn't work out in practice.

The reasons will appear from a study of any typical directorate. Here we find: (a) The paid officials themselves, who are interested in their jobs first and the stockholders second; (b) Investment bankers whose first interest is in underwriting profits; (c) Commercial bankers, whose first interest is in making and protecting loans; (d) Individuals who do business of various kinds with the company; and finally—and almost always in a scant minority—(e) Directors who are interested only in the welfare of the stockholders.

Even the latter are usually bound by ties of friendship to the officers (that is how they came to be nominated), so that the whole atmosphere of a board meeting is not conducive to any assertion of stockholders' rights against the desires of the operating management. Directors are not dishonest, but they are human. The writer, being himself a member of several boards, knows something of this subject from personal experience.

The conclusion stands out that liquidation is peculiarly an issue for the stockholders. Not only must it be decided by their independent judgment and preference, but in most cases the initiative and pressure to effect liquidation must emanate from stockholders not on the board of directors. In this connection we believe that the recognition of the following principle would be exceedingly helpful:

The fact that a company's shares sell persistently below their liquidating value should fairly raise the question whether liquidation is advisable.

Please note we do not suggest that the low price proves the desirability of liquidation. It merely justifies any stockholder in raising the issue, and entitles his views to respectful attention.

It means that stockholders should consider the issue with an open mind, and decide it on the basis of the facts presented and in accordance with their best individual judgment. No doubt in many of these cases— perhaps the majority—a fair-minded study would show liquidation to be unjustified. The going concern value under normal conditions would be found so large as compared with the sum realizable in liquidation, as to warrant seeing the depression through, despite current operating losses.

However, it is conceivable that under present difficult conditions the owners of a great many businesses might conclude that they would fare better by winding them up rather than continuing them. What would be the significance of such a movement to the economic situation as a whole? Would it mean further deflation, further unemployment, further reduction of purchasing power? Would stockholders be harming themselves? Superficially it might seem so, but powerful arguments can be advanced to the opposite effect.

The operation of unsoundly situated enterprises may be called a detriment, instead of an advantage, to the nation. We suffer not only from over-capacity, but still more from the disruptive competition of companies which have no chance to survive, but continue to exist none the less, to the loss of their stockholders and the unsettlement of their industry.

Without making any profits for themselves, they destroy the profit possibilities of other enterprises. Their removal might permit a better adjustment of supply to demand, and a larger output with consequent lower costs to the stronger companies which remain. An endeavor is now being made to accomplish this result in the cotton goods industry.

From the standpoint of employment, the demand for the product is not reduced by closing down unprofitable units. Hence, production is transferred elsewhere and employment in the aggregate may not be diminished. That great individual hardship would be involved cannot be denied, nor should it be minimized but in any case the conditions of employment in a fundamentally unsound enterprise must be precarious in the extreme. Admitting that the employees must be given sympathetic consideration, it is only just to point out that our economic principles do not include the destruction of stockholders' capital for the sole purpose of providing employment.

We have not yet found any way to prevent depression from throttling us in the midst of our superabundance. But unquestionably there are ways to relieve the plight of the stockholders who today own so much and can realize so little. A fresh viewpoint on these matters might work wonders for the sadly demoralized army of American stockholders.

The Ethics of
American Capitalism

Three major points:

1. There has been a great change, amounting to a revolution, in the mechanisms of American capital—applying to both its economic and its ethical aspects.

2. These changes have been worked out by trial and error, without a systematic philosophy. They have been largely opposed by business-men as a class. The final acceptance of the new system perhaps may (have) come in Tuesday's election—especially in the great triumph of [Dwight D.] Eisenhower versus the choice of a Democratic congress.

3. Our new approach to continued prosperity rests on three sup-ports: (a) dynamic growth of American business; (b) responsibility of government to control excesses and meet recession threats to high level employment; (c) acceptance by government of ethical or welfare responsibilities for all the people. It may be that, in the ethical base will be found a more powerful support to our prosperity than the purely economic factors.

I've noticed two recent books with similar titles: *The Great Crash* [1929] by [J. Kenneth] Galbraith and *The Big Change* by F. L. Allen. The first describes a terrible debacle and the second, major progress along many fronts. Yet the two are not contradictory. The development of new American capitalism was undoubtedly accelerated, perhaps made possible at all, by the Great Depression.

Speech, University of California at Los Angeles's Camp Kramer Retreat, November 10, 1956

The American capitalism that culminated in 1929 had several characteristics, viz:

1. *Laissez-faire* principle, which meant full freedom for profit motive, subject only to laws against stealing and against monopoly. Some public utility controls were included.
2. The central position of the tycoon, who amassed not only great wealth, but enormous economic, political, and even social power as well.
3. The principle that welfare activities should be almost exclusively philanthropic, i.e., as the domain of private charity. Poorhouses were the exception that proved the rule, for they provided neither true welfare nor true philanthropy.
4. As a negative consequence of the above, the very minor role of government in both economics and social welfare. Chief exception here was in the field of education.

These aspects are all changed radically as of now, and most of the transformation has taken place since the Crash, beginning perhaps with [President Herbert] Hoover's RFC [Reconstruction Finance Corporation].

There are now a host of limitations on laissez-faire—labor legislation, continuing rent controls, SEC laws, greater public utility regulation, heavy tax rates, etc.

The tycoon, as such, has virtually disappeared. It is still possible to be and even become a multimillionaire and even an empire builder of sorts—[William] Zeckendorf, Wolfson, etc. But the powers of such men are strictly limited to the field of their operations or manipulations. There is no longer a "House on the Corner"—J. P. Morgan—whose wishes every Wall Street firm had to consider if it wanted to stay in business.

We now have huge corporations operated not by single owners but by managers—managementism rather than capitalism.

Human welfare—including all forms of social security—has become a province of federal and local government, and is thus tax supported.

Finally, government has taken over enormous powers and responsibilities in the economic field. Each limitation on *laissez-faire* has meant more interference [in] business—for weal or woe. But also government is now expected to aid business in time of trouble. S. H. Slichter says "free enterprise has been transformed into government-guided enterprise."

Many, perhaps most, changes have been bitterly opposed by businessmen, partly on grounds of true principle, partly because they felt acute pain in the pocketbook nerve, partly from considerations of power and privilege. There is a good theoretical case against the new capitalism, and it is well expressed in [F. A.] Hayek's *The Road to Serfdom*. Hayek argues that each addition to power of government brings us closer to a socialistic state and that in turn, nearer to a communistic state. Against this should be set the persuasive argument of Allen that we have evolved something distinctive and far removed from socialism.

[Graham quoted from Allen here, but the quote is missing from the speech notes.]

I think large responsibility for hostility of business to (the changes in capitalism) must be laid to Franklin D. Roosevelt, because of his political attitude of hostility to business. The questions of the position of FDR in history is a fascinating one. My own view is that he had an instinctive rather than rational understanding of what was necessary to preserve the American way of life. He may have been at heart an enemy of capitalism—that is difficult to judge. But enemy or not, I should go so far as to say that the net result of his imaginative and devious strategies was the salvation of American capitalism.

Carrying this viewpoint further, I see in Eisenhower's social and economic policy, a Roosevelt, without FDR's animus against business. It may be that his victory, contrasted with his party's defeat in Congress, means only that Eisenhower's personality is irresistible. I doubt that. I feel rather that it signalizes definitely the acceptance by a large majority of the people of the country, our radically changed version of American capitalism, including its newer ethics of welfare and responsibility.

Eisenhower's election demonstrates that it is not necessary to be anti-business to win the presidency (as FDR seems to have imagined). On the other hand, I think that the Democrat's success in Congress—even though it was greatly aided by a terrific campaign by the AFL–CIO—indicates that the majority of the country favor the economic-political-social changes that began in 1933, and feel that they are not entirely safe as yet with a Republican congress.

My last section brings me to an idea which perhaps justifies the title of this talk and its delivery here. My point is, that from the standpoint of national policy, "good ethics is good economics." The same is no doubt true for an individual business.

Let us view the question for the moment from the narrow vantage of the businessman's economic position since 1933. For most of that time he has found himself persecuted, handcuffed by regulation, bedeviled by bureaucracy, and taxed at impossibly high rates. Yet he has survived—and not only survived but prospered. What does this paradox signify?

A cynic might say that the upsweep of our economy is due at bottom to war activities—to World War II, Korea, and the Cold War—and that these have brought prosperity to businessmen despite the efforts of the New Deal, etc., to throttle and destroy him.

My own view is a more optimistic one. I think we have found that the basic welfare activities of government—those centering in various forms of social security, including unemployment insurance—are worth to business more than their cost in high taxes. Nothing is more beneficial for business as a whole than the improvement in the living standards and the purchasing power of our poorer people. F. L. Allen makes that point:

[Quote missing from speech notes.]

We seem to have come a long way from the original tenets of *laissez-faire* capitalism as they were developed for our college courses (before 1929)—not so much by Adam Smith as out of his writings. You remember his famous concept of the "invisible hand." Every time, said he, that a businessman sought to make some decision which would bring him a profit, this invisible hand guided him to make a decision which would be good for society as a whole—i.e., he would decide to make the product that society wanted, or found some way to reduce its cost, and therefore its price to society. This point of view still has validity, but not in the unqualified, over-enthusiastic way in which the proponents of *laissez-faire* presented it. It is now being offset by a complementary point of view, expressed by Peter F. Drucker—the apologist for the corporation—as follows:

"No policy is likely to benefit the business itself unless it benefits society."

PART TWO

ABOUT STOCKS AND THE STOCK MARKET

The investor with a portfolio of sound stocks should expect their prices to fluctuate and should neither be concerned by sizable declines nor become excited by sizable advances. He should always remember that market quotations are there for his convenience, either to be taken advantage of or to be ignored.

The Intelligent Investor, Third Edition, 1959

For a man who continually warned investors to pay no attention to stock market fluctuations—it was, after all, the underlying fundamentals of a company that, in the long-term, determined share price—Graham spent a lot of time thinking about price movements and the market as a whole. He contemplated many mysteries of Wall Street. What makes an undervalued share suddenly rise in price? What exactly is speculation and when is speculation acceptable? Some readers will be surprised to learn that while Graham developed some fundamental notions that he stuck to, his thinking wasn't as limited as many people assume. He continued to question, probe, and explore new ideas until the very end of his life, as the following group of essays shows. Of particular interest in this part is "Renaissance of Value," published in 1974. For the second time in his career, Graham announced that the bear market had reached the point that an abundance of bargain stocks were available to those with the courage to buy. When the article appeared in *Barron's*, Graham inspired a market rebound, and those who listened to him were to profit enormously.

The New Speculation in Common Stocks

Address to the Financial Analysts Society
Stock Market Luncheon, 1958

I asked Hartley Smith, in introducing me to you, to lay chief stress upon my advanced age. What I shall have to say will reflect the spending of many years in Wall Street, with their attendant varieties of experience. This has included the recurrent advent of new conditions, or a new atmosphere, which challenge the value of experience itself. It is true that one of the elements that distinguish economics, finance, and security analysis from other practical disciplines is the uncertain validity of past phenomena as a guide to the present and future. Yet we have no right to reflect on the lessons of the past until we have at least studied and understood them. My address today is an effort toward such understanding in a limited field—in particular, an endeavor to point out some contrasting relationships between the present and the past in our underlying attitudes towards investment and speculation in common stocks.

Let me start with a summary of my thesis. In the past the speculative elements of a common stock resided almost exclusively in the company itself; they were due to uncertainties, or fluctuating elements, or downright weaknesses in the industry, or the corporation's individual set-up. These elements of speculation still exist, of course; but it may be said that they have been sensibly diminished by a number of long-term developments to which I shall refer. But in revenge a new and major element of speculation has been introduced into the common-stock arena from *outside* the companies. It comes from the attitude and viewpoint of the stock-buying public and their advisers—chiefly us security analysts. This attitude may be described in a phrase: primary emphasis upon future expectations.

Nothing will appear more logical and natural to this audience than the idea that a common stock should be valued and priced primarily on the basis of the company's expected future performance. Yet this simple-appearing concept carries with it a number of paradoxes and pitfalls. For one thing, it obliterates a good part of the older, well-established distinctions between investment and speculation. The dictionary says that "speculate" comes from the Latin *specula*, a look-out or watch-tower. Thus it was the speculator who looked out from his elevated watch-tower and saw future developments coming before other people did. But today, if the investor is shrewd or well-advised, he too must have his watch-tower looking out on the future, or rather he mounts into a common watch-tower where he rubs elbows with the speculator.

Secondly, we find that, for the most part, companies with the best investment characteristics—i.e., the best credit rating—are the ones which are likely to attract the largest speculative interest in their common stocks, since everyone assumes they are guaranteed a brilliant future. Thirdly, the concept of future prospects, and particularly of continued growth in the future, invites the application of formulae out of higher mathematics to establish the present value of the favored issues. But the combination of precise formulae with highly imprecise assumptions can be used to establish or rather to justify, practically any value one wishes, however high, for a really outstanding issue. But paradoxically, that very fact on close examination will be seen to imply that no one value, or reasonably narrow range of values, can be counted on to establish and maintain itself for a given growth company; hence at times the market may conceivably value the growth component at a strikingly *low* figure.

Returning to my distinction between the older and newer speculative elements in common stock, we might characterize them by two outlandish but convenient words, viz: endogenous and exogenous. Let me illustrate briefly the old-time speculative common stock, as distinguished from an investment stock, by some data relating to American Can and Pennsylvania Railroad in 1912–1913. (These appear in *Security Analysis*, 1940 Edition, pp. 2–3.)

In those three years the price range of "Pennsy" moved only between $53 and $65, or between 12.2 and 15 times its average earnings for the period. It showed steady profits, was paying a reliable $3 dividend, and investors were sure that it was backed by well over its par of $50 in tangible assets. By contrast, the price of American Can ranged between $9 and $47; its earnings between seven cents and $8.86; the ratio of price to the average earnings moved between 1.9 times and 10 times; it paid no dividend at all; and sophisticated investors were well aware that the $100 par value of the common represented nothing but undisclosed "water," since the preferred issue exceeded the tangible assets available for it. Thus American Can common was a representative speculative issue, because American Can Company was then a speculative-capitalized enterprise in a fluctuating and uncertain industry. Actually, American Can had a far more brilliant long-term future than Pennsylvania Railroad; but not only was this fact not suspected by investors or speculators in those days, but even if it had been it would probably have been put aside by the investors as basically irrelevant to investment policies and programs in the years 1911–1913.

Now, to expose you to the development through time of the importance of long-term prospects for investments, I should like to use as my example our most spectacular giant industrial enterprise—none other than International Business Machines, which last year entered the small group of companies with $1 billion of sales.

May I introduce one or two autobiographical notes here, in order to inject a little of the personal touch into what otherwise would be an excursion into cold figures? In 1912, I had left college for a term to take charge of a research project of U.S. Express Co. We set out to find the effect on revenues of a proposed revolutionary new system of computing express rates. For this purpose we used the so-called Hollerith machines, leased out by the then Computing-Tabulating-Recording Co. They comprised card-punches, card-sorters, and tabulators—tools almost unknown to businessmen, then, and having their chief application in the Census Bureau. I entered Wall Street in 1914, and the next year the bonds and common stock of C.-T.-R. Co. were listed on the New York Stock Exchange.

Well, I had a kind of sentimental interest in that enterprise, and besides I considered myself a sort of technical expert on their products, being one of the few financial people who had seen and used them. So early in 1916 I went to the head of my firm, known as Mr. A. N., and pointed out to him that C.-T.-R. stock was selling in the middle 40s (for 105,000 shares); that it had earned $6.50 in 1915; that its book value—including, to be sure, some non-segregated intangibles—was $130; that it had started a $3 dividend; and that I thought rather highly of the company's products and prospects. Mr. A. N. looked at me pityingly, "Ben," said he, "do not mention that company to me again. I would not touch it with a 10-foot pole. (His favorite expression.) Its 6 percent bonds are selling in the low 80s and they are no good. So how can the stock be any good. Everybody knows there is nothing behind it but water." (Glossary: In those days that was the ultimate of condemnation. It meant that the asset-account on the balance sheet was fictitious. Many industrial companies—notably U.S. Steel—despite their $100 par, represented nothing but water, concealed in a written-up plant account. Since they had nothing to back them but earning power and future prospects, no self-respecting investor would give them a second thought.)

I returned to my statistician's cubby-hole, a chastened young man. Mr. A. N. was not only experienced and successful, but extremely shrewd as well. So much was I impressed by his sweeping condemnation of Computing-Tabulating-Recording that I never bought a share of it in my life, not even after its name was changed to IBM in 1926.

Now let us take a look at the same company with its new name in 1926, a year of pretty high stock markets. At that time it first revealed the goodwill item in its balance sheet, in the rather large sum of $13.6 million. A. N. had been right. Practically every dollar of the so-called equity behind the common in 1915 had been nothing but water.

However, since that time the company had made an impressive record under the direction of T. L. Watson, Sr. Its net had risen from $691,000 to $3.7 million—over five-fold—a greater percentage gain than it was to make in any subsequent 11-year period. It had built up a nice tangible equity for the common, and had split it 3.6 for one. It had established a $3 dividend rate for the new stock, while earnings were $6.39 thereon.

You might have expected the 1926 stock market to have been pretty enthusiastic about a company with such a growth history and so strong a trade position. Let us see. The price range for that year was $31 low, $59 high. At the average of $45 it was selling at the same seven times multiplier of earnings and the same 6.7 percent dividend yield as it had done in 1915. At its low of $31 it was not far in excess of its tangible book value, and in that respect was far more conservatively priced than 11 years earlier.

These data illustrate, as well as any can, the persistence of the old-time investment viewpoint until the culminating years of the bull market of the 1920s. What has happened since then can be summarized by using 10-year intervals in the history of IBM. In 1936 net expanded to twice the 1926 figures, and the average multiplier rose from seven to 17.5. From 1936 to 1946 the gain was 2.5 times, but the average multiplier in 1946 remained at 17.5. Then the pace accelerated. The 1956 net was nearly four times that of 1946, and the average multiplier rose to 32.5. Last year, with a further gain in net, the multiplier rose again to an average of 42, if we do not count the unconsolidated equity in the foreign subsidiary.

When we examine these recent price figures with care we see some interesting analogies and contrasts with those of 40 years earlier. The one-time scandalous water, so prevalent in the balance-sheets of industrial companies, has all been squeezed out—first by disclosure and then by write-offs. But a different kind of water has been put back into the valuation by the stock market—by investors and speculators themselves. When IBM now sells at seven times its book value, instead of seven times earnings, the effect is practically the same as if it had no book value at all. Or the small book value portion can be considered as a sort of minor preferred stock component of the price, the rest representing exactly the same sort of commitment as the old-time speculator made when he bought Woolworth or U.S. Steel common entirely for their earning power and future prospects.

It is worth remarking, in passing, that in the 30 years which saw IBM transformed from a seven times earnings to a 40-times earnings enterprise, many of what I have called the endogenous speculative aspects of our large industrial companies have tended to disappear, or at least to diminish greatly. Their financial positions are firm, their capital structures conservative; they are managed far more expertly, and even more honestly, than before. Furthermore, the requirements of complete disclosure have removed one of the important speculative elements of years ago—that derived from ignorance and mystery.

Another personal digression here. In my early years in the street one of the favorite mystery stocks was Consolidated Gas of New York, now Consolidated Edison. It owned as a subsidiary the profitable New York Edison Co., but it reported only dividends received from this source, not its full earnings. The unreported Edison earnings supplied mystery and the hidden value. To my surprise I discovered that these hush-hush figures were actually on file each year with the Public Service Commission of the state. It was a simple matter to consult the records and to present the true earnings of Consolidated Gas in a magazine article. (Incidentally, the addition to profits was not spectacular.)

One of my older friends said to me then: "Ben, you may think you are a great guy to supply those missing figures, but Wall Street is going to thank you for nothing. Consolidated Gas with the mystery is both more interesting and more valuable than ex-mystery. You youngsters who want to stick your noses into everything are going to ruin Wall Street."

It is true that the three M's which then supplied so much fuel to the speculative fires have now all but disappeared. These were Mystery, Manipulation, and (thin) Margins. But we security analysts have ourselves been creating valuation approaches which are so speculative in themselves as to pretty well take the place of those older speculative factors. Do we not have our own 3Ms now—none other than Minnesota Mining and Manufacturing Co.—and does not this common stock illustrate perfectly the new speculation as contrasted with the old? Consider a few figures. When 3M common sold at $101 last year the market was valuing it at 44 times 1956 earnings, which happened to show no increase to speak of in 1957. The enterprise itself was valued at $1.7 billion, of which $200 million was covered by net assets, and a cool $1.5 billion represented the market's appraisal of "goodwill." We do not know the process of calculation by which that valuation of goodwill was arrived at; we do know that a few months later the market revised this appraisal downward by some $450 million, or about 30 percent. Obviously it is impossible to calculate accurately the intangible component of a splendid company such as this. It follows as a kind of mathematical law that the more important the goodwill or future earning-power factor the more uncertain becomes the true value of the enterprise, and therefore the more speculative inherently the common stock.

It may be well to recognize a vital difference that has developed in the valuation of these intangible factors, when we compare earlier times with today. A generation or more ago it was the standard rule, recognized both in average stock prices and informal or legal valuations, that intangibles were to be appraised on a more conservative basis than tangibles. A good industrial company might be required to earn between 6 percent and 8 percent on its tangible assets, represented typically by bonds and preferred stock; but its excess earnings, or the intangible assets they gave rise to, would be valued on, say, a 15 percent basis. (You will find approximately these ratios in the initial offering of Woolworth Preferred and Common stock in 1911, and in numerous others.) But what has happened since the 1920s? Essentially the exact reverse of these relationships may now be seen. A company must now typically earn about 10 percent on its common equity to have it sell in the average market at full book value. But its excess earnings, above 10 percent on capital, are usually valued more liberally, or at a higher multiplier, than the base earnings required to support the book value in the market. Thus a company earning 15 percent on the equity may well sell at 13.5 times earnings, or twice its net assets. This would mean that the first 10 percent earned on capital is valued at only 10 times, but the next 5 percent— what used to be called the excess—is actually valued at 20 times.

Now there is a logical reason for this reversal in valuation procedure, which is related to the newer emphasis on growth expectations. Companies that earn a high return on capital are given these liberal appraisals not only because of the good profitability itself, and the relative stability associated with it, but perhaps even more cogently because high earnings on capital generally go hand and hand with a good growth record and prospects. Thus what one is really paying for nowadays in the case of highly profitable companies is not the goodwill in the old and restricted sense of an established name and a profitable business, but rather for their assumed superior expectations of increased profits in the future.

This brings me to one or two additional mathematical aspects of the newer attitude toward common-stock valuations, which I shall touch on merely in the form of brief suggestions. If, as many tests show, the earnings multiplier tends to increase with profitability—i.e., as the rate of return on book value increases—then the arithmetical consequence of this feature is that value tends to increase directly as the square of the earnings, but *inversely* with book value. Thus in an important and very real sense tangible assets have become a drag on average market value rather than a source thereof. Take a far-from-extreme illustration. If Company A earns $4 a share on a $20 book value, and Company B also $4 a share on $100 of book value, Company A is almost certain to sell at a higher multiplier, and hence at higher price than Company B—say $60 for Company A shares and $35 for Company B shares. Thus it would not be inexact to declare that the $80 per share of greater assets for Company B are responsible for the $25 per share lower market price, since the earnings per share are assumed to be equal.

But more important than the foregoing is the general relationship between mathematics and the newer approach to stock values. Given the three ingredients of (a) optimistic assumptions as to the rate of earnings growth, (b) a sufficiently long projection of this growth into the future, and (c) the miraculous workings of compound interest—and the security analyst is supplied with a new kind of philosopher's stone which can produce or justify any desired valuation for a really good stock.

I have commented in a recent article in the *Analysts Journal* on the vogue of higher mathematics in bull markets, and quoted David Durand's exposition of the striking analogy between value calculations of growth stocks and the famous Petersburg Paradox, which has challenged and confused mathematicians for more than 200 years. The point I want to make here is that there is a special paradox in the relationship between mathematics and investment attitudes on common stocks, which is this: Mathematics is ordinarily considered as producing precise and dependable results; but in the stock market the more elaborate and abstruse the mathematics the more uncertain and speculative are the conclusions we draw therefrom.

In 44 years of Wall Street experience and study, I have never seen dependable calculations made about common-stock values, or related investment policies, that went beyond simple arithmetic or the most elementary algebra. Whenever excalculus is brought in, or higher algebra, you could take it as a warning signal that the operator was trying to substitute theory for experience, and usually also to give to speculation the deceptive guise of investment.

The older ideas of common-stock investment may seem quite naive to the sophisticated security analyst of today. The great emphasis was always on what we now call the defensive aspects of the company or issue—mainly the assurance that it would continue its dividend unreduced in bad times. Thus the strong railroads, which constituted the standard investment commons of 50 years ago, were actually regarded in very much the same way as the public utility commons in recent years. If the past record indicated stability, the chief requirement was met; not too much effort was made to anticipate adverse changes of an underlying character in the future. But, conversely, especially favorable future prospects were regarded by shrewd investors as something to look for but not to pay for.

In effect this meant that the investor did not have to pay anything substantial for superior long-term prospects. He got these, virtually without extra cost, as a reward for his own superior intelligence and judgment in picking the best rather than the merely good companies. For common stocks with the same financial strength, past earnings record, and dividend stability, all sold at about the same dividend yield.

This was indeed a short-sighted point of view, but it had the great advantage of making common-stock investment in the old days not only simple but also basically sound and highly profitable.

Let me return for the last time to a personal note. Somewhere around 1920 our firm distributed a series of little pamphlets entitled "Lessons for Investors." Of course it took a brash analyst in his middle 20s like myself to hit on so smug and presumptuous a title. But in one of the papers I made the casual statement that "If a common stock is a good investment it is also a good speculation." For, reasoned I, if a common stock was so sound that it carried very little risk of loss it must ordinarily be so good as to possess excellent chances for future gains. Now this was a perfectly true and even valuable discovery, but it was true only because nobody paid any attention to it.

Some years later, when the public woke up to the historical merits of common stocks as long-term investments, they soon ceased to have any such merit, because the public's enthusiasm created price levels which deprived them of their built-in margin of safety, and thus drove them out of the investment class. Then, of course, the pendulum swung to the other extreme, and we soon saw one of the most respected authorities declaring (in 1931) that no common stock could *ever* be an investment.

When we view this long-range experience in perspective we find another set of paradoxes in the investor's changing attitude towards capital gains as contrasted with income. It seems a truism to say that the old-time common-stock investor was not much interested in capital gains. He bought almost entirely for safety and income, and let the speculator concern himself with price appreciation. Today we are likely to say that the more experienced and shrewd the investor, the less attention he pays to dividend returns, and the more heavily his interest centers on long-term appreciation.

Yet one might argue, perversely, that precisely because the old-time investor did not concentrate on future capital appreciation he was virtually guaranteeing to himself that he would have it, at least in the field of industrial stocks. And, conversely, today's investor is so concerned with anticipating the future that he is already paying handsomely for it in advance. Thus what he has projected with so much study and care may actually happen and still not bring him any profit. If it should fail to materialize to the degree expected he may in fact be faced with a serious temporary and perhaps even permanent loss.

What *lessons*—again using the pretentious title of my 1920 pamphlets—can the analyst of 1958 learn from this linking of past with current attitudes? Not much of value, one is inclined to say. We can look back nostalgically to the good old days when we paid only for the present and could get the future for nothing—an "all this and heaven too" combination. Shaking our heads sadly we mutter, "Those days are gone forever." Have not investors and security analysts eaten of the tree of knowledge of good and evil prospects? By so doing have they not permanently expelled themselves from that Eden where promising common stocks at reasonable prices could be plucked off the bushes? Are we not doomed always to run the risk either of paying unreasonably high prices for good quality and prospects, or of getting poor quality and prospects when we pay what seems a reasonable price?

It certainly looks that way. Yet one cannot be sure even of that pessimistic dilemma. Recently, I did a little research in the long-term history of that towering enterprise, General Electric, stimulated by the arresting chart of 59 years of earnings and dividends appearing in their recently published 1957 report. These figures are not without their surprises for the knowledgeable analyst. For one thing they show that prior to 1947 the growth of GE was fairly modest and quite irregular. The 1946 earnings, per share adjusted, were only 30 percent higher than in 1902—52 cents versus 40 cents—and in no year of this period were the 1902 earnings as much as doubled. Yet the price-earnings ratio rose from nine times in 1910 and 1916 to 29 times in 1936 and again in 1946. One might say, of course, that the 1946 multiplier at least showed the well-known prescience of shrewd investors. We analysts were able to foresee then the really brilliant period of growth that was looming ahead in the next decade. Maybe so. But some of you remember that the next year, 1947, which established an impressive new high for GE's per-share earnings, was marked also by an extraordinary fall in the price-earnings ratio. At its low of $32 (before the 3-for-1 split) GE actually sold again at only nine times its current earnings, and its average price for the year was only about 10 times earnings. Our crystal ball certainly clouded over in the short space of 12 months.

This striking reversal took place only 11 years ago. It casts some little doubt in my mind as to the complete dependability of the popular belief among analysts that prominent and promising companies will now always sell at high price-earnings ratios; that this is a fundamental fact of life for investors and they may as well accept and like it. I have no desire at all to be dogmatic on this point. All I can say is that it is not settled in my mind, and each of you must seek to settle it for yourself.

But in my concluding remarks I can say something definite about the structure of the market for various types of common stocks, in terms of their investment and speculative characteristics. In the old days the investment character of a common stock was more or less the same as, or proportionate with, that of the enterprise itself, as measured quite well by its credit rating. The lower the yield on its bonds or preferred, the more likely was the common to meet all the criteria for a satisfactory investment, and the smaller the element of speculation involved in its purchase.

This relationship, between the speculative ranking of the common and the investment rating of the company, could be graphically expressed pretty much as a straight line descending from left to right. But nowadays I would describe the graph as U-shaped. At the left, where the company itself is speculative and its credit low, the common stock is of course highly speculative, just as it has always been in the past. At the right extremity, however, where the company has the highest credit rating because both its past record and future prospects are most impressive, we find that the stock market tends more or less continuously to introduce a highly speculative element into the common share through the simple means of a price so high as to carry a fair degree of risk.

At this point I cannot forbear introducing a surprisingly relevant, if quite exaggerated, quotation on the subject which I found recently in one of Shakespeare's sonnets.

It reads

> Have I not seen dwellers on form and favor
> Lose all and more by paying too much rent?

Returning to my imaginary graph, it would be the center area where the speculative element in common-stock purchases would tend to reach its minimum. In this area we could find many well-established and strong companies, with a record of past growth corresponding to that of the national economy and with future prospects apparently of the same character. Such common stocks could be bought at most times, except in the upper ranges of a bull market, at moderate prices in relation to their indicated intrinsic values. As a matter of fact, because of the present tendency of investors and speculators alike to concentrate on more glamorous issues, I should hazard the statements that these middle-ground stocks tend to sell on the whole rather below their independently determinable values. They thus have a margin-of-safety factor supplied by the same market preferences and prejudices which tend to destroy the margin of safety in the more promising issues. Furthermore, in this wide array of companies there is plenty of room for penetrating analysis of the past record and for discriminating choice in the area of future prospects, to which can be added the higher assurance of safety conferred by diversification.

When Phaeton insisted on driving the chariot of the sun, his father, the experienced operator, gave the neophyte some advice which the latter failed to follow—to his cost. Ovid summed up Phoebus Apollo's counsel in three words:

Medius tutissimus ibis
You will go safest in the middle course

I think this principle holds good for investors and their security-analyst advisers.

Stock Market Warning: Danger Ahead!

Based on a Speech Graham Delivered at UCLA, December 17, 1959

The stock market has been advancing with only one significant setback throughout the decade of the 1950s. It has thus established a new record for the length of its rise, although it has not equaled the extent of the record advance of the 1920s: 325 percent in this market versus 450 percent from 1921–1929.

What does this phenomenal upward movement portend for investors and speculators in the future? There are various ways of approaching this question. To answer it, I shall divide the question into two parts. First, what indications are given us by past experience? Second, how relevant is past experience to the present situation and prospects?

As to the first part of my answer, I should be able to make some definite statements—which will be the reverse of encouraging. But as to the applicability of the record of the past to present, I cannot express a categorical judgment. I shall present certain facts on the one side and certain expectations pointing the other way; I shall state my own opinion as to the probable answer; but in the end, each must resolve that part of the question for himself.

INDICATIONS FROM PAST EXPERIENCE

However, in order to judge today's market level, it is desirable—perhaps essential—to have a clear picture of its past behavior. Speculators often prosper through ignorance; it is a cliché that in a roaring bull market knowledge is superfluous and experience a handicap. But the typical experience of the speculator is one of temporary profit and ultimate loss. If experience cannot help today's investor, then we must be logical and conclude that there is no such thing as investment in common stocks and that everyone interested in them should confess himself a speculator. This is just about what has actually happened in recent years—only in reverse. Everyone now calls himself an investor, including a huge horde of speculators.

This point is neatly illustrated by the opening lines of an article in a recent issue of *Business Week* describing the annual convention of Investment Clubs. The writer says: "Like all investors, large and small, they were mainly interested in which way the market—and particular stocks—would move next." If that sentence accurately describes a *bona fide* investor of 1960, then—to use a phrase made famous by a certain Mr. Khrushchev—the shrimps have really begun to whistle on the mountain tops.

BULL MARKET OR NEW MARKET?

The main issue before the investor may be expressed this way: Have we been in a bull market or in a new sort of market? If this is a bull market, then the term itself implies a bear market to follow it some day. What could be the probable extent of a decline in a traditional bear market? Here are some figures, which apply the experience of the 12 bear markets since 1874 to the recent high level of 685 for the Dow Jones Industrial Average. [See Table 3.]

The average of these 12 declines (all taken from Cowles Standard indexes) would indicate a market low of about 400, a fall of over 40 percent from the 685 high. Investors may consider themselves mentally prepared for a 40 percent shrinkage in stock prices, especially if they envisage such a drop as taking place from a level far above today's average. At this point, however, a second factor of past experience becomes relevant. The record shows that declines have tended to be roughly proportional to the previous advances. Thus, the six largest advances averaging 63 percent of the high level reached were followed by declines

TABLE 3

Comparison of Twelve Bear-Market Declines

Time Period	Percent Decline	Equivalent Low from 885
1874–77	36	435
1881–84	26	500
1889–97	40	410
1901–03	44	385
1906–07	45	375
1909–14	29	485
1916–17	36	435
1919–21	44	385
1929–32	85	115
1937–38	44	385
1939–42	39	415
1946–49	27	490

averaging 46 percent while the other six advances averaging 38 percent of the high produced declines averaging 37 percent.

Experience gives us another measure of the possible bear-market decline. This measure is based on the principle that the higher the market advances above a computed normal, the further it is likely to decline below such normal. If this principle—enunciated long ago by Roger Babson—were to hold in the future as in the present, then a further rise of the market from these levels—in itself an alluring probability— would actually carry with it an intensified future penalty.

Let me illustrate this point of experience by some horrifying assumptions—to present the worst of the picture. Let us assume that the market makes everyone happy by advancing fairly soon to that millennial level of 1,000 for the Dow-Jones Industrials, of which some predictions are already on file. Assume further that this is a speculative advance—very like that of the late 1920s—and that the Central Value of the D-J Average at the time is only 400. By applying the old Babson economic law of "action and reaction—equal and opposite," the corrective downswing would carry the average as low as 160, a loss of 84 percent. Impossible, you say, and no doubt you are right. But a condition similar to the one I am assuming actually occurred in 1929, and the ensuring shrinkage in the D-J Average was not 86 percent but 89 percent—from 382 to 42.

There is a paradox in this economic law which makes it virtually impossible for it to find acceptance in practice. For the almost universal optimism that accompanies the great advances in the stock market precludes even the most conservative observer from imagining a decline so drastic as these figures illustrate.

CURRENT OPTIMISM

Let me turn now from this Cassandra-like utterance to the picture of the future stock market that is strongly etched in the minds of most investors and speculators and of their expert advisors. Past experience may not be entirely eliminated from this picture, but it enters in a very muted way. The keynote, of course, is optimism. We are enthusiastic about business prospects for the next decade. In fact, that period received its name in many quarters—the Fabulous Sixties—even before it had begun. Herodotus recounts a saying of Solon the Wise that rich King Croesus sadly recalled before his execution—namely, that no man's life should be accounted a happy one until it is over. Perhaps the more prudent time to characterize the 1960s would be when they are over rather than when they have just begun.

Most people are equally optimistic about the stock market. One of my friends—a brilliant analyst—was quoted recently in the *Wall Street Journal* as saying that the bull market is about to enter its 19th year and soon will be able to vote. Translated, that means he is carrying the bull market both backward in time to include 1942—ignoring the 1946–1949 setback and doldrums—and confidently forward in time to 1963.

The optimism about both business and the stock market is founded on a host of favorable facts and expectations, including an important "favorable factor," the likelihood of continued price inflation. I shall discuss these a little later.

Investors accept in theory the premise that the stock market may have its recessions in the future. But these drops are envisaged in terms of the experience of the past 10 years when the maximum decline was only 19 percent—from 521 to 420 in 1957. The public is confident that such setbacks will be made up speedily, and hence that a small amount of patience and courage will bring great rewards in the form of a much higher price level soon thereafter.

Investors may think they are basing this view of the future on past experience, but in this they are surely mistaken. The experience of the 1949–1959 market—or of all bull markets put together—reflects only the sunny side of the investment. It is one thing to say airily that the market has always come back after declines and made new heights; it is another to reflect on the fact that it took 25 years for the market to reach again the high level of 1929, or that the D-J Average sold at the same high point in 1919 as it did in 1942—23 years later.

THE PRESENT BULL MARKET IN RELATION TO PAST ONES

Up to now I have been talking only in terms of past fluctuations on the one hand, and present confidence and optimism on the other. It is time to fill in the picture with certain financial and economic data which will place the present stock market quantitatively in relation to past bull markets.

We have a number of authoritative measures of the factors of earnings, dividends, and asset values in relation to price, as applied to the market as a whole—with more emphasis placed on the industrial list. My data will apply to the industrials only. There are the figures for the 30 D-J issues published by *Barron's*; on 125 issues of Moody's; and the very comprehensive group of 425 industrials of Standard-Poor's. Rather strangely, all three indexes give very much the same indications, both currently and over the last 30 years. At the high levels of 1959, the dividend yield on all three indices were just about 3 percent, and the ratio of price to earnings of the past 12 months was about 19 times. Let us compare these ratios with some figures for the high levels of the past bull markets. [See Table 4.]

TABLE 4

	Moody's 125 Industrials		Long-Term Bond Yield (Moody's AAA Corporates)	Standard-Poors 425 Industrials	
	Price-Earnings Ratio	Dividend Yield		Price-Earnings Ratio	Dividend Yield
1959 High	19.0x	3.06%	4.55%	18.2x	2.95%
1949 Low	(Av) 7.1	(Av) 6.82	2.65	5.6	7.50
1946 High	15.9	3.58	2.49	16.1	3.55
1937 High	17.3	4.15	2.27	17.6	4.08
1929 High	19.4	3.23	4.95	19.0	3.10

And now compare them with the situation just before this bull market started in 1949. [See Table 5.]

These figures illustrate two important points. The first is that the ratios of price to dividends and to earnings are just about where they were at the top of the markets in 1946, 1937, 1929, and about 2.5 times what these ratios were 10 years ago. The second point is that the actual increase in earnings between 1949 and 1959 was very modest—only about 50 percent or less. During this period, the interest rate on highest grade points advanced from 2.65 percent to 4.55 percent, or about 75 percent. This means that if the proper rate of capitalization of current earnings should vary with long-term interest rates—a not implausible

TABLE 5

	Dow-Jones 30 Industrials			Standard-Poors 425 Industrials		
	Earnings	Dividends	Price	Earnings	Dividends	Price
Cal. Year 1949	23.54	12.79	Low 161	2.46	1.03	13.9
12 mos., Sept. 1959	35.14	20.00	High 678	3.50	1.92	65.3
Percent Increase	49	57	322	42	86	370

theory—then common stocks would actually be worth less now than in 1949, although they are selling four times as high.

The value situation is not as bad as that, however. On the other hand, we find that dividends have increased more than earnings, and have nearly doubled in the 10 years—at least for the Moody's and Standard indexes. Again, if we capitalize average earnings, say of the past 10 years', rather than the last 12 months' earnings, we would find an increase of about 120 percent between the 1940–1949 and the 1950–1959 decades. What is most important, perhaps, is that the 1947–1949 price level was clearly too low. But even making allowance for these three factors, the actual figures would probably not produce an increase of more than 100 percent in value from the 1949 year-end figures of 200 for the D-J Index.

If the rise of interest rates is not taken into account—and most of the valuation methods applied to the D-J Index do not do so—various techniques will produce, for the most part, higher figures. These figures cover a wide range, but they all have one thing in common: they are appreciably lower than the present market price. Let me summarize a few of the valuations referred to in the 1959 edition of *The Intelligent Investor*, which apply to the beginning of that year; Gerstein—383; Molodovsky—560; Value Line—471; Weston—600; Graham—365. Not all these methods have been applied consistently in the past—the high ones are definitely influenced by the new and more favorable attitude toward common stocks. I would estimate that the older valuation methods—i.e., those in use prior to 1955, let us say—would yield a current average figure of no more than 450, or one-third less than the present level.

Two of the large financial counsel firms have made valuations applicable to the year 1963—four years ahead of their valuation date. One found a value for the D-J of 664, the other of 634. These were based on rather optimistic assumptions of earnings growth in the next four years. If we assume that their conclusions are sound, we then should have to observe that the stock market is already paying a full price for the much better earnings and dividends expected in 1963. (Note that these 1963 valuations cannot properly be said to derive from past experience, in the manner of the other figures presented.)

This ends my presentation of the direct implications of past experience as applied to the current market level. My conclusions are not favorable. They would imply that the current bull market is repeating the excesses of the past bull markets and is destined to pay a penalty correspondingly severe. But now I must approach the second part of my review, and raise the companion question: "How relevant and useful is past experience as applied to the present situation?"

NEW ECONOMIC FACTORS

Most investors, businessmen, and economists are convinced that the business world we find ourselves in now is radically different and more favorable than that of the past. The improvement is of two kinds: First, the positive drive towards an expanding economy. This is powered by rising population, more research, more sustained capital investment, broader consumer spending, etc.—in other words, by a confident and aggressive attitude in all the important sectors of the economy. Then we have new defenses against recession, which will guarantee us more stability than in the past. These include the government's obligation to maintain high-level employment, assumed in the 1946 [Employment] Act, and the automatic built-in stabilizers, such as unemployment benefits, social security, farm supports. Two other factors—not as respectable as those just described—are also counted on by many to help maintain and expand the economy. One is price inflation, considered as beneficial to business if not overdone. The other is the Cold War, with the huge defense spending that it entails.

This array of favorable factors is most imposing, and it has captured the imagination of many, perhaps most, experienced economists. The case for very good business in the 1960s is made energetically in a current book, *New Forces in American Business,* by Dexter Keezer and the McGraw-Hill economics staff.

The optimism about business is no doubt the chief factor in producing the present optimism about the stock market. But here the factor of inflation plays a stronger and almost separate role. People tell themselves, on the one hand, that the inescapable inflation of the future guarantees ever-higher earnings and prices for common stocks—and, conversely, that if their funds are held in bonds or other cash equivalents their real value, in terms of purchasing power, will dwindle constantly. This combination of prospects for the 1960s—good business mixed with steady inflation—has produced a powerful stock market cocktail which the public—young and old, experienced and inexperienced—is finding intoxicating and most agreeable.

THE ROSY VIEW OF THE FUTURE

Now what can past experience tell us about the validity and dependability of this rosy view as to the future of business and common stocks? Its verdict cannot be conclusive, because no prediction—whether of a repetition of past patterns or of a complete break with past patterns— can be proved in advance to be right. Nevertheless, past experience does have some things to say that are at least relevant to our problem. The first is that optimism and confidence have always accompanied bull markets; they have grown as the bull market advanced, and they had to grow, otherwise the bull markets could not have continued to their dizzy levels—and they have been replaced by distrust and pessimism when the bull markets of the past collapsed.

As might be expected, the previous period of greatest enthusiasm about the economic prospects of the U.S. coincided with the tumultuous bull market of the late 1920s. Then, as now, nearly everyone was convinced that we had entered a New Era of continued and dynamic prosperity which made all past markets experience worse than useless. You all know that the phrase New Era became almost the official description of the American economy of 1928–1929. It is a bit ironical to note that today nearly everyone is again convinced that we have entered into a new era of sustained and dynamic prosperity, but also that everyone is careful not to use the words New Era, because they would remind us too uncomfortably of what happened in and after 1929.

In the 1920s, also, the new idea that good common stocks are intrinsically sounder than bonds gained ground rapidly. The financial services explained away the apparent dangers of stock yields below bond yields on the ground that the growth factor would eventually more than repay the stock buyer for his present sacrifice of income return.

Influence of Price Inflation

The factor of price inflation did not enter into the market of the 1920s, since the price level remained steady throughout. However, it did enter into the thinking of investors and speculators in 1936–1937; for between the June 1932 low and the March 1937 high, wholesale prices advanced about 90 percent. (This may be compared with an advance of just 19 percent between the 1949 low and the recent 1959 high). You may be interested to know that between 1901 and 1910, wholesale prices advanced steadily to a total of 17.5 percent—quite a bit more than in the 1950s. Nevertheless, in that decade, the market experienced two declines of about 50 percent each, and the rise to March 1937 was also followed by a decline of nearly 50 percent.

Past experience shows us two things about commodity price inflation as a stock market factor. First, inflation has existed most of the time in this century, and often at a much greater average rate than we have seen since 1949. But this has not prevented the stock market from falling disconcertingly after large advances. Secondly, the investor-speculator view as to the significance of inflation has varied greatly in this period. Paradoxically, three of the six *bear* markets since 1914 have been accompanied by *rising* wholesale prices—two of them very substantial. Arnold Bernhard in his recent book, *The Evaluation of Common Stocks*, points out that in the bear market lows of 1949, many financial experts were writing about inflation as an unfavorable factor for common stocks—this at a time when the price level had advanced nearly 40 percent in the three years 1946–1949.

The past record shows clearly that inflation has been chiefly a *subjective* stock market factor. It has exerted an important bullish influence only when wholesale prices and the stock market happened to be rising at the same time. Investors seem to forget about inflation when stocks turn definitely downward.

An arithmetical aspect of the inflation element was brought to my attention recently by William Miller, executive secretary of Town Hall. At current levels, tax-exempt bonds returned fully twice as much to most investors as representative common stocks, after allowing for income tax on the latter. The investor in tax-free bonds could accordingly set aside about 2 percent per annum out of his bond interest as a fund to take care of future inflation, and still remain in as good a net disposable-income position as he would with common stocks today.

There are some factors in our present economy which were not duplicated in previous bull markets. Most of you will think of the great advance in the popularity of common stocks—especially with pension funds and other institutional holders—as one of these new factors. There could be some doubt on this point; for the popularity of common stocks in 1929 may have been not very different from that of today. The New York Stock Exchange points to the approximate doubling of the number of shareholders—from six [million] to 12 million—as an indication of the greatly improved standing of common stocks; this, too, is a phenomenon characteristic of a long bull market. No doubt the number of holders had scored a similar advance in the bull market running from 1921 to 1929. In fact, Simon-pure experience suggests that the increase of small shareholders may be more of a danger than a strength for future stock markets.

INCREASED STABILITY

The factors I would recognize as new relate mainly to economic stability—as exemplified by the government's commitment under the Employment Act of 1946, the institution of unemployment insurance, old age pensions, and the like. There are few predictions I am willing to make—but one is that the intensity of future business recessions or depressions will be less than it has been in the past. And this is an important bullish factor.

Another new factor in today's balance sheet is the Cold War—a really unparalleled phenomenon in former times. My view—not held by many authorities—is that the Cold War has contributed a good deal on balance to stimulating our economy during the 1950s. To what extent it will continue in the 1960s is a matter of opinion; it is also a matter of opinion as to whether or not the related military expenditures will carry the same weight in the total economy as in the last decade.

POSSIBILITIES OF DECLINE

If the last two factors I have mentioned are both new and favorable to the business climate, it is proper to ask whether they also guarantee investors a favorable stock market experience indefinitely in the future—more specifically, whether they guarantee him against those market declines on the order of 40 percent or more which we have had so often in the past. The answer to this question even tentatively requires me to depart to some extent from consideration of past experience and to indulge in some more abstract reasoning. If business is to have more stability in the future than before 1950—as seems likely—then common stock earning and dividends should also be more stable. This, in turn, should entitle them to be valued more liberally than in the past, which means that a higher normal or central value for common stocks generally may well be more justified than would be indicated solely by past experiences. How much higher? If the D-J, judged solely by past experience, is worth 450 today, would it be worth 670 or more in the light of these new stabilizing factors? I don't know—and I don't think anyone else knows. My own guess is that under the bull market conditions of today, most financial experts would be inclined to answer yes—thus justifying the present level. But if the market should decline to 450, the same experts will persuade themselves that the old valuation relationships are still valid and that the new ones were only a bull-market mirage.

In support of this rather cynical opinion, let me refer once more to conditions in 1949 just before our great bull market started. The Employment Act was three years old, but it was completely ignored as a stabilizing factor—indeed, organized business was violently opposed to it. What is more to the point is the fact that, as recently as 10 years ago, the multipliers or valuation rate for stock earnings were the lowest for any three-year period in history since the Cowles records began in 1871, except for the World War I years 1916–1918, when everyone recognized the earnings to be temporary. Now let us see what one of the leading investment services said about the stock market in September 1949—just before the rise began—when confronted with the current price level of less than six times earnings. I summarize their remarks:

"Historically the price earnings ratio is extremely low. Stocks are intrinsically cheap. But the growing factor is public sentiment. Renewal of confidence is needed. Because of these problems, we have for some time recommended that a portion of investment funds be in the form of reserves." The last sentence is a professional way of expressing a generally bearish view on the stock market.

Now let us contrast this analysis of the record low price-earnings ratio of 1959 with the reaction of another leading service to the near-record high multipliers in 1959. This service lists the variations in these ratios from 1929 to 1959, and points out that "stocks are now in the upper reaches of the valuation scale." But then the report adds that business prospects are favorable for 1960, that earnings and dividends should rise further, and "they should support new market pushes." This service does not suggest that during future periods of strength, the investor should move away from stocks to a more balanced position between stocks and bonds. This is a mildly cautionary view, and certainly not to be criticized. But the point I do want to make is how weak and equivocal was the reaction of one service to the record-low price-earnings ratios in 1949 and of the other service to the record-high multipliers of today.

All my experience goes to show that most investment advisers take their opinions and measures of stock values from stock prices. In the stock market, value standards don't determine prices; prices determine value standards.

Let me return to the question of whether new economic conditions justify higher multipliers of earnings and dividends than in the past. Let me assume, as is likely, that the answer is yes. Would that fact assure the investor against a costly and discouraging bear market experience? It seems to me that this is most improbable. The central level of values will be raised, but the fluctuations around these levels may well be just as wide as in the past, in fact, one might expect even wider fluctuations. For since no one has any clear idea of just how the new central values are to be determined, it will be done by a process of trial and error in which speculative excess on the upside and undue pessimism on the downside may play an even greater part than in most market cycles of former years.

SPECULATIVE EXCESSES IN THE
CURRENT MARKET

In this connection, I arrive finally at a "law" about human nature that cannot be repealed and is unlikely to be modified to any great extent. This law says that people without experience or superior abilities may make a lot of money fast in the stock market, but they cannot keep what they make, and most of them will end up as net losers. (This is true even though the long-term trend of stock prices has been definitely upward.) This is a particular application of a much wider natural law, which may be stated simply as: "There is no such thing as a free lunch," that, for those too young to remember, was offered in the good old days to patrons of the corner saloon.

The stock market has undoubtedly reached the stage where there are many people interested in free lunches. The extraordinary price levels of stock of rather new companies in the electronics and similar fields, the spate of new common stock offerings of small enterprises at prices 25 or more times their average earnings and three times their net worth (with immediate price advances upon issuance), the completely unwarranted price discrepancies such as those established by speculators between the three issues of Studebaker-Packard—all indicate reckless elements in the present stock market picture which foretell serious trouble ahead, if past experience means anything at all.

Let me conclude with one of my favorite clichés—"The more it changes the more it's the same thing." I have always thought this motto applied to the stock market better than anywhere else. Now the really important part of this proverb is the phrase, "the more it changes." The economic world has changed radically and will change even more. Most people think now that the essential nature of the stock market has been undergoing a corresponding change. But if my cliché is sound—and a cliché's only excuse, I suppose, is that it *is* sound—then the stock market will continue to be essentially what it always was in the past—a place where a big bull market is inevitably followed by a big bear market. In other words, a place where today's free lunches are paid for doubly tomorrow. In the light of experience, I think the present level of the stock market is an extremely dangerous one.

Renaissance of Value

Rare Investment Opportunities Are Emerging

At a seminar held last week by the Institute of Chartered Financial Analysis, Benjamin Graham, author of several classic works on Wall Street and successful professional investor, spoke on "The Renaissance of Value." What follows is an excerpt from his talk.

The title of this seminar—"The Renaissance of Value"—implies that the concept of value had previously been in eclipse in Wall Street. This eclipse may be identified with the virtual disappearance of the once well-established distinction between investment and speculation. In the last decade, everyone became an investor—including buyers of stock options and odd-lot short-sellers. In my own thinking, the concept of value, along with that of margin of safety, has always lain at the heart of true investment, while price expectations have been at the center of speculation.

At this point let me consider briefly an approach with which we were closely identified when managing the Graham-Newman fund. This was the purchase of shares at less than their working-capital value. That gave such good results for us over a 40-year period of decision-making that we eventually denounced all other common-stock choices based on the usual valuation procedures, and concentrated on these sub-asset stocks. The "renaissance of value," which we are talking about today, involves the reappearance of this kind of investment opportunity. A Value Line publication last month listed 100 such issues in the

From *Barron's*, September 23, 1974. Reprinted by permission of *Barron's*, © 1974 Dow Jones & Company, Inc. All Rights Reserved Worldwide.

non-financial category. Their compilation suggests that there must be at least twice as many sub-working-capital choices in the *Standard & Poor's Monthly Stock Guide*. (However, don't waste $25 in sending for an advertised list of "1000 Stocks Priced at Less Than Working Capital." Those responsible inexcusably omitted to deduct the debt and preferred stock liabilities from the working capital in arriving at the amount available for the common.)

It seems no more than ordinary sense to conclude that if one can make up, say, a 30-stock portfolio of issues obtainable at less than working capital, and if these issues meet other value criteria, including the analysts' belief that the enterprise has reasonably good long-term prospects, why not limit one's selection to such issues and forget the more standard valuation methods and choices? I think the question is a logical one, but it raises various practical issues: How long will such "fire-sale stocks"—as Value Line called them—continue to be available; what would be the consequences if a large number of decision-makers began as of tomorrow to concentrate on that group; what should the analyst do when these are no longer available?

Such questions are actually related to broader aspects of the value approach, involving the availability of attractive investment opportunities if and when most investors and their advisers followed this doctrine.

Some interesting questions relating to intrinsic value versus market price are raised by the takeover bids that are now part of our daily financial fare. The most spectacular such event occurred a few weeks ago, when two large companies actively competed to buy a third, with the result that within a single month the price of ESB Inc. advanced from $17.50 to over $41. We have always considered the value of the business to a private owner as a significant element in appraising a stock issue. We now have a parallel figure for security analysts to think about: the price that might be offered for a given company by a would-be acquirer. In that respect, the ESB transaction and the Marcor one that followed it offer much encouragement to those who believe that the real value of most common stocks is well above their present market level.

There is another aspect of take-overs that I want to bring up here, on a somewhat personal basis, because it relates to an old and losing battle that I have long fought to make stockholders less sheeplike vis-à-vis their managements. You will recall that the first bid of INCO was termed a "hostile act" by the ESB management, who vowed to fight it tooth and nail. Several managements have recently asked stockholders to vote charter changes that would make such acquisitions more difficult to accomplish against their opposition—in other words, make it more difficult for stockholders to obtain an attractive price for their share. The stockholders, still sheeplike, generally approve such proposals. If this movement becomes widespread, it could really harm investors' interests. I hope that financial analysts will form a sound judgment about what is involved here and do what they can to dissuade stockholders from cutting their own throats in such a foolish and reckless fashion. This might well be a subject for the Financial Analysis Federation to discuss and take an official stand on.

There is at least a superficial similarity between the prices offered in takeovers and those formerly ruling in the market for the first-tier issues, as represented by "the favorite 50." The large institutions have acted somewhat in the role of conglomerates extending their empires by extravagant acquisitions. The P-E ratio of Avon Products averaged 55 in 1972, and reached 65 at the high of $140. This multiplier could not have been justified by any conservative valuation formulae. It was not made by speculators in a runaway bull market; it had the active or passive support of the institutions that have been large holders of Avon.

As I see it, institutions have been persuaded to pay outlandish multipliers for shares of the Avon type by a combination of three influences. First, the huge amounts of money they have to administer, most of which they decided to place in equities. Second, the comparatively small number of issues to which their operations were confined, in part because they had to choose multimillion-share companies for their block transactions, and partly by their insistence on high-growth prospects. The third influence was the cult of performance, especially in pension-fund management.

The arithmetic here is deceptively simple. If a company's earnings will increase 15 percent this year, and if the P-E ratio remains unchanged, then presto! the "investment" shows a 15 percent performance, plus the small dividend. If the P-E ratio advances—as it did for Avon in almost every year—the performance becomes that much better. These results are entirely independent of the price levels at which these issues are bought. Of course, in this fantasia, the institutions were pulling themselves up by their own bootstraps—something not hard to do in Wall Street, but impossible to maintain forever.

These institutional policies raise two implications of importance for financial analysts. First, what should a conservative analyst have done in the heady area and era of high-growth, high-multiplier companies? I must say mournfully that he would have to do the near-impossible— namely, turn his back on them and let them alone. The institutions themselves had gradually transformed these investment-type *companies* into speculative *stocks*. I repeat that the ordinary analyst cannot expect long-term satisfactory results in the field of speculative issues, whether they are speculative by the company's circumstances or by the high price levels at which they habitually sell.

My second implication is a positive one for the investing public and for the analyst who may advise a non-institutional clientele. We have many complaints that institutional dominance of the stock market has put the small investor at a disadvantage because he can't compete with the trust companies' huge resources, etc. The facts are quite the opposite. It may be that the institutions are better equipped than the individual to speculate in the market; I'm not competent to pass [judgment] on that. But I am convinced that an individual *investor* with sound principles, and soundly advised, can do distinctly better over the long pull than a large institution. Where the trust company may have to confine its operations to 300 concerns or less, the individual has up to 3,000 issues for his investigations and choice. Most true bargains are not available in large blocks; by this very fact the institutions are well-nigh eliminated as competitors of the bargain hunter.

Assuming all this is true, we must revert to the question we raised at the outset. How many financial analysts can earn a good living by locating undervalued issues and recommending them to individual investors? In all honesty I cannot say that there is room for 13,000 analysts, or a large proportion thereof, in this area of activity. But I can assert that the influx of analysts into the undervalued sphere in the past has never been so great as to cut down its profit possibilities through that kind of over-cultivation and over-competition. (The value analyst was more likely to suffer from loneliness.)

True, bargain issues have repeatedly become scarce in bull markets, but that was not because all the analysts became value-conscious, but because of the general upswing in prices. (Perhaps one could even have determined whether the market level was getting too high or too low by counting the number of issues selling below working-capital value. When such opportunities have virtually disappeared, past experience indicates that investors should have taken themselves out of the stock market and plunged up to their necks in U.S. Treasury bills.)

So far I have been talking about the virtues of the value approach as if I had never heard of such newer discoveries as "the random walk," "the efficient portfolios," the Beta coefficient, and others such. I have heard about them, and I want to talk first for a moment about Beta. This is a more or less useful measure of past price fluctuations of common stocks. What bothers me is that authorities now equate the Beta idea with the concept of "risk." Price variability yes; risk no. Real investment risk is measured not by the percent that a stock may decline in price in relation to the general market in a given period, but by the danger of a loss of quality and earning power through economic changes or deterioration in management.

In the five editions of *The Intelligent Investor*, I have used the example of A&P shares in 1936–1939 to illustrate the basic difference between fluctuations in price and changes in value. By contrast, in the last decade the price decline of A&P shares from $43 to $8 paralleled pretty well a corresponding loss of trade position, profitability, and intrinsic value. The idea of measuring investment risks by price fluctuations is repugnant to me, for the very reason that it confuses what the stock market says with what actually happens to the owners' stake in the business. . . .

The value approach has always been more dependable when applied to senior issues than to common stocks. Its particular purpose in bond analysis is to determine whether the enterprise has a fair value so comfortably in excess of its debt as to provide an adequate margin of safety. The standard calculation of interest coverage has much the same function. There is much work of truly professional caliber that analysts can do in the vast area of bonds and preferred stocks—and, to some degree also, in that of convertible issues. The field has become an increasingly important one, especially since all well-rounded portfolios should have their bond component.

Any security analyst worth his salt should be able to decide whether a given senior issue has enough statistically based protection to warrant its consideration for investment. This job has been neglected at times in the past 10 years—most glaringly in the case of the Penn-Central debt structure. It is an unforgivable blot on the record of our profession that the Penn-Central bonds were allowed to sell in 1968 at the same prices as good public-utility issues. An examination of that system's record in previous years—noting, inter alia, its peculiar accounting and the fact that it paid virtually no income taxes—would have clearly called for moving out of the bonds, to say nothing of the stock even at prices well below its high of $86.

We now have a situation in which all bonds sell at high yields, but many companies have an overextended debt position. Also, many of them do not seem to have sufficiently strong protective provisions in their bond indentures to prevent them from offering new debt in exchange for their own common stock. (A striking example is the current bond for stock operations of Caesar's World.) These widespread present maneuvers seem to me to be so many daggers thrust in the soft bodies of the poor creditors.

Thus security analysts could well advise a host of worthwhile switching in the bond field. Even in the Federal debt structure—where safety is not at issue—the multiplicity of indirect U.S. Government obligations of all sorts, including some tax-exempts, suggests many opportunities for investors to improve their yields. Similarly, we have seen many convertible issues selling at close to a parity price with the common; in the typical case, the senior issue has offered a higher yield than the junior shares. Thus a switch from the common stock into the senior issue in these cases would be a plain matter of common sense. (Examples: Studebaker-Worthington and Engelhard Industries preferred vs. common.)

Let me close with a few words of counsel from an 80-year-old veteran of many a bull and many a bear market. Do those things as an analyst that you know you can do well, and only those things. If you can really beat the market by charts, by astrology, or by some rare and valuable gift of your own, then that's the row you should hoe. If you're really good at picking the stocks most likely to succeed in the next 12 months, base your work on that endeavor. If you can foretell the next important development in the economy, or in technology, or in consumers' preferences, and gauge its consequences for various equity values, then concentrate on that particular activity. But in each case you must prove to yourself by honest, no-bluffing self-examination and by continuous testing of performance, that you have what it takes to produce worthwhile results.

If you believe—as I have always believed—that the value approach is inherently sound, workable, and profitable, then devote yourself to that principle. Stick to it, and don't be led astray by Wall Street's fashions, illusions, and its constant chase after the fast dollar. Let me emphasize that it does not take a genius or even a superior talent to be successful as a value analyst. What it needs is, first, reasonably good intelligence; second, sound principles of operation; third, and most important, firmness of character.

But whatever path you follow as financial analysts, hold on to your moral and intellectual integrity. Wall Street in the past decade fell far short of its once-praiseworthy ethical standards, to the great detriment of the public it serves and of the financial community itself. When I was in elementary school in this city, more than 70 years ago, we had to write various maxims in our copybooks. The first on the list was "Honesty is the best policy." It is still the best policy . . .

The Future
of Common Stocks

B efore I came down to Wall Street in 1914, the future of the stock
market had already been forecast—once and for all—in the famous
dictum of J. P. Morgan the elder: "It will fluctuate." It is a safe prediction for me to make that, in future years as in the past, common
stocks will advance too far and decline too far, and that investors, like
speculators—and institutions, like individuals—will have their periods
of enchantment and disenchantment with equities.

To support this prediction let me cite two watershed episodes—as
I shall call them—that occurred within my own financial experience.
The first goes back just 50 years, to 1924; it was the publication of
E. L. Smith's little book entitled, *Common Stocks as Long-Term Investments*. His study showed that, contrary to prevalent beliefs, equities as
a whole had proved much better purchases than bonds during the
preceding half century. It is generally held that these findings provided the theoretical and psychological justification for the ensuing
bull market of the 1920s. The Dow Jones Industrial Average (DJIA),
which stood at 90 in mid-1924, advanced to 381 by September 1929,
from which high estate it collapsed—as I remember only too well—to
an ignominious low of 41 in 1932.

On that date the market's level was the lowest it had registered for
more than 30 years. For both General Electric and for the Dow, the
highpoint of 1929 was not to be regained for 25 years.

Here was a striking example of the calamity that can ensue when
reasoning that is entirely sound when applied to past conditions is

blindly followed long after the relevant conditions have changed. What was true of the attractiveness of equity investments when the Dow stood at 90 was doubtful when the level had advanced to 200 and was completely untrue at 300 or higher.

The second episode—historical in my thinking—occurred towards the end of the market's long recovery from the 1929 to 1932 debacle. It was the report of the Federal Reserve in 1948 on the public's attitude toward common stocks. In that year the Dow sold as low as 165 or seven times earnings, while AAA bonds returned only 2.82 percent. Nevertheless, over 90 percent of those canvassed were opposed to buying equities—about half because they thought them too risky and half because of unfamiliarity. Of course this was just the moment before common stocks were to begin the greatest upward movement in market history—which was to carry the Dow from 165 to 1050 last year. What better illustration can one wish of the age-old truth that the public's attitudes in matters of finance are completely untrustworthy as guides to investment policy? This may easily prove as true in 1974 as it was in 1948.

I think the future of equities will be roughly the same as their past; in particular, common stock purchases will prove satisfactory when made at appropriate price levels. It may be objected that that is far too cursory and superficial a conclusion; that it fails to take into account the new factors and problems that have entered the economic picture in recent years—especially those of inflation, unprecedentedly high interest rates, the energy crisis, the ecology-pollution mess, and even the movement towards less consumption and zero growth. Perhaps I should add to my list the widespread public mistrust of Wall Street as a whole, engendered by its well-nigh scandalous behavior during recent years in the areas of ethics, financial practices of all sorts, and plain business sense.

Of course these elements—mainly unfavorable to the future values of common stocks—should be taken into account in the formulation of today's investments policies. But it is absurd to conclude from them that from now on common stocks will be undesirable investments no matter how low their price level may fall.

The real question is the same as it has always been in the past, namely: Is this a desirable time or price level to make equity purchases?

We should divide that question, I think, into the following: (a) Is this a desirable level to buy stocks in general, as represented by the DJIA or Standard & Poor's 500? (b) Even if the averages may not be at an attractive level, can investors expect satisfactory results by choosing individual issues that are undoubtedly worth at least what they are selling for?

The distinction I have just made is clearly relevant to the present situation because of the recent advent of the "two-tiered market," resulting from the massive preference of institutions for large, high-growth companies. This in turn has brought about disparities in the P/E ratios for issues of investment character—differences as high as 10 to one—that have been unexampled in all my experience, except perhaps at the height of the 1929 madness with its celebrated blue-chip issues.

My own answer to the double question just posed is as follows: As to the present level of the averages—say, 850 for the Dow and 93 for the S&P 500—the factor most directly affecting current security values and prices is most assuredly the high rate of interest now established for the entire spectrum of bond and note issues. One of the glaring defects of institutional attitudes has been that as recently as early 1973—when they supported the record price level of the averages—they failed to take into account that AAA bonds were then yielding 7.3 percent and had been above 8.5 percent not long before. (As it happened they were destined to surpass the 8.5 percent rate in 1974.) In 1964 the AAA rate averaged 4.4 percent. It seems logical to me that the earning/price ratio of stocks generally should bear a relationship to bond-interest rates. If this thesis is accepted in its simplest form, we must conclude: If $1 of Dow earnings was worth $17 when bond yields were 4.4 percent, that $1 is now worth only 52 percent of $17, or $8.80, with AAA bonds at 8.5 percent. This in turn would suggest a currently justified multiplier of, say, nine for the normal current earnings of the Dow. If you place those earnings at the record 1973 figure of $86, you arrive at a current valuation of only 775 for the DJIA. You may quarrel with this figure on various grounds. One may be your expectation that bond rates will fall in the future. But that prospect is far from certain, while the present 8.5 percent rate is a fact. Also, if bond yields go down appreciably, then bond prices—especially of the low-coupon, large-discount issues—will advance as well as stocks. Hence such bonds could still work out better than the Dow if and when interest rates decline.

Viewing the matter from another angle, I should want the Dow or Standard and Poor's to return an earnings yield of at least four-thirds that on AAA bonds to give them competitive attractiveness with bond investments. This would mean an earnings yield of 11 percent, and it brings us smack back to the valuation of about 775 for the Dow that we found by comparing the early 1974 situation with that 10 years before.

Furthermore, my calculations of growth rates over the past 25 years give an annual figure for the Dow of only 4.5 percent. If this rate were to continue in the future, the expectable combination of growth plus dividends would produce less than a 10 percent overall return, consisting of 4.5 percent growth plus a compounded dividend yield of, say, 5 percent. This second calculation would make my current 775 valuation for the Dow appear overgenerous. Incidentally, a corresponding approach to the S&P 500 Index gives a somewhat less favorable result than for the Dow at current levels. The S&P 425 and 500 indexes have both grown at about a 5 percent rate over the past 25 years. But this advantage appears to be offset by their higher P/E ratios compared with the DJIA.

Selecting Individual Common Stocks

When we come to valuing individual stocks I should like to divide them into three classes, as I find them in the NYSE list. Group I is the growth issues selling at more than 20 times their last 12 months' earnings. Group II is the relatively unpopular stocks selling for less than seven times recent earnings—i.e., at 15 percent earnings yield or better. Group III has multipliers between 7 and 20.

In my count of 1,530 NYSE issues, there were 63, or 4 percent of the total, selling above 20 times earnings, of which 24 passed the 30 times mark. By contrast, more than 500—over a third—sold below seven times earnings, and of these about 150—say, 1 percent of the total— were quoted under five times the last 12 months' profits.

If the earnings on which these multipliers are based can be counted on, more or less, in the future—without any special requirements as to growth—it is evident that many NYSE issues can now compete in attractiveness with bonds at 8.5 percent. In this large area of choice there are many that would be suitable for pension fund investment; many indeed that may be regarded as definitely undervalued. These are especially suited for longer-term commitments as distinguished from short-term speculative purchase. Among the under seven-times-earnings list are huge concerns like Firestone (with $3 billion of sales) and intermediate-sized enterprises like Emhart, which has paid dividends for 72 years and recently sold under its net current asset value.

THE BOOK VALUE APPROACH

The developments that have produced these extraordinarily low multipliers for so many NYSE (and other) issues now present us with another phenomenon—namely, the reestablishment of book value, or net worth, as a point of departure and possible guide to the selection of common stocks. In a large area of the present stock market we could return to a very old-fashioned but nonetheless useful criterion for equity investment—namely, the value of the company as a private enterprise to a private owner, irrespective of market quotations for the shares. If the business has been prosperous, and is at least reasonably promising for the future, it should be worth its net asset value; hence an opportunity to buy an interest therein at a substantial discount from net worth could be considered attractive.

As it happens, about half the NYSE companies were selling last month at less than book value, and about one-quarter, or about 400 issues, at less than two-thirds of net worth. What is equally interesting is that about one-third of all common stocks actually sold both *above* and *below* their net worth in the past 12 months. Certainly more than half fluctuated around this figure in the last five years. For the most part, these issues selling below book are also in the low multiplier group.

I may be so bold as to suggest that this situation makes possible a quite simple approach to equity investment that is open to almost everyone from the small investor to the quite large pension fund manager. This is the idea of buying *selected* common stocks—those meeting additional criteria of financial strength, etc.—obtainable at two-thirds or less of book value, and holding them for sale at their net asset value—to show a non-spectacular but quite satisfactory 50 percent profit. We

cannot predict with assurance how this apparently too-simple investment program will work out in the future. But I can say that my studies
covering the period 1961 to 1974 show the presence of sufficient opportunities of this kind in most years, and also excellent overall results from
the assumed operations.

Since I spoke of three grouping of the NYSE list, I should now give
my views of Groups I and III. Those selling at intermediate multipliers
may present individual opportunities, but they have no special interest
for me as a category. But the first-tier, high-growth issues present a real
challenge to past experience. Obviously they would be wonderful private or market-type investments if obtainable at book value or even
twice that figure. The trouble is, of course, that most of them sell at
more than five times book value—and some more than 10 times. Last
year the ratios were a good deal higher than that. At these levels, they
take on a *speculative character* which is due entirely to their price level,
and in no sense to any weakness of the companies themselves. (I made
this point as long ago as 1958 in an address before the Financial Analysts
Federation; it is reproduced as an Appendix to *The Intelligent Investor*.)
The speculative risks attached to high-growth stocks have been brought
home dramatically in the past 18 months by the price declines in many
of these favorites. (I need not give examples.)

However, I do want to use an instance here in connection with a
brief discussion of a recently launched academic theory about the stock
market, which could have great practical importance if it coincided
with reality. This is the hypothesis of the efficient market. In its extreme form it makes two declarations: (1) The price of nearly every
stock at nearly all times reflects whatever is knowable about the company's affairs; hence no consistent profits can be made by seeking out
and using additional information, including that held by insiders.
(2) Because the market has complete or at least adequate information
about each issue, the prices it registers are therefore "correct," "reasonable," or "appropriate." This would imply that it is fruitless, or at least
insufficiently rewarding, for security analysts to look for discrepancies
between price and value.

I have no particular quarrel with declaration one, though assuredly
there are times when a researcher may unearth significant information
about a stock, not generally known and reflected in the price. But I deny

emphatically that because the market has all the information it needs to establish a correct price the prices it actually registers are in fact correct. Take as my example a fine company such as Avon Products. How can it make sense to say that its price of $140 was "correct" in 1973 and that its price of $32 was also "correct" in 1974? Could anything have happened—outside of stock-market psychology—to reduce the value of that enterprise by 77 percent or nearly $6 billion? The market may have had all the information it needed about Avon; what it has lacked is the right kind of judgment in evaluating its knowledge.

Descartes summed up the matter more than three centuries ago, when he wrote in his *Discours de la Méthode*: "Ce n'est pas assez d'avoir l'esprit bon, mais le principal est de l'appiquer bien." In English: "It is not enough to have a good intelligence"—and I add, "enough information"—"the principal thing is to apply it well."

I can assure the reader that among the 500-odd NYSE issues selling below seven times earnings today, there are plenty to be found for which the prices are not "correct" ones, in any meaningful sense of the term. They are clearly worth more than their current selling prices, and any security analyst worth his salt should be able to make up an attractive portfolio out of this universe.

INFLATION AND INVESTMENT POLICY

Let us turn now to inflation. Do the prospects of continued inflation make equity purchases undesirable at present market prices or indeed at any conceivable level? It is passing strange that this question should even suggest itself. It seems only yesterday that everyone was saying that stocks, even at high prices, were definitely preferable to bonds because equities carried an important measure of protection against future inflation.

But it should be admitted that not only recently, but for many years and perhaps decades past, equities as a whole have failed to provide the protection against inflation that was expected from them. I refer to the natural surmise that a higher general price level would produce a higher value for business assets and hence correspondingly higher profit rates in relation to original costs. This has not been borne out by the statistics.

The rate of return on book equities as a whole—much understated as they must be in terms of reproduction costs—has at best held constant at around the 10 to 12 level. If anything, it has declined from the 1948 to 1953 period when the Dow was selling at only seven times earnings.

It is true of course that the earnings on the DJIA and the S&P 425 Industrials have tripled from 1947–1951 to 1969–1973. But in the same period the book value of both indexes has quadrupled. Hence we may say that all the increase in post-war earnings may be ascribed to the simple building up of net worth by the reinvestment of undistributed profits, and none of it to the more than doubling of the general price level in those 28 years. In other words, inflation as such has not helped common-stock earnings.

This is a good reason—and there are others—not to be enthusiastic about equities at every market level. This caution is part of my long-held investment philosophy. But what about the current situation? Should inflation prospects dissuade an investor from buying strong companies on a 15 percent earnings return? My answer would be "no."

What are the investors' real choices—whether as an institution or as an individual? He can elect to keep his money in short-term obligations, at a good yield, expecting that future inflation will eventually produce lower market levels for all kinds of stocks, including those with low multipliers. This choice would be justified when the investor is convinced that stocks are selling above their true value, but otherwise it is only a kind of bet on future market movements. Or he may conceivably decide on an entirely new sort of investment policy—namely, to move from stocks or bonds into things: real estate, gold, commodities, valuable pictures, and the like. Let me make three observations here.

The first is that it is impossible for any really large sums of money—say billions of dollars—to be invested in such tangibles, other than real property, without creating a huge advance in the price level, thus creating a typical speculative cycle ending in the inevitable crash. Secondly, this very type of hazard is already manifest to us in the real estate field, where numerous new ventures, financed through a combination of borrowing and quoted common-stock issues, have encountered problems of all sorts, including large stock-market losses for their investors.

My third observation is on the positive side. I think all investors should recognize the possibility—though not necessarily the probability—of future inflation at the recent 11 percent rate, or even higher, and should introduce what I shall call a "concrete-object factor" in their overall financial approach. By this I mean that they should not be content to have an overwhelming proportion of their wealth represented by paper money and its equivalents, such as bank deposits, bonds and receivables of all sorts. For the shorter or longer pull—who can really tell?—it may turn out to be wiser to have at least an indirect interest—via the common-stock portfolio—in such tangibles as land, buildings, machinery, and inventories. This is relatively easy to accomplish in the execution of an ordinary common-stock investment policy. My point is only that it would be worthwhile to introduce the concept as a specific and measured criterion in analyzing one's resources. That idea is as readily applicable to pension funds as to other portfolios.

It should be obvious from my overall approach to the future of equities that I do not consider such much-publicized problems as the energy crisis, environmental pressures, foreign exchange instability, etc. as central determinations of financial policy. They enter into the value-versus-price equation in the same general fashion as would any such other adverse factors as (1) a tendency towards lower profit margins, and (2) the higher debt burden and the higher interest rate thereon. Their weight for the future may be assessed by economists and security analysts, presumably with the same accuracy, or lack of it, as has characterized such predictive work in the past.

INSTITUTIONAL DOMINANCE, EFFICIENT MARKETS, AND THE PROSPECTS FOR SECURITY ANALYSIS

Is there an equity bias among money managers? My answer is that there has undoubtedly been such a bias in the past decade, and that it was a powerful force in establishing price levels for the stock market generally that were out of line with bond yields. It may well have contributed to these high yields themselves, for it deprived the bond market of billions of dollars that went instead into buying shares from former holders at advancing P/E rates. Since concern is now expressed about institutional disenchantment with equities, it may well be that the bias of recent years is not only rapidly disappearing but is being reversed and that it is now the function of real old timers like myself to caution against taking on an equally unjustified bias *against* stocks at low price levels.

What will be the effect on performance of having, say, $200 billion of institutional money in equities, plus, say 11,000 working security analysts, all trying to "beat the averages?" The reader will pardon a reference here to a couplet by Heinrich Heine à propos of the appointment of 45 German professors to some commission of inquiry 150 years ago. He wrote:

> Funf-und-vierzig Professoren
> Vaterland, du bist verloren!
>
> (Forty-five Professors
> Fatherland, you're ruined!)

If only 45 professors can present such a menace, how about 11,000 analysts?

Seriously, the effect of large-scale participation by institutions in the equity market, and the work of innumerable financial analysts striving to establish proper valuation for all sorts, should be to stabilize stock-market movements, i.e., in theory at least, to dampen the unjustified fluctuation in stock prices.

I must confess, however, that I have seen no such result flowing from the preponderant position of the institutions in market activity. The amplitude of price fluctuations has, if anything, been wider than before the institutions came into the market on a grand scale. What can be the reason? The only one I can give is that the institutions and their financial analysts have not shown any more prudence and vision than the general public; they seem to have succumbed to the same siren song—expressed chiefly in the cult of "performance." They, too, have largely put aside the once vital distinction between investment and speculation. (This leads me to ask whether some day soon we shall see some legal problems for certain banking institutions growing out of their accountability for the results of *trust* investments made from 1968 to 1973 that failed to meet the strict judicial requirements of the prudent man rule.)

Let me give a concrete example of my statement that institutional investment does not appear to have contributed either stability or rationality to stock prices—American Airlines. The *Standard & Poor's Monthly Stock Guide* shows the holdings of this and other concerns by about 2,000 insurance companies and investment funds, though not by banks and their trust departments. In 1970, the canvassed institutions owned 4.3 million shares of American Airlines, or 22 percent of the total. The company reported a deficit of $1.30 per share in 1970, then earnings of 13 cents in 1971 and a magnificent 20 cents in 1972. In response, our so-called efficient stock market advanced the price from a 1970 low of $13 to a new all-time high of $49.84 in 1972. This was 250 times that year's profits.

Now what did our financial institutions do to hold down this insane speculative binge in the shares? Did they sell out their holdings somewhere along the line, to cash in a profit and rid their portfolios of a clearly overvalued issue?

On the contrary. The guide showed that during this period they actually *increased* their ownership to 6.7 million shares, or by a full 50 percent, held by 143 companies. And the latest figures, in 1974, show that 117 funds etc. still owned 5.7 million shares or 20 percent of the total. (In the meantime the company reported a record deficit of $48 million in 1973, and price collapsed from $50 in 1972 to $7.50 in 1974.)

This story hardly suggests that the institutions have been valiant contributors to "efficient markets" and correct stock prices.

More and more institutions are likely to realize that they cannot expect better than market-average results from their equity portfolios unless they have the advantage of better-than-average financial and security analysts. Logically this should move some of the institutions towards accepting the S&P 500 results as the norm for expectable performance. In turn this might lead to using the S&P 500 or 425 lists as actual portfolios. If this proves true, clients may then find themselves questioning the standard fees most of them are paying financial institutions to handle these investments. (Incidentally, if my half-serious prophecy of a movement towards actual S&P Index portfolios is realized we should have an ironical return to a form of investment in equities that existed here 50 years ago. The first investment funds were actual trusts and fixed trusts at that. The portfolios were set up, on a once-and-for-all basis, from the very beginning. Changes could be made only under compulsory conditions.)

A modification of my fixed-fund suggestion would leave more leeway for the work of financial analysts. This modification would base equity portfolios initially on an actual or presumed imitation of the S&P Index, or—more simply—the DJIA. The operating manager or decision maker would be permitted to make substitutions in this list, but only on a persuasive showing that the issues substituted had distinctly more intrinsic value per dollar of price than the ones to be dropped. Combined with fairly heavy accountability for the results of such departures from the original list, such a program might well improve the actual performance. In any case it would give the financial analysts' profession something to do.

There has indeed been a strong intimation in this article that the DJIA and the S&P indexes are now selling too high in relation to many issues now purchasable at low P/E ratios. If this view is correct, any competent analyst has an excellent present opportunity to earn his pay by recommending desirable substitutes for certain companies in these averages.

Please bear in mind that while I have been making a case for equity investment now—despite, or perhaps because of, institutional disillusionment with them—I am not proposing a 100 percent stock position for any investor. On the contrary, I think that everyone's total portfolio should always have a minimum component of 25 percent in bonds, along with a complementary minimum holding of 25 percent in equities. The remaining half of the funds may be divided between the two, either on a standard 50–50 basis (adjusted to reflect changes caused by significant price movements) or in accordance with some consistent and conservative policy of increasing the bond proportion above 50 percent when bonds appear more attractive than equities, and vice versa when equities appear more attractive than bonds.

Do equities win by default because there is no assumed liquidity in other alternatives? There are various answers to this query. The first is, of course, that the alternative of putting funds into short- or longer-term debt obligations does not diminish the liquidity factor. Secondly, I could argue that liquidity is itself a minor desideratum in a true investment program, and that too many value considerations have been sacrificed to an assumed need for quick marketability. But thirdly, I could not say to what extent the liquidity factor should enter into consideration of non-income-producing objects—such as paintings, commodities, etc.—as alternatives to common stocks. My hunch is that the absence of income—as against 8.5 percent annually on bonds—should be more important here for your investment decisions than the liquidity factor.

AN INDEXED ECONOMY
AND A MANAGED ECONOMY

What are the implications of an "indexed economy"? I have already stated views of inflation's effect on equities. I feel that an indexed economy—in the full sense of Milton Friedman's recent proposal—is too impractical and remote to warrant serious discussion here. We have it in part in cost-of-living adjustments in union contracts, including to some degree pension plans. There was once an indexed bond issue, put out by Remington-Rand Corporation at the insistence of Irving Fisher (then a director), which varied the coupon payments with the cost-of-living index. Conceivably—though not probably—that idea may be revived. However, we have a growing number of debt obligations that vary the coupon rates with changes in current bond yields or bank lending rates. The floodgates seem to be opening here with the offering of $650 million of Citicorp floating rate notes due in 1989.

We have all become so familiar with a more or less managed economy since the Roosevelt era beginning 40 years ago, that we should be quite inured to its effect on everything including equities. Basically, the intervention of government in the economy has had two opposite effects on common stock values. It has benefitted them greatly through its virtual guarantee against the money panics and large-scale depressions of the pre-1935 decades. But it has hurt profits through the maze of restrictions and the numerous other burdens it has imposed on business operations. Up to now, the net effect seems to have been favorable to equity values—or at least to their prices. This can be seen at first glance by comparing the Dow or S&P Index lines on a chart before and after 1949. In such comparisons the price declines in 1969 to 1970 and 1973 to 1974 appear like minor downturns in a massive upward sweep.

Experience suggests therefore that the various threats to equities implied in the last question are not very different from other obstacles that common stocks have faced and surmounted in the past. My prediction is that stocks will surmount them in the future.

But I cannot leave my subject without alluding to another menace to equity values not touched on my terms of reference. This is the loss of public confidence in the financial community growing out of its own conduct in recent years. I insist that more damage has been done to stock values and to the future of equities from inside Wall Street than from outside Wall Street. Edward Gibbon and Oliver Goldsmith both wrote that, "History is little more than a register of the crimes, the follies and the misfortunes of mankind." This phrase applies to Wall Street history in the 1968 to 1973 period, but with more emphasis to be given to its crimes and follies than to its misfortunes.

I have not time even to list all the glaring categories of imprudent and inefficient business practice, of shabby and shoddy ethics perpetrated by financial houses and individuals, without the excuse of poverty or ignorance to palliate their misdemeanors. Just one incredible example: Did anyone ever hear of a whole industry almost going bankrupt because it was accepting more business than it could handle? That is what happened to our proud NYSE community in 1969, with their back-office mix ups, missing securities, etc. The abuses in the financial practice of many corporations during the same period paint the same melancholy picture.

It may take many years—and new legislation—for public confidence in Wall Street to be restored, and in the meantime stock prices may languish. But I should think the true investor would be pleased, rather than discouraged, at the prospect of investing his new savings on very satisfactory terms. To pension-fund managers, especially with large and annual increments to invest, the prospects are especially inviting. Could they have imagined five years ago that they would be able to buy AAA bonds on an 8 percent to 9 percent basis, and the shares of sound companies on a 15 percent or better earnings yield? The opportunities available today afford a more promising investment approach than the recent absurd idea of aiming at, say, 25 percent market appreciation by shifting equities among institutions at constantly higher price levels—a bootstrap operation if there ever was one.

Let me close with a quotation from Virgil, my favorite poet. It is inscribed beneath a large picture panel at the head of the grand staircase of the Department of Agriculture building in Washington. It reads: *O fortunate nimium . . . Agricolae!*

Virgil addressed this apostrophe to the Roman farmers of his day, but I shall direct it at the common-stock buyers of this and future years:

"Oh enviably fortunate investors, if only you realized your current advantages!"

PART THREE

About the Profession of Investing

We have no scoring system for security analysts, and hence no batting averages. Perhaps that is just as well. Yet it would be anomalous indeed if we were to devote our lives to making concrete recommendations to clients without being able to prove, either to them or to ourselves, whether we were right in any given case. The worth of a good analyst undoubtedly shows itself decisively over the years in the sum total results of his recommendations.

The Analysts Journal
First Quarter, 1946

When Ben Graham testified before the Fulbright Committee—the Senate Committee on Banking and Currency—his testimony provided rare insight into how Wall Street operated. Senator James W. Fulbright was frankly naive about the investment world, and he asked many of the questions that many of us would have liked to have the opportunity to ask Graham. In simple and direct language, Graham described what he and other professional investors do, how they do it, and what he personally thought of the process.

Whenever we catch Ben speaking (as opposed to writing) he catches fire. It's plain to see why he was such a popular teacher. And in his senate testimony, and in the other writings of this part, Graham delivered a revolutionary message for the day. He wanted the work of security analysis to have professional status, and he thought he knew how to achieve that.

Before Graham began his campaign for a training, testing, and credentialing program for financial analysts, the job of a security analyst was just that—a job. Graham knew the work required special skills, that it should have standards of performance and an ethics code, and until it did, it would never be fully respected. He worked tirelessly toward this end, and plenty of people opposed him. Today, thanks to Graham's perseverance and the hard work of many of his students, the shingle of Certified Financial Analyst (CFA) is displayed with justifiable pride.

Toward a Science
of Security Analysis

Proceedings, Fifth Annual Convention,
National Federation of Financial Analysts Societies

Messrs. Chairmen, members, ladies and gentlemen, the National Federation has conferred a signal honor upon me in assigning me this prominent place at the annual convention. In return, I should launch immediately into my sober and serious subject. However, I am afraid that neither you nor I are feeling very serious and sober at the moment. This western hospitality has become overwhelming. At the Dean Witter cocktail party I heard one of the ladies say to her husband, "Tom, don't you dare take another drink. Your face is beginning to blur already." (*Laughter*) But, as for me, I am in the position of the security analyst who boarded that special train in Chicago, carrying a Bible, and his friend said to him, "Jim, what are you doing with a Bible?" He said, "Well, our schedule calls for us to stop Saturday, May 15, at New Orleans. I have heard a lot about that city—the shows, women, liquor, and the gambling—it is going to be wonderful." His friend said: "What are you going to do with the Bible?" He replied, "If it is as good as they say it is, I may stay over Sunday." (*Laughter*)

Now, figuratively speaking, you all are staying over Sunday, for I am launching into my sermon, "Toward a Science of Security Analysis."

With this week's elaborate and enthusiastic proceedings one is tempted to say that security analysts and security analysis have finally come of age and are entering upon their full patrimony of dignity and power. But it is not my present purpose to compliment the societies on

---

their progress—impressive as it has been—but rather to summon you to deeper efforts and wider accomplishments. Since college days, I have carried as my favorite motto the words that Goethe put in the mouth of Orestes:

> The little done soon vanishes from the gaze that looks ahead and sees how much there remains to do.

My topic was chosen nearly a year ago, but it happens to coincide neatly with the theme of the last issue of *The Analysts Journal*, which was devoted to "The Effect of Science on Securities." There the emphasis was placed on what science is accomplishing for the various industries in which we invest. Our theme tonight seeks to carry the scientific concept into the processes and conclusions of security analysis itself. None of you, I am sure, expects me to expound a full-blown, completely articulated "science of security analysis." No—as my modest title suggests, you must be satisfied with a rapid survey of the field, with the raising of a number of questions which are left for the future and for yourselves to answer, and perhaps with a few constructive ideas that may assist my fellow workers in our fascinating vineyard. My apologies in advance for the absence of humor in this talk. In this field it seems impossible to be entertaining and reasonably scientific at the same time.

THE SCIENTIFIC METHODS

As H. D. Wolfe pointed out in his paper in the last journal (Science as a Trustworthy Tool), scientific method includes among its factors the wide observation and recording of events, the construction of rational and plausible theories or formulas, and their validation through the medium of reasonably dependable predictions. There are many varieties of scientific or quasi-scientific disciplines, and the character of the predictions based on them will vary greatly from one to another.

At one extreme take this microphone. An electrical engineer, having rigged it up carefully, can predict that a word spoken into it will be immediately amplified. The prediction is precise; the verification prompt and unquestionable. At the other extreme let us take psychoanalysis—a discipline sometimes compared with our own security analysis. Here prediction and verification are less definite. A layman who finances psychoanalytical treatment for one of his family is apt to be slightly in the dark about such details as the nature of the illness, the method and duration of the treatment, and the extent of the cure, if any. About the only thing he can predict with certainty is how much it will cost per hour. Between these two extremes lies actuarial science, which to my mind is more relevant than the others to the scientific possibilities of security analysis. The life insurance actuary makes predictions concerning mortality rates, the rate of earnings on invested reserves, and factors of expense and profit—in all instances based largely on carefully analyzed past experience, with allowance for trends and new factors. Out of these predictions, with the aid of mathematical techniques, he fashions suitable premium schedules for various types of insurance. What is most important for us about his work and his conclusions is that he deals not with individual cases but with the probable *aggregate result* of a large number of similar cases. Diversification is of the essence in actuarial science.

Thus our first practical question about "scientific security analysis" is whether it is actuarial in character, and has diversification as its essential ingredient. One plausible answer may be that diversification is essential for certain types and objectives of security analysis but not for others. Let us classify the things that security analysis tries to do and see how the element of diversification applies to each. At the same time we may raise other questions concerning the scientific methods and predictions operating in each of the classes.

I suggest that the end product of our work falls into four different categories, as follows:

1. The selection of safe securities, of the bond type.
2. The selection of undervalued securities.
3. The selection of growth securities, that is, common stocks that are expected to increase their earning power at considerably better than the average rate.
4. The selection of "near-term opportunities," that is, common stocks that have better-than-average prospects of price advance, within, say, the next 12 months.

This list does not include stock market analysis and predictions based thereon. Let me comment briefly on this point. If security analysis is to be scientific, it will have to be so in its own right and not by depending on market techniques. It is easy to dismiss this point completely by saying that, if market analysis is good, it doesn't need security analysis; and, if it isn't good, security analysis doesn't want *it*. But this may be too cavalier an attitude toward an area of activity that engages the interest of a host of reputable security analysts. That stock market analysis and security analysis combined may be able to do a *better* job than security analysis by itself is at least a conceivable proposition and perhaps a plausible one. But the burden is on those who would establish this thesis to demonstrate it to the rest of us in unequivocal and convincing fashion. Certainly the published record is far too meager, as yet, to warrant conceding a scientific standing to a combination of the two analyses.

FOUR CATEGORIES

To return to our four categories of security analysis. Choosing safe bonds and preferred stocks is certainly the most respectable if not the most exciting occupation of our guild. Not only has it major importance of its own, but also it can offer useful analogies and insights for other branches of our work. The emphasis of bond analysis is on past performance, tempered by a conservative view of future changes and dangers. Its chief reliance is on a margin of safety that grows out of a small ratio of debt to total real value of the enterprise. It requires broad diversification to assure a representative or average overall result. These viewpoints have made bond investment, as practiced by our financial institutions, a soundly scientific procedure. In fact, bond investment now appears to be almost a branch of actuarial science. There are interesting similarities (as well as differences) between insuring a man's life for $1,000 against a premium of $34 [*note*: this should probably be $35] per year, and lending $1,000 on a long-term bond also paying $35 per year. The calculated mortality rate for men aged 35 is about four out of a 1,000, or $4/10$ percent per year. A comparable "mortality rate" might be applied to corporate enterprises in the best financial and operating health, to estimate the risk attaching to high-grade bond investment. Such a figure, say a half percent, might then properly measure the risk and yield differential between the strongest corporate bonds and U.S. Government obligations.

BOND INVESTMENT
AS A SCIENTIFIC PROCEDURE

Bond investment should take on more of the character of a scientific procedure when the monumental corporate bond study, carried on by the National Bureau of Economic Research and other agencies, is finally completed and the mass of statistical data and findings is made available to security analysts. The greatest weakness of our profession, I have long believed, is our failure to provide really comprehensive records of the results of investments initiated or carried on by us under various principles and techniques. We have asked for unlimited statistics from others covering the results of their operations, but we have been more than backward in compiling fair and adequate statistics relating to the results of our own work. I shall have a suggestion to make on that point a little later.

SELECTION OF UNDERVALUED SECURITIES

The selection of undervalued securities appears next on my list because of its logical relationship to investment in safe bonds or preferred stocks. The margin-of-safety concept is the dominant one in both groups. A common stock is undervalued, typically, if the analyst can soundly establish that the enterprise as a whole is worth well above the market price of all its securities. There is a close analogy here with bond selection, which also requires an enterprise value well in excess of the debt. But the rewards for establishing that a common stock is undervalued are, of course, incomparably greater; for in the average case all or a good part of the margin of safety should eventually be realized as a profit to the buyer of a truly undervalued issue.

In this connection I want to throw out a broad and challenging idea—that from a scientific standpoint common stocks *as a whole* may be regarded as an essentially undervalued *security form*. This point grows out of the basic difference between individual risk and overall or group risk. People insist on a substantially higher dividend return and a still larger excess in earnings yield for common stocks than for bonds, because the risk of loss in the average *single* common stock issue is undoubtedly greater than in the average *single* bond. But the comparison has not been true historically of a *diversified group* of common stocks, since common stocks as a whole have had a well-defined upward bias or long-term upward movement. This in turn is readily explicable in terms of the country's growth, plus the steady reinvestment of undistributed profits, plus the strong net inflationary trend since the turn of the century.

FIRE AND CASUALTY RATES

The analogy here is with fire and casualty insurance rates. People pay about twice as much for fire insurance as their own actuarially determined exposure would indicate—because they cannot soundly afford to carry the individual risk themselves. For similar reasons the overall return on common stocks appears to have been at least twice as much as their true overall risk has required. An interesting relationship at this point appears from the Keystone chart showing the trend of the Dow Jones industrial average since 1899. Both the upper and lower lines happen to rise at the rate of one-third every 10 years. You will recognize this as the 2.90 percent rate of compound interest realized on U.S. Savings Bonds, Series E. What this means is the consistent Dow Jones investor has obtained the same increase in *principal value* as the savings bonds offer in lieu of interest; and in addition the Dow Jones stock investor has obtained all the annual dividends from his holdings as a bonus above the government bond interest rate.

The reasoning I have just indulged in is, I believe, both scientifically valid and psychologically dangerous. Its validity depends on the maintenance in the stock market of the substantial disparity between bond yields and the price-earnings ratios on stocks. If—as happened in the 1920s—this very thesis is twisted into the slogan that common stocks are attractive investments, regardless of how high they sell, then we would find ourselves beginning as scientists and ending as heedless and ill-starred gamblers. It may be a fair generalization to assert that the top levels of most "normal" bull markets are characterized by a tendency to equate stock risks with bond risks. These high valuations may indeed have some justification in pure theory, but the important thing for us to bear in mind as practicing analysts is that, when you pay full value for common stocks, you are in great danger of later appearing to have paid too much.

INDIVIDUAL UNDERVALUATIONS

Turning now to the field of *individual* undervaluations, we find ourselves on more familiar ground. Our work with this group readily admits of the scientific processes of wide observation and the testing out of predictions or hypotheses by their sequels. The theory of undervalued issues must necessarily require an explanation of their origin. The explanations are in truth quite varied and taken together from what may be called a "pathology of market prices." They range from obvious causes, such as an unduly low dividend or a temporary setback in earnings, to more subtle and special conditions such as too much common stock in the capital structure or even too much cash in the bank. In between lie numerous other causes such as the presence of important litigation, or the combination of two dissimilar businesses, or the use of the now discredited holding company setup.

ORIGINS OF UNDERVALUATIONS UNDERSTOOD

The origins of undervaluation are pretty well understood by now and could no doubt be set forth in an acceptably scientific study. We do not know as much about the cure of undervaluations. In what proportion of cases is the discrepancy corrected? How or why does the correction occur? How long does the process take? These questions remind us somewhat of those we raised about psychoanalysis at the outset. But one thing of importance we do know, and that is that the purchase of undervalued issues on a diversified basis does produce consistently profitable results. Thus we have a worthwhile field for more scientific cultivation. Here inductive studies carried on intelligently and systematically over a period of years are almost certain to be rewarding.

SELECTION OF GROWTH STOCKS

The third objective of security analysis is the selection of growth stocks. How scientific a procedure is this now, and how scientific can it be made to be? Here I enter difficult waters. Most growth companies are themselves tied in closely with technological progress; by choosing their shares the security analyst latches on, as it were, to the coattails of science. In the 40 or more plant inspections that are on your scheduled field trips for this convention week, no doubt your chief emphasis will be placed on new products and new process developments; and these in turn will strongly influence your conclusions about the long-pull prospects of the various companies. But in most instances this is primarily a *qualitative* approach. Can your work in this field be truly scientific unless it is solidly based on dependable *measurements*, that is, specific or minimum projections of future earnings, and a capitalization of such projected profits at a rate or multiplier that can be called reasonably conservative in the light of past experience? Can a definite *price* be put on future growth—below which the stock is a sound purchase, above which it is dear, or in any event speculative? What is the risk that the expected growth will fail to materialize? What is the risk of an important downward change in the market's evaluation of favorable prospects? A great deal of systematic study in this field is necessary before dependable answers to such questions will be forthcoming.

STOCK INVESTMENTS
IN THE PRE-SCIENTIFIC STAGE

In the meantime I cannot help but feel that growth stock investment is still in the pre-scientific stage. It is at the same time more fascinating and less precise than the selection of safe bonds or undervalued securities. In the growth stock field, the concept of margin of safety loses the clarity and the primacy it enjoys in those other two classes of security analysis. True, there is safety in growth, and some of us will go so far as to declare that there can be no real safety except in growth. But these sound to me more like slogans than scientifically formulated and verified propositions. Again, in the growth field the element of selectivity is so prominent as to place diversification in a secondary and perhaps dubious position. A case can be made for putting all your growth eggs in the one best or a relatively few best baskets. Thus in this branch of security analysis the actuarial element may be missing, and that circumstance undoubtedly militates against truly scientific procedures and results.

INVERTED RELATIONSHIP

There is undoubtedly an organic but inverted relationship between the growth stock concept and the theory of undervalued securities. The attraction of growth is like a tidal pull which causes high tides in one area, the assumed growth companies, and low tides in another area, the assumed nongrowth companies. We can measure, in a sense, scientifically the distorting effect of this influence by using as our standard the *minimum business value* of enterprises in the nonfavored group. By way of illustration let us apply that thought to three California concerns. The shares of Roos Brothers, a local retail enterprise, will in the nature of things tend to sell below their analytically determined value for basically the same reasons that are bound to produce overvaluations in the shares of Superior Oil or Kern County Land.

I come finally to the standard occupation of brokerage house analysts and advisory services, namely, the selection of issues favorably situated for a near-term market advance. The usual assumption here is that, if the earnings will improve or the dividend will be raised, then the price will improve. Thus the process consists essentially of locating and recommending those companies that are likely to increase their earnings or dividends in the near term. You all know the three basic hazards encountered in this work: that the expected improvement will not take place, that it is already discounted in the current price, that for some other reason or for no known reason the price will not move the way it should.

SEARCHING SELF-EVALUATION

This brings me to my conclusion and my one concrete proposal. Security analysis has now reached the stage where it is ready for a continuous and searching self-examination by the use of established statistical tools. We should collect the studies and recommendations of numerous analysts, classify them in accordance with their objectives (perhaps in the four groups suggested in this paper), and then do our best to evaluate their accuracy and success. The purpose of such a record would not be to show who is a good security analyst and who is a poor one, but rather to show what methods and approaches are sound and fruitful and which ones fail to meet the test of experience.

This suggestion was originally made in the article published under the pseudonym of Cogitator in *The Analyst Journal* six years ago. At that time I wrote: "It is unlikely that security analysis could develop professional stature in the absence of reasonably definite and plausible tests of the soundness of individual and group recommendations." The New York Society is now taking the first positive steps to establish a quasi-professional rating or title for security analysts who meet specified requirements. It is virtually certain that this movement will develop ultimately in full-fledged professional status for our calling. The time may well be ripe for the Federation and its constituent societies to begin a systematic accumulation of case histories, which should make possible the transmission of a continuous, ever-growing body of knowledge and technique from the analysts of the past to those of the future.

When this work is well under way security analysis may begin—modestly, but hopefully—to refer to itself as a scientific discipline.

Testimony Before the Committee on Banking and Currency, United States Senate

On Factors Affecting the Buying and Selling of Equity Securities

Eighty-Fourth Congress, First Session,
Friday, March 11, 1955

THE CHAIRMAN: The next witness is Mr. Benjamin Graham, chairman and president of Graham-Newman Corp., of New York. Mr. Graham, we are very happy to have you this morning and are looking forward to your testimony.

Would you care to read your statement or would you rather summarize it?

MR. GRAHAM: I would prefer to summarize it if I may.

THE CHAIRMAN: Fine.

MR. GRAHAM: But in the first place may I make a correction?

THE CHAIRMAN: Yes.

MR. GRAHAM: The correction is to the effect that I am not president of Graham-Newman Corp., but chairman of the board. I

From *Stock Market Study,* Extract from Hearings Before the Committee on Banking and Currency, United States Senate, Eighty-Fourth Congress, First Session, on Factors Affecting the Buying and Selling of Equity Securities, including the Statement of Benjamin Graham, Chairman of the Board, Graham-Newman Corp., New York, Friday, March 11, 1955, Washington, D.C.: U.S. Government Printing Office.

would like to add, if I may, I am also chairman of the Government Employees Insurance Co. of this city, which is a smaller but rather vigorous competitor of General Wood's Allstate Insurance Co., and we have paid Sears, Roebuck the compliment of patterning our profit-sharing plan very closely on theirs.

I have tried in the statement to deal with three factors: First, the question of the present level of stock prices from the standpoint of the relationship between price and value. Secondly, causes of the rise in the market since September 1953; and, thirdly, feasible methods of controlling excessive speculation in the future.

With respect to the present level of stock prices, my studies lead to the impression that leading industrial stocks are not basically overvalued, but they are definitely not cheap; and they are in danger of going over into an unduly high level.

I would like to add on this point, while I deal in my statement with leading industrial stocks, I am going to be criticized for not taking into account the fact that the stock market is made up of many hundreds of issues which have different price patterns. The fact remains in the last year or so the market pattern has been more uniform, I think, than it has been in most markets, and the level of advance in the market price has been fairly evenly distributed over all types of stocks—both the leaders and secondary issues.

With respect to the causes of the rise in the market since September 1953, my statement indicates I would emphasize very much the change in investment and speculative sentiment, more than any change in basic economic factors. I wanted to point out that that carries an element of danger because a change of sentiment for the better may be followed by change in sentiment for the worse.

Finally, in regard to the feasible methods of controlling excessive speculation in the future, I am in sympathy with the action of the Federal Reserve in increasing margin requirements as speculative activity increases.

I feel in general speculation on margin is expensive to the public, and is sound only when it is practiced by people who have a great deal of experience and a great deal of ability.

I also have an idea with respect to temporary modification of the capital-gains tax if it appears desirable to increase the supply of stocks for a temporary period of time.

I would rather answer questions from this point on instead of going into more detail about my statement.

THE CHAIRMAN: Thank you very much, Mr. Graham. In connection with your own company, does it invest in a representative sample of the best stocks in the market, or does it use some other guide for investment?

MR. GRAHAM: No. We have not been purchasing the market leaders. Our business has been something of a specialty business. We have emphasized the purchase of securities selling under intrinsic value, and have gone to what is generally known as a special situation.

THE CHAIRMAN: Would you describe that for us—for our information. You understand you are talking to a committee—at least the members who you notice are present now—who know very little about this. Would you tell us what specialty situations are and how you approach it? How do you determine whether a special situation is undervalued or not?

MR. GRAHAM: There is a slight distinction between an overvalued security as such, and a special situation. I shall try to make that distinction clear.

In the first place, with respect to a special situation as it is known in Wall Street. That is a security which upon study is believed to have a probability of increasing in value for reasons not related to the movement of stock prices in general, but related to some development in the company's affairs. That would be particularly a matter such as recapitalization and reorganization, merger and so forth.

For example, the typical example of the special situation is a company in trusteeship undergoing reorganization. Because of the fact that it is in trusteeship, the securities tend to sell at less than their intrinsic value. When the reorganization is completed, the proper value is established and there will normally be a profit in the purchase of such securities. There are other examples of that kind. The public utility breakups were a very interesting generic group of securities, because we had an underlying situation in which these holding companies, being in ill favor in general with the investing public, tended to sell at less than the value of their constituent companies, and when they were broken up the value of the constituent companies in the market greatly exceeded the value of the holding company shares.

With respect to undervalued securities in general, not special situations, that would be based upon a process of security analysis, which shows by a study of the company's balance sheet and income account that it is selling for considerably less than its intrinsic value, which in general can be defined as considerably less than the value of the company to a private owner.

THE CHAIRMAN: How do you evaluate management?

MR. GRAHAM: Management is one of the most important factors in the evaluation of a leading company and it has a great effect upon the market price of secondary companies. It does not necessarily control the value of the secondary companies for the long pull because if the management is comparatively poor there are forces at work which tend to improve the management and thereby improve the value of the company.

THE CHAIRMAN: When you go into special situations and buy large blocks, do you usually try to get control of the company

MR. GRAHAM: No; that is very exceptional. I would say out of about 400 companies that we may have invested in in the last few years, there would not be more than three or four in which we would have had any interest in acquiring control.

THE CHAIRMAN: You would have if you thought the management was bad, would you not? I mean that would be one of the principal elements in that case?

MR. GRAHAM: That could be a reason for our seeking control, hoping to improve the management situation.

THE CHAIRMAN: How do you go about acquiring large blocks without disturbing the market too much? Do you do it in your own name, or what is the procedure?

MR. GRAHAM: Well, there are two procedures. One is to acquire shares in the open market over a period of time. The other is by making a bid for a specified or unspecified number of shares, which is made public and which all stockholders have an opportunity to accept.

THE CHAIRMAN: What I mean is, I assume that you specialize in special situations. You analyze it and after considerable work, I take it, you decide that it is undervalued and it is a good special situation. You start buying in the market, and you reveal your interest and everyone knows what you are doing. I wondered how you proceed.

MR. GRAHAM: That could happen, but very often it does not. May I give you an example of that, Senator. In a book I wrote, *The Intelligent Investor*, I gave an example of an undervalued security, the Northern Pacific Railroad stock, which at the time of my first analysis sold at $20 and later went down to $14. We decided to buy a fair amount of stock. I should say that after reading the book once or twice I convinced myself the share should be bought. We went ahead and acquired about 50,000 shares of that stock in the market with comparatively little effect upon the price.

THE CHAIRMAN: Were there a lot of shares of that?

MR. GRAHAM: There were about 2.5 million shares altogether.

THE CHAIRMAN: That is a pretty big company.

MR. GRAHAM: Yes, indeed, but that was a large investment for us. But there are other instances in which, where companies are smaller, it is not equally feasible to acquire shares in the open market, and it might be desirable to make a bid or offer, as it is generally called, to acquire shares in some public way.

THE CHAIRMAN: You make no effort to conceal your interest in a special situation or to deal through trust companies or other accounts?

MR. GRAHAM: Well, in most of our purchases, the vast majority of them, we purchase shares the same way as anyone else would through brokerage houses, who act for us, and there is no concealment.

THE CHAIRMAN: To your knowledge are there many instances of concealment of the purchaser in acquisition of stock?

MR. GRAHAM: Well, you might say that virtually all of the companies that are acquired in the open market—I mean where control is acquired in the open market, in virtually all these cases there is some degree of concealment. That is to say, nobody publishes the fact that he and his group are acquiring control in the open market. It would obviously be unwise from a business point of view. Sometimes the news gets around, but it is generally unofficial. There have been a few instances, comparatively few, in which efforts are made to acquire control of a company generally through a reputable bank or trust company where the name of the purchaser is not revealed; in other cases it is revealed.

THE CHAIRMAN: We have had suggestions that this is done, and I was wondering what the process is and whether or not you do it or have done it. I wonder if you could describe for us the way you can acquire control without revealing your identity, not applicable to yourself necessarily. How would anyone do it?

MR. GRAHAM: Well, outside of the method of acquiring control in the open market, which as I said before is the more customary way, the other method would be to ask a bank or trust company to communicate to the stockholders an offer to buy the shares, generally at a price above the market, and state that the acquisition is being made for clients of the trust company, without giving their names.

THE CHAIRMAN: There is no requirement if a trust company purchases stock on the exchange to reveal the beneficial owners; is that right? They do not have to say "We are buying this for Mr. Jones or Mr. Smith?"

MR. GRAHAM: No, obviously not, sir.

THE CHAIRMAN: So that would be the usual way, simply to use an established firm which is in and out of the market, for your agent to purchase for you?

MR. GRAHAM: Yes. That would not be a trust company. Normally that would be a brokerage firm.

THE CHAIRMAN: Does a broker have to reveal who his principal is?

MR. GRAHAM: No. On the contrary, it is one of the basic principles of Wall Street that the relationship between the broker and the client is confidential and the name should not be revealed except to authorities who have a legitimate reason to ask for the information.

THE CHAIRMAN: Well, that is an important exception. What about a trust company? If the Chase National Bank purchases shares and they are asked by the president of the exchange whom they are buying for, do they tell him? Is it same as the broker?

MR. GRAHAM: The president of the New York Stock Exchange has no authority over anyone except members of the New York Stock Exchange.

THE CHAIRMAN: Well, then, there is a difference. As to the brokers, he has access to the beneficial owner, but he does not have as to the trust company. Is that right?

MR. GRAHAM: That would be true with respect to the president of the stock exchange, yes.

THE CHAIRMAN: Who would have control, the SEC?

MR. GRAHAM: As a reservation, I am not certain the constitution of the stock exchange gives the president the power to ask the brokers for the names of their clients or their dealings, but I assume that in the investigations that the stock exchange makes into its own dealings, including such things as manipulation and so forth, such information is asked for and given.

THE CHAIRMAN: I understood that with regard to the members for disciplinary purposes they have the right to inquire, but I would not be too certain about that.

MR. GRAHAM: I believe that is so, but I am not sure.

THE CHAIRMAN: When there is a battle for control of a company, the stockholders who intend to remain with the company would want to know whether they should participate in the battle or should sell out, and the identity of the purchaser would be important to them in such circumstances, would it not?

MR. GRAHAM: Well, if you are speaking of a battle for control in terms of a proxy battle, of course, the identity of the people who are endeavoring to obtain a majority of the votes by proxy solicitation is absolutely vital, and the proxy rules require that complete disclosure be made of the identity of such person. With respect to purchases of shares, however, that is an entirely different matter, and the theory of the stock market is that people are allowed to purchase shares anonymously. It will be a little embarrassing for many people if each time they bought or sold shares their identity would have to be revealed.

THE CHAIRMAN: Of course, it is not done customarily, but it is subject to being revealed in an investigation at any time, is it not?

MR. GRAHAM: As far as I know, the revelations of purchasers of shares have been limited pretty much to criminal activities. I do not recall cases in which the names of buyers have been revealed, even though they may be known to the authorities, merely because these people happen to have bought stock.

THE CHAIRMAN: Do you recall the Lawrence Portland Cement Co.? Did you make an attempt to gain control of that company?

MR. GRAHAM: Yes; in association with other people, who at that time, I believe, were either the largest or second-largest holders, we made a bid for a specified number of shares.

THE CHAIRMAN: How did that work out?

MR. GRAHAM: It did not succeed. The price advanced above our bid price, and consequently we did not get any quantity of stock.

THE CHAIRMAN: Do you think that was an instance of their having known that you were interested and having great respect for your judgment, and it went up before you could get control?

MR. GRAHAM: No. On the contrary, what happened was that the company itself went into the market and forced the price up above our bid price.

THE CHAIRMAN: Well. I do not know how it could have been otherwise. You could not have purchased that amount in open market, could you?

MR. GRAHAM: No, but we made a blanket offer to the stockholders to turn in their stock to us at a given price, which was above the market at the time the offer was made.

THE CHAIRMAN: What was your offer?

MR. GRAHAM: I think it was $26 a share.

THE CHAIRMAN: When was that?

MR. GRAHAM: Four years ago, perhaps.

THE CHAIRMAN: What is it selling for now?

MR. GRAHAM: I do not know.

THE CHAIRMAN: Has it been split?

MR. GRAHAM: It has advanced, and the name has been changed.

THE CHAIRMAN: What is the name of it now?

MR. GRAHAM: Dragon Portland Cement.

THE CHAIRMAN: I am told that, allowing for the split, it is now selling for $130 a share. That vindicates your judgment, does it not?

MR. GRAHAM: I wish we had been able to buy it; yes.

THE CHAIRMAN: Was it true that in that case you got no stock at all?

MR. GRAHAM: No; because our offer was a contingent offer. We made an offer to the stockholders to buy their share at a price above the then marker, provided a sufficient number of shares would be deposited. What happened then was, as I said before, that the officers of the company, not wishing this bid to succeed, went into the market and pushed the price of the stock above our price. As a result, people did not turn in any number of shares to speak of, and we dropped the whole thing.

THE CHAIRMAN: I am not sure—do you wish to discuss these individual cases or not?

MR. GRAHAM: Well, I have no strong feeling on the matter. I do not know to what extent it would be useful to the committee. If it is useful to the committee, I have no objection.

THE CHAIRMAN: I do not wish to embarrass you about it. I had understood that it was quite all right. The only purpose is that we have had a number of people here who have discussed general principles. None of them, I believe, were what we call active traders. I suppose that is what you are, is it not?

MR. GRAHAM: Well, we do not consider ourselves as traders in the ordinary sense. Technically you might call us that.

THE CHAIRMAN: What I was trying to do was to illustrate procedures that are followed by people actually in the market. If you do not care to be questioned about individual cases, I would not want to press the matter.

MR. GRAHAM: I have no sensitiveness on the subject at all. We are very proud of our achievements in our company.

THE CHAIRMAN: I thought maybe you were a little reluctant in the case of the Dragon Cement to discuss the details.

MR. GRAHAM: I am not a reluctant dragon, Senator, except I do not remember the details too well. I was not active personally in the matter.

THE CHAIRMAN: Can you think offhand of other similar examples of the intent to gain control?

MR. GRAHAM: You mean examples similar to the one made in Lawrence?

THE CHAIRMAN: Yes.

MR. GRAHAM: Well, there was one recently.

THE CHAIRMAN: What is that?

MR. GRAHAM: I am trying to remember the name. I remember that a trust company in Boston—

THE CHAIRMAN: The Atlantic Gulf and West Indies Steamship Co.?

MR. GRAHAM: No, that was a different situation. You are referring now to our own experience. The Atlantic Gulf and West Indies was quite a different situation. At that time we made an arrangement with the chief stockholder of that company to purchase, I think, the greater part of his holdings, and made a corresponding bid to everybody else to buy their shares at the same price, which was considerably above the market at the time we began our negotiations.

THE CHAIRMAN: Was that a negotiated sale you were trying to effect off the exchange, or was it a listed stock?

MR. GRAHAM: Yes, it was a listed stock. The negotiation was done with the large stockholder, and the rest was an offer extended to all the stockholders on the same terms.

THE CHAIRMAN: Was that negotiation directly with the stockholder?

MR. GRAHAM: That is correct.

THE CHAIRMAN: Did it succeed?

MR. GRAHAM: Yes, it did.

THE CHAIRMAN: You did not use an intermediary in that case?

MR. GRAHAM: No, that offer went over our name, I believe. The difference was this: At the time we had already arranged to buy a large amount of this stock, and we felt that, for one thing, that should be a matter of record and was made a matter of record.

THE CHAIRMAN: So that is an illustration of the successful way to purchase control of a company?

MR. GRAHAM: Yes. It is much more desirable to buy it by negotiation to begin with.

THE CHAIRMAN: Do you think there is any serious problem from the public's point of view with regard to the anonymous purchase of stock, especially with regard to gaining control of a company?

MR. GRAHAM: Senator, I have observed this thing for the last 40 years. I cannot think of a single instance in which the public has been hurt by offers to buy control whether the names were revealed or not revealed. In every such instance the public has been helped because they have been able to get a higher price for their shares than they would have been able to get if no such bid had been made.

THE CHAIRMAN: You see nothing wrong with the procedure? I am not arguing with you. I am only asking you.

MR. GRAHAM: I have had occasion to think about that matter for a long time, Senator, and it seems to me that the true arguments are all, from the public's standpoint, in favor of not preventing bids being made to the public at higher than the prices previously ruling.

THE CHAIRMAN: Is your company an open-end or closed-end company?

MR. GRAHAM: We are technically an open-end company, and practically a closed-end company. Let me explain that.

THE CHAIRMAN: I will be very happy for you to.

MR. GRAHAM: We are registered under the Investment Company Act of 1940 as an open-end company, which means that we are contractually obligated to repurchase shares at any time at the net asset value when presented to us. However, no such shares have been presented to us for a great many years. Our shares have sold consistently at well over their net asset value. Furthermore, we have not sold any shares of stock to the public at any time and have not increased our capitalization for many years, so that we operate actually as a closed-end company, namely, with a fixed capitalization.

THE CHAIRMAN: What is the capital? Are these trade secrets or not?

MR. GRAHAM: Not at all. They would not be a secret in any case, Senator, but as it happens our figures are made public. They are filed with the Securities and Exchange Commission. We have 5,000 shares of stock with a present asset value on the order of $1,100 a share and with a market price rather considerably above that.

THE CHAIRMAN: A market price above that?

MR. GRAHAM: That is right.

THE CHAIRMAN: But the shares sell very seldom, I understand?

MR. GRAHAM: That is true. There are very infrequent sales. Nonetheless, there are quite a number of them in the course of a year or two.

THE CHAIRMAN: When was your company started?

MR. GRAHAM: The company was incorporated in 1936, but it was a continuation of a business which was set up in 1926.

THE CHAIRMAN: To what do you attribute your great success in this business?

MR. GRAHAM: Well, Senator, that is assuming that we have made a great success.

THE CHAIRMAN: Would you not consider it a success?

MR. GRAHAM: I will admit that we think it is, but I did not want to be in the position of passing over your question as taking for granted that we have made a great success.

THE CHAIRMAN: I will take responsibility for saying you obviously have made a success.

MR. GRAHAM: I think our success is due to our having established sound principles of purchase and sale of securities, and having followed them consistently through all kinds of markets.

THE CHAIRMAN: I take it that ordinary members of the public cannot buy your shares; is that right?

MR. GRAHAM: Well, they cannot buy them in unlimited amounts, but they can buy them over the counter in small amounts.

THE CHAIRMAN: Are they quoted over the counter?

MR. GRAHAM: They are quoted over the counter; yes, sir.

THE CHAIRMAN: At what, $1,100?

MR. GRAHAM: I would say probably around $1,250 or $1,300 a share now.

THE CHAIRMAN: Above the asset value?

MR. GRAHAM: That is correct, sir.

THE CHAIRMAN: Is it customary for open-end companies to be selling above their asset value?

MR. GRAHAM: Well, it is unusual for any investment company to sell above its asset value, but there are a number of instances. The best-known instance is the Lehman Corp., which for a good part of the time sells above its asset value. That, however, is a closed-end company. It is impossible for an open-end company to sell at more than the selling premium over its asset value as long as it offers shares of stock to the public. That is obvious. In some instances a company like State Street Investment has followed a policy like ours and has not offered shares generally to the public, and the shares have sold at a premium.

THE CHAIRMAN: Do you personally control your company?

MR. GRAHAM: No; I am a comparatively small stockholder.

THE CHAIRMAN: You are?

MR. GRAHAM: Yes, sir.

THE CHAIRMAN: Does your family control it?

MR. GRAHAM: No. We have a comparatively small number of shares.

THE CHAIRMAN: Does any one family or person control it, or is it distributed rather evenly?

MR. GRAHAM: The shares are distributed fairly evenly. I would say there is a family with whom we have no relationship that represents the largest stockholding at the present time.

THE CHAIRMAN: If someone wishes to sell their shares, they still can demand what from you?

MR. GRAHAM: They can demand the net asset value.

THE CHAIRMAN: Which, of course, they do not do, because they can get more?

MR. GRAHAM: That is correct. We have not taken in any shares for many years.

THE CHAIRMAN: What inspired you to form an investment company? You did start this investment company; did you not?

MR. GRAHAM: Yes. May I say that I entered the brokerage business in 1914 and became a junior member of a stock-exchange firm, and in 1923 I believed that sound investing principles would be successful, and I started a private fund in 1923, which was changed around in 1926.

THE CHAIRMAN: What is a private fund?

MR. GRAHAM: A private fund would be one in which no offering was made to the general public through advertisements, circulars, or any other way, but merely to friends who were permitted or asked to contribute.

THE CHAIRMAN: How large was that company?

MR. GRAHAM: It was about a half million dollars at the beginning.

THE CHAIRMAN: Just you and your friends?

MR. GRAHAM: That is correct, sir. My own participation was very small. I had very little money.

THE CHAIRMAN: You started buying stock; is that right?

MR. GRAHAM: Stocks and bonds; yes.

THE CHAIRMAN: I would be interested, if you do not mind telling us, to have the history of this development.

MR. GRAHAM: Well, Senator, if you feel there is any value in this.

THE CHAIRMAN: There is, because we like to get some feel of how these trust companies develop. However, I do not wish to embarrass you. If you think it puts you at a disadvantage with competitors or anyone else, you do not have to.

MR. GRAHAM: No, Senator. I have been accused of telling all my secrets. I have written a number of books, and I reveal them all in these books.

THE CHAIRMAN: I was particularly interested to know what happened to you in 1932.

MR. GRAHAM: We had rough going.

THE CHAIRMAN: You first started at the beginning with a half million dollars. What happened then up until 1929?

MR. GRAHAM: We were quite successful, and the fund grew to $2.5 million at the beginning of 1929.

THE CHAIRMAN: In stocks, I take it?

MR. GRAHAM: In stocks and bonds.

THE CHAIRMAN: What did you do in 1929?

MR. GRAHAM: In 1929 we lost money.

THE CHAIRMAN: Well, a lot? Did you go down with the market or see it coming or what?

MR. GRAHAM: We did pretty well in 1929 alone, but the real difficulty we experienced in 1930 and 1931 when the market went much further downward than we had anticipated. We had pretty well anticipated the 1929 decline. And so our resources were shrunk pretty much. I do not think they shrank as much as General Woods' pension fund did, which he mentioned before, but they went down fairly low, and it was not until 1936 that a person who had been with us in 1929 and had held on would find himself even, but by 1936 he was even in our business.

THE CHAIRMAN: You said you changed. When did it become a registered investment company?

MR. GRAHAM: It became a registered investment company in 1941 after the passage of the Investment Company Act.

THE CHAIRMAN: What happened in 1936? Did not some change occur?

MR. GRAHAM: We incorporated, for a very peculiar reason. We had originally operated as a joint account, and the individual members reported on a partnership basis.

THE CHAIRMAN: Each participant in the fund?

MR. GRAHAM: That is correct, reported his share of the results. But before 1936 the Treasury claimed that we were an association taxable as a corporation, and we had considerable problems as to where we stood, whether we were or were not a corporation. So our counsel said, "You had better incorporate and settle this matter once and for all, because the Treasury will get you either way.

THE CHAIRMAN: This was the original group of friends; is that right?

MR. GRAHAM: That is correct.

THE CHAIRMAN: That is all that were in it in 1936?

MR. GRAHAM: There were accretions on a private basis. I had more friends in 1936 than I had in 1923.

THE CHAIRMAN: When did you make them, during the depression?

MR. GRAHAM: Not so many as afterward.

THE CHAIRMAN: Go ahead. You incorporated in 1936 and in 1941 you registered. When did you sell any stock to the public, or did you ever sell any? You have 5,000 shares, you say?

MR. GRAHAM: Yes. May I say that we originally had more shares, that is, we sold stock up to 50,000 shares with a nominal par value and stated value of $100 a share.

THE CHAIRMAN: When did you do that?

MR. GRAHAM: Well, we did that in series by offering rights primarily to our older stockholders, and that built our capital up to $5 million, consisting of 50,000 shares worth about $100 a share. But we discovered—this may interest you, Senator—that we were beginning to get a great many one-share stockholders, people we had never heard of who came in and invested a hundred-odd dollars and then got our reports and found out what we were doing and imitated it. So to deal with that situation we perpetrated a reverse split-up in which we issued 1 share for 10, increased the unit value in the market to about $1,200 or $1,300 a share, and from that time on we did not get quite so many one-share stockholders.

THE CHAIRMAN: What do you charge for managing the investment company? You are the manager of the company, is that right?

MR. GRAHAM: I am one of three managers. The other two managers are Mr. Jerome A. Newman, who has been a partner of mine since 1927, and his son, Mr. Howard A. Newman.

THE CHAIRMAN: Is it public knowledge what you charge?

MR. GRAHAM: Yes. We charge a great deal. We pay ourselves salaries on the order of $25,000 and $15,000, and we also have a profit-sharing plan under which after a $40-a-share dividend is earned and paid in any year the management as a whole receives 20 percent of the additional amount earned and paid.

THE CHAIRMAN: Are your earnings largely capital gains?

MR. GRAHAM: Yes; very largely capital gain. As a matter of fact, you might say they are almost exclusively so.

THE CHAIRMAN: I hope it is clear that if you do not wish to say, if it is a matter that you do not wish to discuss, particularly your own compensation, I am not trying to fish. That is just illustrative of what I assume is a typically successful man, and if you do not care to answer, I hope you will feel free to say so.

MR. GRAHAM: I would just like to make two remarks about that. In the first place, I have no hesitation whatever in telling you things that the investors in my fund know, obviously; but, secondly, I think it is a misconception to consider that we are typical managers of a successful firm. Our arrangement is very unusual.

THE CHAIRMAN: I want to clear up the misconception. That is exactly why you are here. Why is it not typical? I would like you to describe what is a typical situation.

MR. GRAHAM: The difference is first, that our compensation arrangement is much more liberal than that received by other investment funds. This 20 percent which we receive on excess earnings is a very large percentage.

THE CHAIRMAN: But that depends on what you pay. You said $40 a share, which struck me as a rather liberal dividend.

MR. GRAHAM: That is just the base dividend. We paid $340 a share last year.

THE CHAIRMAN: That is still better than General Motors paid.

MR. GRAHAM: Yes. I just want to make two things clear, sir. One is that our compensation arrangement is much more liberal in its terms than the standard arrangement. Secondly, we believe, and I think our stockholders believe, that we earn our compensation because our results to them after deducting compensation have been good.

THE CHAIRMAN: I assumed that or you would not be there. I was trying to get a picture of this business. You are helping us a great deal, I may say. Can you put it in a little different terms so that we can compare your situation with the managers of some of the well-known firms? I would appreciate it if you would put that in the record so that we will have it.

MR. GRAHAM: Oh, yes. The difference is tremendous between our own situation and that of a typical investment fund. Let us take the largest one, Massachusetts Investors Trust.

THE CHAIRMAN: Yes.

MR. GRAHAM: Their capital may be a hundred times ours. Their expenses are much less than a hundred times ours. Their expense burden is very little, percentagewise, as compared with ours. The trustees receive compensation on the order of maybe one-fourth of 1 percent on capital.

THE CHAIRMAN: Wait a minute. Of earnings or capital?

MR. GRAHAM: This would be capital.

THE CHAIRMAN: Per year? One-quarter of 1 percent?

MR. GRAHAM: No, I think I have overstated it. It might have been that much at one time. I think it is less now. As the capital grows the percentage of compensation to the trustees has diminished. Frankly speaking, I should not be talking about this because I do not know it well enough, but I do know in general that their rate of compensation is very conservative in relation to the funds that they handle.

THE CHAIRMAN: What percentage of the capital invested in your fund is represented by the compensation to management? Can you express it in terms that would be comparable? Would it be 1 percent?

MR. GRAHAM: Well, let us put it this way: Over a period of years we have tended to earn about 20 percent on capital per year before compensation and about 3 percent of that has been paid to management as compensation, leaving 17 percent to the stockholders.

THE CHAIRMAN: Three percent of the earnings?

MR. GRAHAM: No; 3 percent on capital out of the 20 percent earned on capital.

THE CHAIRMAN: I do not follow you there. You earn 20 percent on the invested capital per year; is that right?

MR. GRAHAM: That is roughly true on an average.

THE CHAIRMAN: What percentage of that 20 did you get as management?

MR. GRAHAM: We got about 15 percent, the reason being that there is a 4 percent deduction first.

THE CHAIRMAN: Fifteen percent of the 20 percent earned?

MR. GRAHAM: That is right.

THE CHAIRMAN: I see.

MR. GRAHAM: Not 15 percent of 20, leaving 5; but 15 percent of 20—

THE CHAIRMAN: Leaving 85 percent for the stockholders of the 20?

MR. GRAHAM: That is right.

THE CHAIRMAN: I understand that. Maybe this is a silly question and you never do it, but is it ever translated into a percentage of the capital invested per year?

MR. GRAHAM: Well, these figures I am giving you start with the percentage of capital invested.

THE CHAIRMAN: No, that is earnings.

MR. GRAHAM: Well, we earn 20 percent on capital. May I summarize once again. Taking that as a typical result on capital, the stockholders have gotten 17 percent on their capital and we have gotten an amount equivalent to three percent on their capital.

THE CHAIRMAN: I see, whereas the normal or average investment company, I take it, is less than 1 percent; is that right?

MR. GRAHAM: Yes, that is certainly true.

THE CHAIRMAN: You get three times as much as the average, or better?

MR. GRAHAM: That is true.

THE CHAIRMAN: Well, I take it you are worth it. You manage it more effectively than they do. Is that not correct?

MR. GRAHAM: Well, naturally we have to believe that, and our stockholders believe that.

THE CHAIRMAN: I take it you approach this whole business in quite a different way. Those big funds do not look for special situations. They go into the market and just buy the run of the mine, do they not—the blue chips and the bonds, and so on. Is that not correct?

MR. GRAHAM: Well, that is correct in a general way, but not completely. Some of the bigger funds, particularly like the Lehman Corp., which is a large fund, has always had a rather keen interest in special situations, and a certain amount of their capital—by no means the major amount—has gone into special situations.

THE CHAIRMAN: When you say "large," how large is Lehman?

MR. GRAHAM: Lehman would be over $100 million.

THE CHAIRMAN: Of invested capital?

MR. GRAHAM: At present market values.

THE CHAIRMAN: As compared to yours?

MR. GRAHAM: Ours is on the order of $6.5 million.

THE CHAIRMAN: On market value. That is not the original investment. That is the capital as now valued on the market; is that correct?

MR. GRAHAM: That is right. We have paid back to our stockholders virtually all the earnings that have been made, so that in a sense our present value is very similar to the amount of money paid in.

THE CHAIRMAN: You do not seek to increase the invested capital, I take it. Any particular reason for that?

MR. GRAHAM: The basic reason, Senator, has been that we have not believed that we could get the same satisfactory results on very large capital as we can get on a moderate amount of capital.

THE CHAIRMAN: Why is that?

MR. GRAHAM: Because if you deal with special situations and undervalued securities, the markets in those for the most part are not very large. It is not possible to acquire an unlimited amount without affecting the market price, and if we had 10 times as much capital it would be very difficult for us to invest it the same way as our present capital.

THE CHAIRMAN: I know some who have undervalued stocks down in Arkansas in my hometown who might talk to you about it.

MR. GRAHAM: We are always open to suggestions, Senator.

THE CHAIRMAN: There is no market for them. I believe you said in your statement that as far as whether the market is too high or too low right now, you could not say it is too high or too low. I take it that you think it is a period that requires caution, and you do not believe in jumping in and purchasing stocks?

MR. GRAHAM: Well, let us put it this way, Senator: Quantitatively the market seems to be about right, but qualitatively I consider it to be on the high side and getting into a dangerous situation.

THE CHAIRMAN: Well, that is, I think, a very understandable statement. That ought to be plain to anyone. If it is about right, that means it is not likely to go up or down? It is about on dead center?

MR. GRAHAM: On the contrary, Senator, it may be about right, but that is likely to be accidental. A year from now—pardon me, sir.

THE CHAIRMAN: I take it you meant the relationship between prices and earnings and income is at a figure that is not clearly undervalued or overvalued; is that right?

MR. GRAHAM: I would say that is true for the most representative stocks as a whole.

THE CHAIRMAN: There will always be exceptions both ways?

MR. GRAHAM: Yes, indeed.

THE CHAIRMAN: I am not trying to tell you, you understand. I am rephrasing it only for the purpose of trying to understand what you said. I haven't any idea about whether it is high or low. I am trying to put it in language so I could understand what I thought you said.

Did you notice the testimony of Mr. Galbraith the other day regarding the tendency of the market and speculators losing their relationship to reality, that the market generates enthusiasm all its own for capital gains? Did you notice that testimony?

MR. GRAHAM: Yes, indeed, sir.

THE CHAIRMAN: Would you agree with it?

MR. GRAHAM: Yes; I would agree with it in general terms.

THE CHAIRMAN: That is interesting, because he is purely an academic figure and you are a practical one, and yet this is one point upon which you agree.

MR. GRAHAM: I should say, Senator, that I am something of an academic man myself.

THE CHAIRMAN: I did not know that.

MR. GRAHAM: I have the title of adjunct professor of finance at Columbia University, and I give a course in the evaluation of common stocks.

THE CHAIRMAN: I saw you on television in an Ed Murrow show, but I did not understand that you were a professor. I thought they had brought you in as a practical operator to tell them how it was done. I misunderstood.

MR. GRAHAM: They made me a professor because I am a practical operator.

THE CHAIRMAN: That is very unusual, is it not?

MR. GRAHAM: Yes. The Columbia School of Business has about four or five such practicing professors.

THE CHAIRMAN: I see. I think that it is interesting that you agree that it is a dangerous element when the market becomes too overenthusiastic and loses, as Professor Galbraith says, contact with reality. You think there is a tendency to that at the present time?

MR. GRAHAM: Yes, there are some tendencies, undoubtedly.

THE CHAIRMAN: Then you would say, as he put it, I believe, that there is too much speculative activity in the market?

MR. GRAHAM: Well, "too much" is a difficult phrase to define. I think if the market continued pretty much as it has been doing now in regard to the total amount of speculative activity, I would not be too concerned about the outcome. I am afraid of the cumulative effect of more and more speculative activity.

THE CHAIRMAN: I am not sure that is different from the way he put it. I think he was careful to say he did not think the level of prices was too high, but that during the past year there had been too rapid a rise. That there had not been any developments in the business world, productivity or all the other things that would justify that rapid rise. It was the rapidity of the rise and the tendency to generate a sentiment, as he put it, of over enthusiasm that disturbed him. He recommended, as you know, an increase in the margin requirements. Would you recommend an increase in margin requirements?

MR. GRAHAM: I would like to duck the responsibility to this extent: I said in my statement that I feel the Federal Reserve should have no hesitation about increasing margin requirements further if it became increasingly concerned over the extent of speculation. I do not think it is necessary for me to make the decision for my friend Bill Martin, but I think the Federal Reserve has as good judgment as anyone in that connection.

THE CHAIRMAN: That is a proper answer. I see nothing wrong with that. It is not your responsibility. Some, though, have taken the position that it would be discriminatory and a bad thing to increase the margin requirements to 100 percent.

Do you think if the capital gains tax were eliminated and there was no tax upon capital gains that would increase the attractiveness of speculation or decrease it:

MR. GRAHAM: On the whole it would increase the attractiveness of speculation.

THE CHAIRMAN: If it did, that would tend to increase the level of prices; would it not?

MR. GRAHAM: That is my best judgment. It is true that there would be some unfreezing of shares now held by long-time owners, but my own feeling is that very likely the net result would be an increase in speculative enthusiasm.

THE CHAIRMAN: Is it fair to ask you now whether your own company—and you do not have to answer if you do not want to—is buying or selling stocks? You can be perfectly free to say you do not care to answer.

MR. GRAHAM: We have been selling on balance from our general portfolio of undervalued securities and endeavoring to put our money into special situations which are not at the risk of the market.

THE CHAIRMAN: Has it happened that in the past year or two you have made any particular study of any industry which is primarily dependent upon defense contracts for its business?

MR. GRAHAM: No; we have had no occasion to study them in any detail. We just have a general knowledge of the picture.

THE CHAIRMAN: Would you care to elaborate at all about your knowledge of the defense industry picture?

MR. GRAHAM: Well, it is common knowledge, of course, that the aircraft-manufacturing companies are largely dependent on the defense program.

THE CHAIRMAN: Would the fact that a company which is wholly dependent upon a defense contract had profits which increased in the last six months of 400 [percent to] 500 percent over the preceding year or similar period mean anything to you at all with regard to the Government's contracts with that company?

MR. GRAHAM: Senator, I did not state in my statement that I was chairman of the research committee of the War Contracts Price Adjustment Board during the war. That is the renegotiation board, and we had to consider principles of renegotiation, including the profits of aircraft-manufacturing concerns. The mere increase in profits as such is not an indication that the contracts are improvident, but there is a prima facie suggestion that they be examined into.

THE CHAIRMAN: Do you not think that 400 [percent to] 500 percent is a rather unusual increase in profits in the course of 12 months?

MR. GRAHAM: I do not recall any particular instances in which that ratio existed, but if it should exist I am sure the renegotiation people will study that with care.

THE CHAIRMAN: Do you think the Renegotiation Act ought to be reenacted? It expired, you know, at the end of December.

MR. GRAHAM: I am convinced that it should be, or something similar.

THE CHAIRMAN: The administration has not requested it, has it?

MR. GRAHAM: I am not part of the administration, Senator.

THE CHAIRMAN: I understand they did last weekend; yes. It was also in the State of the Union message. I had forgotten that. If nothing else happens in these hearings, maybe that is worthwhile. But you are in favor of the reenactment of that?

MR. GRAHAM: Yes, indeed.

THE CHAIRMAN: Would you mind commenting upon the situation which I notice recurs in many instances—there was a notable one this morning in the case of Du Pont, one of our big companies, and the same thing is true with General Motors—where so many of them have shown during 1954 a substantial increase in profits on a decreased volume. In some instances, of course, as we saw in the figures of General Motors, it was the difference in excess-profits tax, but I believe in many cases that plays a relatively minor part. What do you think is going on in our big industries that accounts for that?

MR. GRAHAM: Well, of course, the first point is what you have mentioned—that the good showing for 1954 earnings in the large companies (approximately equal to the 1953 earnings in the aggregate) is due to a considerable degree to the repeal of the excess-profits tax. To some extent it is also due to the fact that corporations, both large and small, have been getting somewhat better control over their costs in recent years. That I would say is more true actually in the case of the small companies than it is in the big ones, because the small companies suffered most from the costs getting out of hand.

THE CHAIRMAN: Would such a circumstance indicate a lack of competition?

MR. GRAHAM: I do not think so, because for one thing the margin of profit in and of itself is no larger now than it was in previous years. In the case of General Motors, for example, their profit margin last year, I think, after taxes was about 8.2 percent. I imagine that in 1936 it was probably around 14 percent to 15 percent after smaller taxes, but before taxes I would say the profit margin is approximately the same, maybe somewhat less now than it was in 1936.

THE CHAIRMAN: You do not see anything to criticize about General Motors carrying all of the reductions in taxes in profit rather than decreasing the prices?

MR. GRAHAM: My own view on that may seem peculiar to you, Senator, but I think that General Motors does not care to reduce its prices substantially because the effect on the competitive situation would be disastrous, and they would—

THE CHAIRMAN: Why?

MR. GRAHAM: Well, the point is this: General Motors has to make a very good profit in order that other automobile companies can exist at all. If it made a small profit, some of the other automobile companies would go out of business completely.

THE CHAIRMAN: Why do you want to subsidize these other automobile companies at the expense of the poor farmer, who is struggling along on a starvation diet now?

MR. GRAHAM: Senator, I did not suggest that.

THE CHAIRMAN: The prices for these Chevrolets are enormous. If they could cut them $800, it would help a lot.

MR. GRAHAM: I would like to make my point of view clear again. I am not expressing my own opinion as to what should or should not be done. I am only telling you what I think is General Motors' policy, and that General Motors itself cannot dare in the present state of the economy and the political sentiment to reduce its prices to a point where other companies were forced out of business and General Motors had almost a monopoly of the business.

THE CHAIRMAN: Well, in another way you are saying there is no competition in the automobile business; are you not?

MR. GRAHAM: No, sir, that is not true either, because in the first place the competition between General Motors and Ford is very keen, and the competition between General Motors and Chrysler used to be very keen and is now again becoming keen.

THE CHAIRMAN: To show you how innocent I am, I do not understand it at all. I always thought price happened to be the principal element in competition, that you could not have competition if you did not care what the price was, and that all the rest was shadow boxing and just make-believe. If you were really competitive and you desired to have the market, I had thought one of the first things to do was sell cheaper. That used to be the orthodox doctrine. This idea that the competition is just in advertising, to keep the price up, makes no sense to an old-fashioned man. It sounds exactly like the cartel system in Germany—"We split up the market and all take our part, and then we advertise and make people believe we are competing"—and there is no real competition. If General Motors really is competing and is desirous of obtaining the market, she would get it, would she not, by cutting the prices?

MR. GRAHAM: Well, Senator, my view of this thing may be wrong, but it differs quite a bit from yours. I think the competition that existed between General Motors and Chrysler, for example, was very intense, and its effect on Chrysler was almost disastrous. Chrysler lost virtually all its earning power last year, and although its business remained high in terms of dollars, it lost out on sales of cars to a point where the earnings almost disappeared and tremendous effort was necessary by Chrysler to improve its cars and to improve its selling practice. Now, that, as far as I can see, is more or less a classical example of the actual working of competition.

THE CHAIRMAN: I am afraid I gave a false impression. I am not now at least trying to express an opinion for or against it. I am trying to develop whether or not there is competition in the automobile field. I am unable to see that there is, in view of your statement that all General Motors needs to do to put them all out of business is lower the prices to where it could still get along and it would not go broke but it could break its competitors. In orthodox competitive business that is what happens, is it not? In the old days that is what happened, was it not?

MR. GRAHAM: Well—

THE CHAIRMAN: I do not say I disagree with you that would be a bad thing socially, and politically it is dangerous. That is a different thing from saying that it is really competitive. Do you really feel that it is competition or do you feel that it would be inadvisable to permit competitive forces to have their full sway?

MR. GRAHAM: Could I try to summarize my view by saying that I believe there is a great deal of competition in the automobile industry today, but it is not competition carried to its final conclusion, which would mean the destruction of the weaker companies.

THE CHAIRMAN: It is sort of superficial competition?

MR. GRAHAM: It is a limited-objective competition.

THE CHAIRMAN: Some of the bureaucrats, or somebody, developed a term called "administered prices." Is that not what it is? They sort of get together and decide if you go below a certain amount you will destroy Chrysler, and it is not wise to destroy Chrysler?

MR. GRAHAM: As long as you are speaking of economic principle, you must remember there is such a thing as the optimum or maximization of profits, and it is quite possible that General Motors by cutting its prices could do more business but at the same time earn less money. There is no reason in the world why General Motors as an ordinary business should not charge such prices as will give it maximum profits.

THE CHAIRMAN: If it ran them all out with a monopoly, they could charge what they like?

MR. GRAHAM: No, sir. The United States would interfere.

THE CHAIRMAN: That is what I am talking about. You are getting into a different field and leaving old-fashioned competition when you talk about interference by the government and what the social and political effects may be. I am not saying it is a good or bad thing. I have heard it said before and I was interested that you confirmed that General Motors could make a reasonable profit—I think that is the language—and still destroy all its competition because of the way it is set up and its efficiency, if you like that term, or at least its distribution and volume. I would gather you would agree with that?

MR. GRAHAM: I do not know that situation intimately, but I feel that probably that is so.

THE CHAIRMAN: I think it is important simply because as your economy changes these different aspects arise which do involve things beyond the immediate profits of a company. I think it would be a great catastrophe if all the other companies were put out of business. I would agree with you on that, but at the same time I do not like to kid myself that they are out there fighting for the business because they are not. General Motors could get it if it thought it wise to do it and still not really injure itself. Of course, its own personal advantage or disadvantage regardless of the nation would be another matter.

Mr. Graham, if you do not mind, our staff director would like to ask you a few questions.

MR. WALLACE: Mr. Graham, in buying a company do you confer with management and obtain information about the company which is not generally available?

MR. GRAHAM: Well, where the purchase was made by agreement with large stockholders who are part of the management, we would ordinarily get, say, a copy of the audit report and material of that kind which is not published, largely, I think, because it is just a matter of inconvenience to publish it. But I should add, in order to avoid a misconception, that I can think of no instance in which we have gotten any information of importance which had any effect on our judgment, which information was not given to the stockholders in connection with the offer to buy.

MR. WALLACE: To the degree that reports are published quarterly, you might get a report on earnings in between these reports, for example, which was not published?

MR. GRAHAM: Well, that is conceivable, a monthly report, but it would be very unusual if it had any effect. I might give you an example of that. When we made our offer to purchase the Atlantic Gulf and West Indies stock—and, incidentally, I might say the offer was made through the Manufacturers Trust Co.—we published, and I think, at the suggestion of the Securities and Exchange Commission, with whom we had discussed the matter before, a semi-annual balance sheet which had been supplied to us by management and had not been made public. It did not give any particular information of value, but it was published as a matter of general policy.

MR. WALLACE: In general, when you buy a block of stock, do the people from whom you buy the stock have the same information that you have?

MR. GRAHAM: As far as any important pieces of information are concerned, I would say yes.

MR. WALLACE: But if you were to buy stock on the open market on the basis of information that you had gotten in conferring with management, would this be considered trading on the basis of inside information?

MR. GRAHAM: No, sir; because, as I understand the interpretation of the rules, trading on inside information applies only to those who have a fiduciary relationship toward the stockholders, namely, officers, directors, and major stockholders.

MR. WALLACE: Is it not illegal for an officer of a corporation to divulge to you any inside information which is not available to the public?

MR. GRAHAM: I would like to clear that point up a little, because I am on both sides of that fence. I am an officer and director of a number of corporations, and I think it is worthwhile for the senators to get a realistic view of the way corporate affairs actually operate. A good deal of information from day to day and month to month naturally comes to the attention of directors and officers. It is not at all feasible to publish every day a report on the progress of the company in the newspapers or send out letters to the stockholders. On the other had, as a practical matter, there is no oath of secrecy imposed upon the officers or directors so that they cannot say anything about information that may come to their attention from week to week. The basic point involved is that where there is a matter of major importance it is generally felt that prompt disclosure should be made to all the stockholders so that nobody would get a substantial advantage in knowing that. But there are all degrees of importance, and it is very difficult to determine exactly what kind of information should or must be published and what kind should just go the usual grapevine route.

MR. WALLACE: Of course, the SEC Act itself makes it illegal for an officer of a corporation to trade on the basis of inside information himself. At least, if he does trade on the basis of inside information, the corporation or stockholders may sue to get his profits back?

MR. GRAHAM: Yes. That is defined in the law in relation to six-months' trades, and I imagine that there is a general idea of the law that it applies to any other kind of trade.

MR. WALLACE: Am I to understand that an officer of a corporation can reveal inside information which would enable a person to trade in stocks on the basis of such information which is not available to the public?

MR. GRAHAM: I believe you are right about that, Mr. Wallace, and it is an interesting area for consideration. It has given me a great deal of thought.

MR. WALLACE: I was going to ask you what your opinion was of the adequacy of the present law. As I understand it, in talking with Mr. Wood when he was here, of the National Association of Securities Dealers, he said that it was not illegal for a director of a corporation whose stock is not listed to do all the trading he wants on the basis of inside information. The question I am raising with you in the case of listed stock is trading on the basis of inside information, not by the director himself but by the director divulging information to someone else. For example, if there is consideration of a merger that is not generally known about, but the officer knows about it and he can tell whether the merger may come off, or on earnings reports he may be in a position to know the dividend will be higher than it was originally thought, or a stock dividend or a stock split, the officer is in a position to have inside information. He is prohibited from trading on a six-months' basis himself, but I would like to ask your opinion if you think the law should be tightened up with respect to his divulging information which is not available to the public generally.

MR. GRAHAM: Well, if a feasible method of tightening the law could be devised which would get that objective without countervailing disadvantages of many sorts, I would be for it. But my experience in these things makes me hesitate to endorse the idea because of gradations of knowledge between the mere beginning of a possibility of something and its finalization. That would be particularly true with respect to a merger. When a merger is only a gleam in a person's eye, it is undesirable, of course, to make any public statement of it. On the other hand, it is very difficult for people to be so discreet that not a word can leak out from anybody when somebody has sat down with somebody else, and from that earliest idea to the later point the gradations are so numerous that it seems very difficult to me to control the passing out of information by officers to other people.

MR. WALLACE: There are how many stockholders of publicly held corporations—between 6.5 million and 7.5 million?

MR. GRAHAM: That seemed to be the figure published by the stock exchange in its study.

MR. WALLACE: Is it your opinion that these 6.5 million or 7.5 million stockholders realize and understand that it is possible to trade on the basis of inside information which they do not have?

MR. GRAHAM: Some do and some do not. I think that the average experienced person would assume that some people are bound to know more about the company than he would, and possibly trade on the additional knowledge.

MR. WALLACE: Now, Mr. Graham, just for the record. You are an expert in this field. Could you explain some terms to us? Could you tell us what is meant by the term "profit taking"?

MR. GRAHAM: Well, profit taking is very simple. It means that people who have a paper profit in their share realize on their paper profit by selling, and the general inference is that there is some pressure on prices as a result of that which puts the market down when that happens. There is some profit taking going on all the time.

MR. WALLACE: Profit taking would have in general an effect of depressing the market slightly for a temporary period?

MR. GRAHAM: Well, profit taking as it is used in markets means there is enough profit taking to depress prices, because there is profit taking all the time in the market even while it is going up.

MR. WALLACE: Is that similar to a sell off?

MR. GRAHAM: Well, a sell off is simply a decline, presumably temporary, in the market, for any number of reasons. Profit taking may be the reason advanced, or a war scare, or something that happens in this committee room or anything else.

MR. WALLACE: Or a technical adjustment is another term?

MR. GRAHAM: The technical adjustment is very likely related to profit taking.

THE CHAIRMAN: You do not think anything we have been doing here has accounted for any fluctuations in the stock market, do you?

MR. GRAHAM: Yes, sir.

THE CHAIRMAN: You do?

MR. GRAHAM: I do, yes. I think that the market, being at a rather sensitive level, is subject to a vast number of influences which might put the market down or up, and among those influences are these hearings.

MR. WALLACE: Mr. Graham, one of the reasons I was discussing these questions is that the market reached a pretty high level on Friday last, did it not? The total market was pretty strong last Friday?

MR. GRAHAM: Yes.

MR. WALLACE: Over the weekend the President announced he was going to extend the Renegotiation Act, did he not?

MR. GRAHAM: Yes.

MR. WALLACE: The foreign picture was in the news considerably, was it not?

MR. GRAHAM: Well, I saw rather minor reference to it in the news.

MR. WALLACE: Then you have this tendency for profit taking, sell offs, technical adjustments, following on a relatively high market, do you not?

MR. GRAHAM: Yes.

MR. WALLACE: So that would you not say that all these factors entered into what happened to the market on Monday and Tuesday—all these factors had some bearing and you cannot really decide which one had the most bearing. But there are many, many factors influencing the market, including the feeling of the stockholder and whether his ulcers are acting up?

MR. GRAHAM: I agree with that, and I tried to convey that impression in my previous answer.

MR. WALLACE: This study then, has some effect on the market only as one of a great, great many factors?

MR. GRAHAM: I might leave out one of the "greats," but it is one of a number of factors.

MR. WALLACE: Thank you.

THE CHAIRMAN: I am impressed that they are taking notice that we are interested in and concerned with what goes on in the market. I do not see any reason why the study should necessarily put the market down. That is what everybody is blaming the committee for, or at least when I say "everybody" we received quite a large number of telegrams the other day—I guess 15 or 20—complaining bitterly that we were putting the market down, rocking the boat, and all that. You would not agree to that, would you?

MR. GRAHAM: No. I think I can say something that would be reassuring to you, Senator, and put it this way: If the study actually does put the market down, then the market was due to go down and should go down.

THE CHAIRMAN: That is a very fair observation, it seems to me. It is a mighty weak market that this hearing could put down, is it not?

MR. GRAHAM: I would agree on that.

THE CHAIRMAN: Now one or two things that have occurred to me. Did you notice Mr. Eccles' proposal yesterday on capital-gains tax? Was it brought to your attention?

MR. GRAHAM: I read it in this morning's paper.

THE CHAIRMAN: Does it appeal to you at all?

MR. GRAHAM: Yes. I had a proposal of my own. I guess all of us have proposals on this thing. I think Mr. Baruch will make one when he appears. We all have proposals. Mr. Eccles' proposal basically is, I think, a sound one, to differentiate more than the law now differentiates between various holding periods.

THE CHAIRMAN: Your proposal, I thought, was simply a temporary device and then, I assumed, a return to what we have?

MR. GRAHAM: Yes; that would be true.

THE CHAIRMAN: Which is certainly worthy of consideration. The effect is that if you hold it really a long time, beyond, say, five years—he was not dogmatic about the precise ending of it—that there would be no capital gains. Does that appeal to you?

MR. GRAHAM: On the whole it does, Senator. You may recall that a number of years ago we had a capital-gains tax of that type, and that the amount of the tax went down to about 10 percent, I think, on holdings between 5 and 10 years, and zero I think after 10 years. So these gradations are largely a matter of judgment, but I think the principle is sound. The theoretical objection to the capital-gains tax is that it is taxing something which does not appear anywhere in the national income or the gross national product, and so on. This theoretical objection could be met in part by this gradation.

THE CHAIRMAN: This is a rather technical question, but perhaps you can help us. While I realize it is difficult to generalize, would you give us your best estimate as to how much the market value of a dollar of retained earnings in comparison to a dollar of dividends paid—how much market value in dollars?

MR. GRAHAM: That takes a few sentences to answer. In the first place, I have made studies on that subject and have written on the subject, and in the past it was possible to show that a dollar of paid-out earnings had four times the value of a dollar of retained earnings in their effect on the market for the average stock, the exception being stocks that were bought mainly for their long-term prospects and were treated in the market in a separate category. I have a feeling, however, that we are now going through a transition period on the question of the weighting of dividends as against retained earnings. I think the transition is going on fairly rapidly. I cannot tell you just where we stand at this minute, but I will predict that in a few years from now the weight of retained earnings will be better, considerably better, than it had been as against distributed earnings.

THE CHAIRMAN: Is that not very largely influenced by the tax structure—the difference between capital gains and normal and surtax rates?

MR. GRAHAM: Well, no, sir; it has not been influenced in the past. On the contrary, the behavior of investors and speculators has been very illogical. In theory they should have preferred retained earnings by successful companies, because those earnings were subject to only one tax to begin with and ultimately only to a capital-gains tax in addition, whereas the distributed earnings were subject to two large taxes immediately. However, the ingrained desire of investors for dividends was so great that it has not yet adjusted itself to the facts of life in the tax structure. It is only beginning now to do so.

THE CHAIRMAN: I see. What you mean is they will slowly catch up?

MR. GRAHAM: They have been extremely slow, and I think extremely unintelligent.

THE CHAIRMAN: That is a very understandable statement. Incidentally, do you think that stock options are largely motivated by the desire to compensate directors by capital gains rather than salaries?

MR. GRAHAM: Well, sir, it is the desire to compensate officers by capital gains. There is no doubt about that at all. That is the admitted purpose of stock options.

THE CHAIRMAN: No, it is not admitted by some of the people that we have had on the stand. They say, "Oh, it is just to inspire loyalty. It has nothing to do with the retaining of earnings." You do not subscribe to that?

MR. GRAHAM: I do not, sir.

THE CHAIRMAN: I agree with your views quite often.

MR. GRAHAM: Senator, I have no intention of shaping my views with the expectation of your agreement.

THE CHAIRMAN: I did not accuse you of that. I was only impressed with your wisdom.

MR. GRAHAM: Thank you, Senator.

THE CHAIRMAN: I used to be a professor. Maybe that is my weakness. You noticed this morning that Sears, Roebuck has found a way to compensate the ordinary employees by capital gains, which I never realized before. Is that not the effect of that pension plan?

MR. GRAHAM: It is provided you have got a Sears, Roebuck type of company. If you had the ordinary company—let me add this, because this is very important. If you took the ordinary company at random on the New York Stock Exchange and tried to put in a Sears, Roebuck type of plan, not only would it be true that in the long run the returns would be comparatively small as against Sears, Roebuck, but I think it would be impossible to maintain such a plan because of the variations in results and in stock prices from year to year. The people just would not have the guts to keep up a plan of that kind in the ordinary company.

THE CHAIRMAN: Well, a company like General Motors could do it, could it not?

MR. GRAHAM: I think so, yes.

THE CHAIRMAN: Do you know whether other funds have this system of paying into a pension fund as much as 10 percent of their income before taxes as a compensation really to their employees, without paying the normal tax rate?

MR. GRAHAM: Well, the only difference is the 10 percent figure that you are mentioning. Ten percent is a fairly high figure, but it is by no means unexampled. I wish I could think of the other companies, but there have been instances I know of with more than 10 percent of the earnings going to a combination of executive and run-of-the-mine employee compensation.

THE CHAIRMAN: I do not believe the compensation to the executives was included in this morning's testimony.

MR. GRAHAM: The executives are part of this, but they are limited to this $500-a-year figure or whatever the maximum is.

THE CHAIRMAN: I meant in addition to that they have bonuses and stock options, which is in addition to the participation in the pension fund.

MR. GRAHAM: That is correct, sir.

THE CHAIRMAN: Which may result in an overall figure beyond 10 percent.

MR. GRAHAM: Yes.

THE CHAIRMAN: What do you think of that?

MR. GRAHAM: There are two parts to it. In the first place, I think it is a remarkably good device for establishing the proper relationship between the business and its employees and a fair treatment of profits. As I said at the beginning, we have a similar approach in our Government Employees Insurance Company, and it has worked out very well for us and our employees. The tax status, of course, is another matter. It is a very favorable tax status in these plans that the congress adopted, and I am sure knowing full well what the consequences would be with the intention of encouraging this kind of development in corporate business and in the position of corporate employees. I think personally even at the cost of some loss of revenue to the Treasury it would be very desirable to encourage this development of medium-size capitalists or, in any event, happy and prosperous employees at the end of their working career.

THE CHAIRMAN: I agree with you as far as you go. It is a fine thing if you look only at that. What do you say about these people who have no way of adjusting their income to capital gains and have to pay the straight tax? What is your answer to them? Do you say, "Well, it is too bad," or how do you justify one set of employees receiving compensation and paying only capital-gains rates and another set doing almost the same thing paying the other rate? If you were in my place and they blamed you for all governmental policies, what would you say to them?

MR. GRAHAM: I would say that what we are talking about is a marginal part of the total compensation of employees. The Sears, Roebuck case, of course, is not so marginal, because you have had this extraordinary success for the corporation itself. But if you take a typical corporation, which sets aside 10 percent of its earnings for this purpose, the amount of additional gains and income to the employees would represent not an inconsiderable part of their earnings, but at least a minor part of their earnings, and the tax advantage I should think should be accepted philosophically because of the desirable consequences that flow from it.

THE CHAIRMAN: Supposing they devoted 50 percent? Supposing they reduced everybody's wages and transferred that to a 50 percent payment into the fund. If you accept the principle, why could you not pay them all on a capital-gains basis?

MR. GRAHAM: No; the principle cannot be accepted to an unlimited application, and the present act, if I understand it correctly, imposes a limitation on that. The amounts which can be put to the benefit of employees in pension funds and profit-sharing funds I believe are limited to 15 percent of the compensation in each year.

THE CHAIRMAN: I wonder if you would give us your views in a broad sense about the economic future of the next few years. Do you see any culmination of a business cycle, or do you subscribe to this view that I read the other day of one of your colleagues in the investment field in New York that a final blowout is necessary?

MR. GRAHAM: Is not necessary?

THE CHAIRMAN: I read into the record an opinion that it always must come, that we have to have this final orgy of buying. I wonder if you would give us an idea of your views for the next few years. How has your mind been working?

MR. GRAHAM: I will do it with the proviso that these views should not be taken too seriously.

THE CHAIRMAN: I do not believe you are infallible.

MR. GRAHAM: As a matter of fact, I have never specialized in economic forecasting or market forecasting either. My own business has been largely based on the principle that if you can make your results independent of any views as to the future you are that much better off. Nevertheless, as an economist of a sort I have studied this question, and I will be glad to give you my view on the matter.

I think that in all probability we would have some economic recession of an appreciable amount, not necessarily a very serious amount, in the natural course of events, which means such things as the inventory situation, the consumer credit situation, the housing situation, capital goods situation, all of which tend on the whole to operate in cycles, and which on the whole could not be continued, in my opinion, indefinitely at the rate at which we see them developing right now. And of course I am now expressing merely the view of an experienced, conservative economist who expects history to repeat itself or the pattern of history to repeat itself.

You have an unknown factor, which is government intervention. The government, it seems to me, is committed now through both parties to intervene perhaps nationally to prevent any serious decline in the business activity which is accompanied by substantial unemployment. I might say that you could have substantial unemployment with an increase in the gross national product and with apparent prosperity, merely because of the development of productivity. And we are approaching an interesting period, in which, I believe, the intentions of the government vis-à-vis employment will be tested out. Last year we expected that it would be tested out, but it was not. We were all very pleasantly surprised. I think in the next five years such a test will take place, and I think you will see, in all probability, the government taking action of an important kind to prevent large-scale unemployment.

THE CHAIRMAN: You think the government should add an element of stability to the normally fluctuating economy?

MR. GRAHAM: The government will try.

THE CHAIRMAN: It will depend upon the wisdom of the government's policy?

MR. GRAHAM: Yes; I guess if you judge wisdom in terms of results.

THE CHAIRMAN: How do you judge wisdom?

MR. GRAHAM: I have an a priori test of wisdom in most cases, but I think in economics it is very difficult to tell what is wise until you have been through it.

THE CHAIRMAN: I suppose I should not ask you to look back and see what happened in the twenties to see who was wise in administration of government; should I?

MR. GRAHAM: I think not.

THE CHAIRMAN: What is your commodity reserve plan? I understand you have one.

MR. GRAHAM: I can put it in a very few words. It is related to your question as to the future of our economic system. In the last 20 years I have been identified with a concept of stabilizing the economy by stabilizing the price level of raw materials taken as a whole and not in individual commodities. The objective has been to permit individual commodities to fluctuate but to establish a narrow range of fluctuation and virtual stability for the value of a market basket of the important commodities. I have added to it the very important factor, quite radical, that those commodities would represent a sound backing for our money, because they represent the things that we need and use, and by so doing they would become commodity reserves and would be self-financing in the same way our gold reserves are self-financing. The consequence would be that by stabilizing pretty well the general level of raw materials prices you would add a very important degree of stability to the general economy.

THE CHAIRMAN: I do not think I quite understood what the limitation of the commodities involved would be?

MR. GRAHAM: These are major storable commodities for the most part, those dealt in on commodity exchanges, but not absolutely.

THE CHAIRMAN: What agricultural commodities, if any, would it include?

MR. GRAHAM: They would include such products as wheat, corn, cotton, sugar, and rubber.

THE CHAIRMAN: Rubber and cotton would be storable indefinitely?

MR. GRAHAM: They would be storable indefinitely through rotation.

THE CHAIRMAN: I forgot to mention one thing. With regard to government policy and interference, do you regard tax policy as of major importance in this element of interference in the economic system?

MR. GRAHAM: It could be. That is to say that one of the means by which the government could intervene to an important degree in the economy would be through a tax-reduction plan. Another method would be through an increase of its expenditures.

THE CHAIRMAN: Did you hear Mr. Eccles yesterday? I am not using him as a model, but simply to save the time of describing the situation, because it does take time. Do you remember his proposal yesterday on taxes?

MR. GRAHAM: I have forgotten it.

THE CHAIRMAN: Well, it does not matter. One other question and I will desist. When you find a special situation and you decide, just for illustration, that you can buy for $10 and it is worth $20, and you take a position, and then you cannot realize it until a lot of other people decide it is worth $30, how is that process brought about—by advertising, or what happens?

MR. GRAHAM: That is one of the mysteries of our business, and it is a mystery to me as well as to everybody else. We know from experience that eventually the market catches up with value. It realized it in one way or another.

THE CHAIRMAN: But do you do anything to help that? Do you advertise, or what do you do?

MR. GRAHAM: On the contrary, we try, as matter of fact, to keep our operations as confidential as we can.

THE CHAIRMAN: Even after you buy?

MR. GRAHAM: Even after we have acquired our shares.

THE CHAIRMAN: Why?

MR. GRAHAM: Basically for the reason that we just are not interested in other people knowing about our business, and we have no interest in endeavoring to persuade people to buy stocks in which we have an ownership. We have never done it and we never will do it.

THE CHAIRMAN: That is rather unusual. Since you make your capital gains, a lot of people have got to decide it is worth 30.

MR. GRAHAM: We have been very fortunate in our experience by finding that people decide that stock that you mention is worth 30 without the necessity of our doing anything about it on the advertising side. We might conceivably at times intervene in a managerial policy. We might suggest some change in the procedure, but that of course is merely because we are substantial stockholders.

THE CHAIRMAN: I think that is about all. There are many other things we could ask you about, I am sure. However, you have other things to do, and the hour is late.

I would like to express the appreciation of the committee for your having taken your time to come down here and volunteer this information. I am sure it is not very pleasant for you to have to talk about these things, but I know no other way we can learn about them. I do appreciate the contribution you have made to our knowledge of the market.

MR. GRAHAM: If I have made a contribution, I do not mind the discomfort.

THE CHAIRMAN: If you have any further suggestions that occur to you which you think we ought to know about we will welcome your writing them to us. Thank you very much for coming.

(Mr. Graham's full prepared statement is as follows:)

STATEMENT OF BENJAMIN GRAHAM, CHAIRMAN OF GRAHAM-NEWMAN CORP.

My name is Benjamin Graham. I live in Scarsdale, NY. I am chairman of Graham-Newman Corp., a registered investment company or investment fund. I am also adjunct professor of finance at the Graduate School of Business, Columbia University.

This statement will address itself mainly to three points:

1. The present level of stock prices from the standpoint of the relationship between price and value.
2. Causes of the rise in the market since September 1953.

3. Feasible methods of controlling excessive speculation in the future.

With regard to the present level of stock prices, common stocks look high and are high, but they are not as high as they look. The market level of industrial stocks is far above the 1929 high as shown by the Standard & Poor's index of 420 industrials. The present figure is above 300 as compared with the 1929 high of 195. The industrials average at about 410 is now only moderately above its 1929 high of 382, but the difference would be much larger except for the substitutions made in the average. However, the railroad and utility issues as a whole are well below their 1929 highs.

The true measure of common stock values, of course, is not found by reference to price movements alone, but by price in relation to earnings, dividends, future prospects and, to a small extent, asset values.

Present concepts of common stock valuation turn largely on estimating average future earnings and dividends and applying thereto a suitable capitalization rate or multiplier. Since these elements are all matters of prediction or judgment, there is room for a wide difference of informed opinion as to the proper value for a single stock or group of stocks at any time. Uninformed or speculative opinion will, of course, cover an even wider range as the market swings from the depth of pessimism to the heights of optimism.

As a guide to identifying the present level of stock prices in the light of past experience, I have made two sets of comparisons—one relating to the industrial average, the other to General Electric, a component of that average and an outstanding blue chip issue. I have related the present prices and the high prices in 1929, 1937, and 1946 to earnings of the preceding year, the preceding 5 years, and the preceding 10 years. This information, together with certain other data, appears on the appended table.

The Dow Jones Industrials are now at a lower ratio to their average earnings in the past than they were at their highs in 1929, 1937, and 1946. The same applies to General Electric as an individual stock. It is clear that the issues referred to—which may be considered as reasonably representative of the larger industrials as a whole—have a considerable way to go before reaching the ratios shown at their former tops. It should be pointed out also that high-grade interest rates are now definitely lower than in previous bull markets except for 1946. Lower basic interest rates presumably justify a higher value for each dollar of dividends or earnings.

Much has been made of these relationships as indicating that the market is still on safe ground. However, such comparisons fail to take into account the extent of the subsequent declines from past bull market highs. Since the Dow Jones average lost 90 percent of its price from 1929 to 1932, it is evident not only that 381 was much too high in 1929, but that the market had entered dangerous ground at a point far below that figure.

I have found it useful to estimate the central value of the Dow Jones Industrial Average by the simple method of capitalizing 10-year average earnings at twice the interest rate for high-grade bonds. This technique presupposes that the average past earnings of a group of stocks presents a fair basis for estimating future earnings, but with a conservative bias on the low side. It also assumes that by doubling the capitalization rate presented by high-grade bonds, we allow properly for the differential in imputed risk between good bonds and good stocks. Although this method is open to serious theoretical objections, it has in fact given a reasonably accurate reflection of the central value of industrial common stock averages since 1881. It may be interesting to note that the central value found by this method in 1929 was 120, which happens to be about the geometric mean between the high of 381 and the subsequent 1932 low of 41. Similarly, the central value in 1936 was 138, higher than in 1938, and this proved to be about the mean between the 1937 high of 194 and the low of 99 in 1938.

This mechanical method applied to the situation in the beginning of 1955 yields a central value for the Dow Jones Industrials of 396, or only slightly under their present value. Such a figure, if reliable, would have to be regarded as rather reassuring. It would indicate that the market in terms of value is no higher now than it was in early 1926, or in early 1936, or late 1945. However, the validity of this central value figure may be open to question if we observe that the 10 years ending in 1954, used to obtain average earnings, did not include any period of real depression. In a sense, therefore, the soundness of this appraisal of central value is bound up with our ability to escape serious business depression in the future as we have in the recent past. It is probably fair to say that the market is not too high today if we have really managed to lick the business cycle.

Although such a development would involve a revolutionary break with the past, I am not prepared to deny its possibility. There is some reason for concluding that in the future serious depressions will be prevented, if not by the natural vitality of American business, then by governmental intervention and possible inflationary moves. The above analysis is by no means unfavorable to the present level of stock prices. However, in reaching my overall conclusion on the subject, I am inclined to hark back to the analysis I made of the stock market in October 1945 at a time when the Dow Jones average stood at 185. This was published in *The Commercial and Financial Chronicle*, October 18, 1945. I should like to quote intact the summary appearing at the end of that article and state that it expresses my view with respect to the stock market today.

The three different approaches used in judging the present level of stock prices have yielded diverse indications. From the first, or historical, approach the market appears distinctly on the high side and vulnerable to a substantial setback. Contrariwise, our second category—that of appraisal based on figure and formula—about supports the present level, and suggests that the familiar bull-market enthusiasm might well carry prices considerably higher. Our third approach, through guesses and projections as to future developments, supplies plenty of material but no definite verdict.

What is the net significance of this analysis for the speculator and the prudent stock investor? Let us define the speculator as one who seeks to profit from market movements, without primary regard to intrinsic values; the prudent stock-investor as one who (a) buys only at prices amply supported by underlying value, and (b) determinedly reduces his stock holdings when the market enters the speculative phase of a sustained advance.

This speculative stage, we are convinced, is now at hand. Hence, the principles of the prudent investor will require him to lighten significantly his holdings of common stocks—the precise selling policy to depend, of course, on his individual position and methods. For the stock speculator we can say little that is helpful. We think he has a 50–50 chance—or perhaps a little better—of seeing the market attain substantially higher than present heights, subject to the probability of intervening reactions. But his chance of eventually holding on to the profits he makes beyond the current level, we should term no better than in former bull markets—and that is none too good.

As to reasons for the market rise since September 1953, in general I agree with the answers by President Funston, of the New York Stock Exchange, to question one of the committee's questionnaire. However, I should like to emphasize more than he did the role of investment and speculative sentiment in determining the wide variations in stock market prices.

In my view, the fundamental reason for the rise was the swing from doubt to confidence—from emphasis on the risks in common stocks to emphasis on the opportunities in common stocks.

There has been no change of importance in the earnings of the Dow Jones Industrial Average since 1949. Actually, however, earnings of most secondary companies fell a great deal in 1953–1954 from the levels of the previous five years. But prior to 1954, the public was expecting a substantial setback and was braced for a large falling off in earnings when business turned down after the middle of 1953. It was the mildness of the shrinkage—especially in gross national product and disposable incomes—that reversed the tide of sentiment and gave currency to the view that we no longer have to fear deep depressions.

This change in sentiment produced a change in the public's valuation of stocks, especially in what it considered suitable multipliers of current earnings. In effect, the multiplier advanced from about 8 for the Dow Jones industrials in 1948–1950 to 10 in 1953, and to a current 14, which is slightly less than the 1936–1940 average.

My studies have led to the conclusion that sentiment alone, not supported by any visible change in value, will produce a swing on the order of $100 to $250 or $100 to $300 in price. It is interesting to note that while American Telephone & Telegraph has paid a uniform dividend of $9 since 1922, and while its earnings have fluctuated comparatively little, its price advanced from $115 in 1922 to $310 in 1929, declined to $70 in 1932, and since then it has fluctuated between lows of about $110 and highs of about $200.

Among the secondary companies, the present situation is more complicated. Prices were very low as against earnings prior to 1953, but many of these companies had poor earnings results in 1953–1954. The price behavior of this large group lagged behind the blue chip advance until July 1954. Recently the rise in secondary issues has more than kept pace with that of the leaders. Bargains are fast disappearing and there are numerous instances of overspeculation in this field. On the whole, however, the typical second-grade stock appears less overvalued today than it was in early 1946.

Regarding feasible ways of controlling undue speculation in the future, I believe the committee should consider carefully and cautiously whether any plan of control is feasible. Speculation has not gone too far as yet, but there may be a grave danger that it will do so. Assuming that measures could be found that are useful and feasible, it would be wise to agree to such measures in advance of the necessity for their use—rather than to begin discussing them while the fire is raging.

It should be recognized that any form of intervention by Washington in the stock market is risky and controversial. You cannot be sure that what you are doing is the right thing and won't cause more harm than good. In this respect your problem corresponds to the public's own quandary in deciding whether to buy or sell or sit tight in the present market. Yet, despite the hazards of any intervention, a certain responsibility is there. It is actually being assumed—for example, by the Federal Reserve in varying margin requirements to correspond somewhat with the state of speculation.

On balance, I am inclined to favor strict controls for margin trading and a fairly rapid advance to the 100-percent-margin limit—that is, no borrowing at all—as the Federal Reserve becomes increasingly concerned about the extent of speculation. My reason is that it is basically unsound for nonprofessionals to borrow money to speculate in stocks—or in anything else. It is unsound for them and for the economy as a whole. Responsibility should also be placed upon our commercial banks to avoid, in general, the direct lending of money to the public for the purpose of speculating in stocks.

Much has been made of the capital gains tax as a deterrent to the selling of stocks. It is urged that this tax be abolished or cut in two, in order to increase the supply of stocks by unfreezing holdings showing large profits. There is some merit in this contention, and I shall have a suggestion to make along these very lines. But I regret that the issue has usually been presented by Wall Street—of which I am proud to consider myself a part—in an incomplete and rather one-sided fashion.

Taxes on capital gains have been imposed since the modern income tax began in 1913. Thus the problem of their impact on speculative markets is by no means a new one. The evidence hardly suggests that the capital gains tax has by itself produced unduly high prices or unduly wide fluctuations. Impressive arguments may be made against capital gains taxes as inequitable in theory and unsound in practice. But there are also impressive arguments against permitting capital gains to go untaxed while imposing high rates on other forms of profit. Although I believe the present capital gains tax system is open to improvement, I would not consider it basically inequitable in relation to our tax burden as a whole. Finally, while a lightening of the tax might well increase the supply of common stocks by persuading holders to take large profits, it might at the same time stimulate further speculative buying, attracted by the new tax advantage. The net result of such a move cannot be foretold.

The objections to reducing the capital gains tax would be overcome, in my opinion, if such a policy were adopted for a limited period of time only and for the specific purpose of dealing with a dangerous stock market situation. For example, the tax might well be reduced from the present 25 percent maximum to a 12.5 percent maximum on securities owned at least two years, such reduction to be effective for a specified period only—say six months. I believe such an arrangement would have the desired effect of increasing the supply of common stocks at a time when such increase is deemed necessary. From the standpoint of the Treasury, the result might well be that a larger revenue would be realized, in spite of the reduced tax rate, because of the inducement to sell locked-up shares. Whatever its effect on the level of stock prices, bona fide investors could not be harmed by such a concession, even if it ran for a limited period.

My proposal would require legislation by Congress, as would any other change in the capital gains tax. Perhaps the best method would be to give the President the power to make changes in the effective rate, within specified limits, upon advice from the Board of Governors of the Federal Reserve System. We have precedents for such powers in our tariff laws.

In conclusion, may I say that while Congress should not ordinarily meddle with the stock market, there are times when it deserves attention from Congress. We are probably in such a time at present.

CERTAIN PRICE-EARNINGS RATIOS FOR THE DOW JONES INDUSTRIAL AVERAGE AND FOR GENERAL ELECTRIC COMMON STOCK

TABLE 6
Dow-Jones Industrial Average

Date	Price	Ratio to Earnings for the Preceding 1 Year	Ratio to Earnings for the Preceding 5 Years	Ratio to Earnings for the Preceding 10 Years	Yield on AAA Bonds (Moody's)	Subsequent Low Price of Average
					Percent	
1955 (March)	414	15X	15X	18X	2.95	—

PART FOUR

INVESTMENT STRATEGIES

*The applicability of history almost always appears after
the event. When it is all over, we can quote chapter and
verse to demonstrate why what happened was bound to
happen because it had happened before. This is not really
very helpful. The Danish philosopher, Kirkegaard, made
the statement that life can only be judged backwards,
it must be lived forwards. That certainly is true with
respect to our experiences in the stock market.*

> Benjamin Graham
> "Will Market Grow to the Sky?
> Some Problems Ahead,"
> *The Commercial and Financial
> Chronicle,* February 1, 1962

This part consists of excerpts from Graham's 1946–1947 lectures to
the New York Institute of Finance, which at that time was owned
and operated by the New York Stock Exchange (NYSE). Later, the
NYSE decided to discontinue the courses and the institute was sold off.
Graham's lectures were transcribed, typed up, reproduced, and sold for
$5 for a set of 10 lectures entitled "Current Problems in Security Analy-
sis." Many of the investment issues addressed by Graham indeed were
current, such as how to analyze a company that was in transition from
a producer of war goods to that of a peace-time producer. U.S. government credits for war-time inventory and expansion costs had to be
taken into consideration when analyzing a company.

There is no question that reading the lectures can sometimes feel like
hacking through dense underbrush. Many readers will want to browse
through this section, dipping in where a subject has particular appeal.
Those who do patiently make their way through historic examples of

investment analysis will be rewarded with some of Graham's most enduring nuggets of timeless wisdom. In the midst of a complex explanation, Graham's words can seem to fly off the page and flutter right into the reader's mind. Graham's classes both at the New York Institute of Finance and at Columbia University never failed to draw a crowd.

Please note that the selected lectures have been edited, in some cases only slightly. In certain instances I have clarified the meaning of words, acronyms, or phrases that readers may not recognize. Those notes appear in brackets. Also removed were a few examples, particularly tax discussions that are outdated and have little or no relevance to a contemporary reader. The use of the ornamental symbol in the middle of a lecture means some material has been edited out. For those who would like to read the material in an unedited form, the lectures have been placed on the John Wiley & Sons website, www.wiley.com/bgraham.

Current Problems
in Security Analysis

LECTURE NUMBER ONE

May I welcome you all to this series of lectures. The large enrollment is quite a compliment to the Institute, and perhaps to the lecturer; but it also poses something of a problem. We shall not be able to handle this course on an informal or round-table basis. However, I should like to welcome as much discussion and as many intelligent questions as we can get, but I shall have to reserve the right to cut short discussion or not to answer questions in the interest of getting along with the course. You all understand our problem, I am sure.

I hope you will find that your time and money will be profitably spent in this course; but I want to add that the purpose of this course is to provide illustrative examples and discussions only, and not to supply practical ideas for security market operations. We assume no responsibility for anything said along the latter lines in this course; and so far as our own business is concerned we may or we may not have an interest in any of the securities that are mentioned and discussed. That is also a teaching problem with which we have been familiar through the years, and we want to get it behind us as soon as we can.

The subject of this course is Current Problems in Security Analysis, and that covers a pretty wide field. Actually, the idea is to attempt to bring our textbook *Security Analysis* up to date, in the light of the experience of the last six years since the 1940 revision was published.

The subject matter of security analysis can be divided in various ways. One division might be in three parts: First, the techniques of security

---

Excerpts from Lectures, 1946–1947, New York Institute of Finance.

analysis; secondly, standards of safety and common stock valuation; and thirdly, the relationship of the analyst to the security market.

Another way of dividing the subject might be to consider, first, the analyst as an investigator, in which role he gathers together all the relevant facts and serves them up in the most palatable and illuminating fashion he can. And then to consider the analyst as a judge of values, or an evaluator. This first division of the subject is rather useful, I think, because there is a good field in Wall Street for people whose work it will be mainly to digest the facts, and to abstain from passing judgment on the facts, leaving that to other people.

Such sticking to the facts alone might be very salutary; for the judgment of security analysts on securities is so much influenced by market conditions down here that most of us are not able, I fear, to express valuation judgments as good analysts. We find ourselves almost always acting as a mixture of market experts and security experts. I had hoped that there would be some improvement in that situation over the years, but I must confess that I haven't seen a great deal of it. Analysts have recently been acting in Wall Street pretty much as they always have, that is to say, with one eye on the balance sheet and income account, and the other eye on the stock ticker.

It might be best in this introductory lecture to deal with the third aspect of the security analyst's work, and that is his relationship to the security market. It is a little more interesting, perhaps, than the other subdivisions, and I think it is relevant as introductory material.

The correct attitude of the security analyst toward the stock market might well be that of a man toward his wife. He shouldn't pay too much attention to what the lady says, but he can't afford to ignore it entirely. That is pretty much the position that most of us find ourselves in vis-à-vis the stock market.

When we consider how the stock market has acted in the last six years, we shall conclude that it has acted pretty much as one would expect it to, based upon past experience. To begin with, it has gone up and it has gone down, and different securities have acted in different fashion. We have tried to illustrate this simply, by indicating on the blackboard the behavior of some sample stocks since the end of 1938. Let me take occasion to point out some of the features in this record that may interest security analysts.

There are two elements of basic importance, I think, that the analyst should recognize in the behavior of stocks over the last six years. The first is the principle of continuity, and the other is what I would call the principle of deceptive selectivity in the stock market.

First, with regard to continuity: The extraordinary thing about the securities market, if you judge it over a long period of years, is the fact that it does not go off on tangents permanently, but it remains in continuous orbit. When I say that it doesn't go off on tangents, I mean the simple point that after the stock market goes up a great deal it not only comes down a great deal but it comes down to levels to which we had previously been accustomed. Thus we have never found the stock market as a whole going off into new areas and staying there permanently because there has been a permanent change in the basic conditions. I think you would have expected such new departures in stock prices. For the last thirty years, the period of time that I have watched the securities market, we have had two world wars; we have had a tremendous boom and a tremendous deflation; we now have the Atomic Age on us. Thus you might well assume that the security market could really have been permanently transformed at one time or another, so that the past records might not have been very useful in judging future values.

These remarks are relevant, of course, to developments since 1940. When the security market advanced in the last few years to levels which were not unexampled but which were high in relation to past experience, there was a general tendency for security analysts to assume that a new level of values had been established for stock prices which was quite different from those we had previously been accustomed to. It may very well be that individual stocks *as a whole* are worth more than they used to be. But the thing that doesn't seem to be true is that they are worth so much more than they used to be that past experience—i.e., past levels and patterns of behavior—can be discarded.

One way of expressing the principle of continuity in concrete terms would be as follows: When you look at the stock market as a whole, you will find from experience that after it has advanced a good deal it not only goes down—that is obvious—but it goes down to levels substantially below *earlier* high levels. Hence it has always been possible to buy stocks at lower prices than the highest of *previous* moves, not of the current move. That means, in short, that the investor who says he does not wish to buy securities at high levels, because they don't appeal to him on a historical basis or on an analytical basis, can point to past experience to warrant the assumption that he will have an opportunity to buy them at lower prices—not only lower than current high prices, but lower than previous high levels. In sum, therefore, you can take previous high levels, if you wish, as a measure of the danger point in the stock market for investors, and I think you will find that past experience would bear you out using this as a practical guide. Thus, if you look at this chart of the Dow Jones Industrial Average, you can see there has never been a time in which the price level has broken out, in a once-for-all or permanent way, from its past area of fluctuations. That is the thing I have been trying to point out in the last few minutes. (Ed. Note: The chart is missing from the text, but Graham is referring to a chart of the Dow-Jones Industrial Average prior to 1946.)

Another way of illustrating the principle of continuity is by looking at the long-term earnings of the Dow Jones Industrial Average. We have figures here running back to 1915, which is more than 30 years, and it is extraordinary to see the persistence with which the earnings of the Dow Jones Industrial Average return to a figure of about $10 per unit. It is true that they got away from it repeatedly. In 1917, for example, they got up to $22 a unit; but in 1921 they earned nothing. And a few years later they were back to $10. In 1915 the earnings of the unit were $10.59; in 1945 they were practically the same. All of the changes in between appear to have been merely of fluctuations around the central figure. So much for this idea of continuity?

The second thing that I want to talk about is selectivity. Here is an idea that has misled security analysts and advisers to a very great extent. In the few weeks preceding the recent break in the stock market I noticed that a great many of the brokerage house advisers were saying that now that the market has ceased to go up continuously, the thing to do is to exercise selectivity in your purchases; and in that way you can still derive benefits from security price changes. Well, it stands to reason that if you define selectivity as picking out a stock which is going to go up a good deal later on—or more than the rest—you are going to benefit. But that is too obvious a definition. What the commentators mean, as is evident from their actual arguments, is that if you buy the securities which apparently have good earnings prospects, you will then benefit market-wise; whereas if you buy the others you won't.

History shows this to be a very plausible idea but an extremely mis-leading one; that is why I referred to this concept of selectivity as decep-tive. One of the easiest ways to illustrate that is by taking two securities here in the Dow Jones Average, National Distillers and United Aircraft. You will find that National Distillers sold at lower average prices in 1940–1942 than in 1935–1939. No doubt there was a general feeling that the company's prospects were not good, primarily because it was thought that war would not be a very good thing for a luxury type of business such as whiskey is politely considered to be.

In the same way you will find that the United Aircraft Company through 1940–1942, was better regarded than the average stock, because it was thought that here was a company that had especially good pros-pects of making money; and so it did. But if you had bought and sold these securities, as most people seem to have done, on the basis of these obvious differential prospects, you would have made a complete error. For, as you see, National Distillers went up from the low of 1940 more than fivefold recently, and is now selling nearly four times its 1940 price. The buyer of United Aircraft would have had a very small profit at its best price and would now have a loss of one-third of his money. This principle of selectivity can be explored in various other ways.

Now my point in going at these two things in such detail is to try to bring home to you the fact that what seems to be obvious and simple to the people in Wall Street, as well as to their customers, is not really obvious and simple at all. You are not going to get good results in security analysis by doing the simple, obvious thing of picking out the companies that apparently have good prospects—whether it be the automobile industry, or the building industry, or any such combination of companies which almost everybody can tell you are going to enjoy good business for a number of years to come. That method is just too simple and too obvious—and the main fact about it is that it does not work well. The method of selectivity which I believe does work well is one that is based on demonstrated value differentials representing the application of security analysis techniques which have been well established and well tested. These techniques frequently yield indications that a security is undervalued, or at least that it is definitely more attractive than other securities may be, with which it is compared.

As an example of that kind of thing, I might take the comparisons that were made in the *Security Analysis* 1940 edition, between three groups of common stocks. They were compared as of the end of 1938, or just before the war. Of these groups one contained common stocks said to be speculative because their price was high; the second contained those said to be speculative because of their irregular record; and the third contained those said to be attractive investments because they met investment tests from a quantitative standpoint. Let me now mention the names of the stocks, and indicate briefly what is their position as of today. Group A consisted of General Electric, Coca-Cola, and Johns-Manville. Their combined price at the end of 1938 was $281, and at recent lows it was $303.50 which meant that they have advanced 8 percent.

The second group (about which we expressed no real opinion except that they could not be analyzed very well) sold in the aggregate for $124 at the end of 1938 and at recent lows for $150, which was an advance of 20 percent.

The three stocks which were said to be attractive investments from the quantitative standpoint sold at $70.50 at the end of 1938—that is for one share of each—and their value at the recent lows was $207, or an increase of 190 percent.

Of course, these performances may be just a coincidence. You can't prove a principle by one or two examples. But I think it is a reasonably good illustration of the results which you should get on the average by using investment tests of merit, as distinct from the emphasis on general prospects which plays so great a part in most of the analysis that I see around the Street.

I want to pass on finally to the most vulnerable position of the securities market in the recent rise, and that is the area of new common stock offerings. The aggregate amount of these offerings has not been very large in hundreds of millions of dollars, because the typical company involved was comparatively small. But I think the effect of these offerings upon the position of people in Wall Street was quite significant, because all of these offerings were bought by people who, I am quite sure, didn't know what they were doing and were thus subject to very sudden changes of heart and attitude with regard to their investments. If you made any really careful study of the typical offerings that we have seen in the last 12 months you will agree, I am sure, with a statement made (only in a footnote unfortunately) by the Securities and Exchange Commission on August 20, 1946. They say that: "The rapidity with which many new securities, whose evident hazards are plainly stated in a registration statement and prospectus, are gobbled up at prices far exceeding any reasonable likelihood of return gives ample evidence that the prevalent demand for securities includes a marked element of blind recklessness. Registration cannot cure that."

That is true. Among the astonishing things is the fact that the poorer the security the higher relatively was the price it was sold at. The reason is that most of the sounder securities had already been sold to and held by the public, and their market price was based on ordinary actions of buyers and sellers. The market price of the new securities has been largely determined, I think, by the fact that security salesmen could sell any security at any price; and there was therefore a tendency for the prices to be higher for these new securities than for others of better quality.

I think it is worthwhile giving you a little resume of one of the most recent prospectuses, which is summarized in the *Standard Corporation Record* of September 13, about a week ago. I don't think this stock was actually sold, but it was intended to be sold at $16 a share. The name of the company is the Northern Engraving and Manufacturing Company, and we have this simple set-up: There are 250,000 shares to be outstanding, some of which are to be sold at $16 for the account of stockholders. That meant that this company was to be valued at $4 million in the market.

Now, what did the new stockholder get for his share of the $4 million? In the first place, he got $1,350,000 worth of tangible equity. Hence he was paying three times the amount of money invested in the business. In the second place, he got earnings which can be summarized rather quickly. For the five years 1936–1940, they averaged 21 cents a share; for the five years ended 1945, they averaged 65 cents a share. In other words, the stock was being sold at about 25 times the prewar earnings. But naturally there must have been some factor that made such a thing possible, and we find it in the six months ending June 30, 1946, when the company earned $1.27 a share. In the usual parlance of Wall Street, it could be said that the stock was being sold at six and a half times its earnings, the point being the earnings are at the annual rate of $2.54, and $16 is six or seven times that much.

It is bad enough, of course, to offer to the public anything on the basis of a six months' earnings figure alone, when all the other figures make the price appear so extraordinarily high. But in this case it seems to me the situation is extraordinary in another respect—that is in relation to the nature of the business. The company manufactures metal nameplates, dials, watch dials, panels, etc. The products are made only against purchase contracts and are used by manufacturers of motors, controls, and equipment, and so forth.

Now, we don't stress industrial analysis particularly in our course in security analysis, and I am not going to stress it here. But we have to assume that the security analyst has a certain amount of business sense. Surely he would ask himself, "how much profit can a company make in this line of business—operating on purchase contracts with automobile and other manufacturers—in relation both to its invested capital and its sales?"

In the six months ended June 1946 the company earned 15 percent on its sales after taxes. It had previously tended to earn somewhere around 3 or 4 percent on sales after taxes. It seems to me anyone would know that these earnings for the six months arose from the fact that any product could be sold provided only it could be turned out, and that extremely high profits could be realized in this kind of market. I think it would have been evident that under more sound conditions this is the kind of business which is doomed to earn a small profit margin on its sales and only a moderate amount on its net worth, for it has nothing particular to offer except the know-how to turn out relatively small gadgets for customer buyers.

That, I believe, illustrates quite well what the public had been offered in this recent new security market. There are countless other illustrations that I could give. I would like to mention one that is worth referring to, I think, because of its contrast with other situations.

The Taylorcraft Company is a maker of small airplanes. In June, 1946, they sold 20,000 shares of stock to the public at $13, the company getting $1; and then they voted a four-for-one split up. The stock is now quoted around $2.5 or $2.75, the equivalent of about $11 for the stock that was sold.

If you look at the Taylorcraft Company, you find some rather extraordinary things in its picture. To begin with, the company is today selling for about $3 million, and this is supposedly in a rather weak market. The working capital shown as of June 30, 1946, is only $103,000. It is able to show even that much working capital, first, after including the proceeds of the sale of this stock, and secondly, after not showing as a current liability an excess profits tax of $196,000 which they are trying to avoid by means of a Section 722 claim. Well, practically every corporation that I know of has filed Section 722 claims to try to cut down their excess profits taxes. This is the only corporation I know of that, on the strength of filing that claim, does not show its excess profits tax as a current liability.

They also show advances payable, due over one year, of $130,000, which of course don't have to be shown as current liabilities. Finally, the company shows $2.3 million for stock and surplus, which is not as much as the market price of the stock. But even here we note that the plant was marked up by $1.15 million, so that just about half of the stock and surplus is represented by what I would call an arbitrary plant mark-up.

Now, there are several other interesting things about the Taylorcraft Company itself, and there are still other things even more interesting when you compare it with other aircraft companies. For one thing, the Taylorcraft Company did not publish reports for a while and it evidently was not in too comfortable a financial position. Thus it arranged to sell these shares of stock in an amount which did not require registration with the SEC. But it is also a most extraordinary thing for a company in bad financial condition to arrange to sell stock to tide it over, and at the same time to arrange to split up its stock four for one. That kind of operation—to split a stock from $11 to $3—seems to me to be going pretty far in the direction of trading on the most unintelligent elements in Wall Street stock purchasing that you can find.

But the really astonishing thing is to take Taylorcraft and compare it, let us say, with another company like Curtiss Wright. Before the split-up, Taylorcraft and Curtiss Wright apparently were selling about the same price, but that doesn't mean very much. The Curtiss Wright Company is similar to United Aircraft in that its price is now considerably lower than its 1939 average. The latter was $8.75, and its recent price was $5.75. In the meantime, the Curtiss Wright Company has built up its working capital from a figure perhaps of $12 million to $130 million, approximately. It turns out that this company is selling in the market for considerably less than two-thirds of its working capital.

The Curtiss Wright Company happens to be the largest airplane producer in the field, and the Taylorcraft Company probably is one of the smallest. There are sometimes advantages in small size and disadvantages in large size; but it is hard to believe that a small company in a financially weak position can be worth a great deal more than its tangible investment, when the largest companies in the same field are selling at very large discounts from their working capital.

During the period in which Taylorcraft was marking up its fixed assets by means of this appraisal figure, the large companies like United Aircraft and Curtiss Wright marked down their plants to practically nothing, although the number of square feet which they owned was tremendous. So you have exactly the opposite situation in those two types of companies.

The contrast that I am giving you illustrates to my mind not only the obvious abuses of the securities market in the last two years, but it also illustrates the fact that the security analyst can in many cases come to pretty definite conclusions that one security is relatively unattractive and other securities are attractive. I think the same situation exists in today's market as has existed in security markets always, namely, that there are great and demonstrable discrepancies in value—not in the majority of cases, but in enough cases to make this work interesting for the security analyst.

When I mentioned Curtiss Wright selling at two-thirds or less of its working capital alone, my mind goes back again to the last war; and I think this might be a good point more or less to close on, because it gives you an idea of the continuity of the security markets.

During the last war, when you were just beginning with airplanes, the Wright Aeronautical Company was the chief factor in that business, and it did pretty well in its small way, earning quite a bit of money. In 1922 nobody seemed to have any confidence in the future of the Wright Aeronautical Company. Some of you will remember our reference to it in *Security Analysis*. That stock sold then at $8 a share, when its working capital was about $18 a share at the time. Presumably the market felt that its prospects were very unattractive. That stock subsequently, as you may know, advanced to $280 a share.

Now it is interesting to see Curtiss Wright again, after World War II, being regarded as presumably a completely unattractive company. For it is selling again at only a small percentage of its asset value, in spite of the fact that it has earned a great deal of money. I am not predicting that Curtiss Wright will advance in the next 10 years the way Wright Aeronautical did after 1922. The odds are very much against it. Because, if I remember my figures, Wright Aeronautical had only about 250,000 shares in 1922 and Curtiss Wright has about 7.25 million shares, which is a matter of great importance. But it is interesting to see how unpopular companies can become, merely because their immediate prospects are clouded in the speculative mind.

I want to say one other thing about the Curtiss Wright picture, which leads us over into the field of techniques of analysis, about which I intend to speak at the next session. When you study the earnings of Curtiss Wright in the last 10 years, you will find that the earnings shown year by year are quite good; but the true earnings have been substantially higher still, because of the fact that large reserves were charged off against these earnings which have finally appeared in the form of current assets in the balance sheet. That point is one of great importance in the present-day technique of analysis.

In analyzing a company's showing over the war period it is quite important that you should do it by the balance sheet method, or at least use the balance sheet as a check. That is to say, subtract the balance sheet value shown at the beginning from that at the end of the period, and add back the dividends. This sum—adjusted for capital transactions—

will give you the earnings that were actually realized by the company over the period. In the case of Curtiss Wright we have as much as $44 million difference between the earnings as shown by the single reports and the earnings as shown by a comparison of surplus and reserves at the beginning and end of the period. These excess or unraveled earnings alone are more than $6 a share on the stock, which is selling today at only about that figure.

LECTURE NUMBER TWO

Those of you who are familiar with our textbook know that we recommend the comparative balance sheet approach for various reasons, one of which is to obtain a check on the reported earnings. In the war period just finished that is particularly important because the reported earnings have been affected by a number of abnormal influences, the true nature of which can be understood only by a study of balance sheet developments.

I have put on the blackboard a simple comparative example to illustrate this point. It is not particularly spectacular. It occurred to me because I observed that early this year Transue and Williams and Buda Company both sold at the same high price, namely $33.50 a share; and in studying the companies' record I could see that buyers could easily have been misled by the ordinary procedure of looking at the reported earnings per share as they appear, let us say, in *Standard Statistics* reports.

Now, as to procedure: First, the balance sheet comparison is a relatively simple idea. You take the equity for the stock at the end of the period, you subtract the equity at the beginning of the period, and the difference is the gain. That gain should be adjusted for items that do not relate to earnings, and there should be added back the dividends paid. Then you get the earnings for the period as shown by the balance sheet.

In the case of Transue Williams the final stock equity was $2,979,000, of which $60,000 had come from the sale of stock, so that the adjusted equity would be $2,919,000. The indicated earnings were $430,000, or $3.17 a share. The transfer to a per share basis can be made at any convenient time that you wish. Dividends added back of $9.15 give you earnings per balance sheet of $12.32. But if you look at the figures that I have in the *Standard Statistics* reports, you would see that they add up to $14.73 for the 10 years, so that the company actually lost $2.41 somewhere along the line.

The Buda situation is the opposite. We can take either the July 31, 1945 date or the July 31, 1946 date. It happens that only yesterday the July 31, 1946 figures came in, but it's a little simpler to consider July, 1945 for this purpose.

We find there that the equity increased $4,962,000 or $25.54 per share, the dividends were much less liberal—$4.20; indicated earnings per balance sheet, $29.74, but in the income account only $24.57. So this company did $5.17 better than it showed, if you assume that the reserves as given in the balance sheet are part of the stockholder's equity and do not constitute a liability of the company.

If you ask the reason for the difference in the results in these two companies, you would find it, of course, in the treatment of the reserve items. The Transue and Williams Company reported earnings after allowances for reserves, chiefly for renegotiation, each year (reserves added up to $1.24 million for 1942–1945) and then almost every year they charged their actual payments on account of renegotiation to the reserves. It turned out that the amounts to be charged were greater than the amounts which they provided. The reserves set up by Transue and Williams, consequently, were necessary reserves for charges that they were going to have to meet; not only were they real, but they actually proved insufficient on the whole. I think I should perhaps correct what I said in this one respect: It may be that Transue and Williams called their reserve a reserve for contingencies, but actually it was a reserve for renegotiation which, as I said, proved insufficient.

In the case of Buda you have the opposite situation. The Buda Company made very ample provision for renegotiation, which they charged to earnings currently, and in addition to that they set up reserves for contingencies. These apparently did not constitute in any sense real liabilities, because in July 1946 the reserves of a contingency nature remained at about $1 million.

In the case of Transue, their reserves got up very high but the end of 1945 saw them down to $13,000, which indicated how necessary were the Transue reserves.

Now, let me pause for a moment to see if there is any question in your mind about this explanation as to why you get different earnings on the two bases, and why Buda shows larger earnings than reported and Transue shows smaller earnings that reported.

[Editor's Note: In the remainder of Lecture Number Two, Graham similarly compares the balance sheet of Curtiss Wright Company to that of United Aircraft, then goes on to discuss depreciation of railroad assets, using the Denver and Rio Grande Railroad as an example. The unabridged lecture can be found on the John Wiley & Sons website, www.wiley.com/bgraham.]

LECTURE NUMBER THREE

Now there is one other item that came to my attention a few days ago which has a bearing on war accounting and that is a reference to what is known as LIFO, which means last-in, first-out. I presume most of you are familiar with that accounting principle. It has had a rather important effect upon the balance sheet figures of some corporations, but not quite so important on their income accounts.

LIFO is an accounting method, permitted by new income tax regulations beginning about 1942, under which instead of considering that the first purchased merchandise is sold or used up in manufacture, the corporation is permitted to assume that the last purchased merchandise is sold or used up. As a result, the inventory is kept down during a period of rising prices because it is not necessary to mark up the value of the quantities of inventory owned at the time that the rising prices began. The result of using that method is (a) to reduce inventory values below market values, and in some cases by a very considerable amount; (b) to reduce accordingly the reported profits; and (c) most important, perhaps, to reduce the amount of taxes which have to be paid.

What you have, then, in the balance sheets is either an understatement of the true value of the inventory, if you want to consider it that;

or a cushion to absorb declines in inventory values without effecting a cash loss if you wish more conservatively to consider LIFO that way.

In the case of the Federated Department Stores, their report which appeared a few days ago gives some details on LIFO which they find necessary to do because of a tax problem facing them. That company showed that since 1942 they had the benefit of a reduction in inventory and taxable profit of $3,875,000 by using LIFO instead of using the usual first-in, first-out method. That enabled them to reduce their taxes by $2.59 million; and it reduced their profits after taxes for the five and a half years by roughly $1.15 million.

The difficulty that they refer to is the fact that in department stores it is practically impossible to identify the items that are sold in relation to just when they were bought. Consequently the department stores have tried to use something called an "index of retail price changes" to determine what would be the effect of LIFO on their accounting. And they now are in a controversy with the Treasury because the Treasury says that the LIFO section does not permit the use of estimates by means of an index as to what last-in, first-out means, and therefore they must go back to their old method of first-in, first-out.

The significance of LIFO is interesting, when you reflect upon it, because it is very similar to the wartime amortization of plant facilities which we discussed two weeks ago. There, you recall, the companies had the opportunity to write down their fixed assets, which were recently acquired, to zero, and to get the benefit of tax credits, the effect of which, however, was to reduce their earnings somewhat. You have exactly the same effect here in LIFO. You write down your inventory, save a great deal of money in taxes, but reduce your apparent earnings somewhat.

I think that for the analyst the significant thing is that the LIFO method is one of the additional conservative elements that have come into corporate accounting in the last five or six years. These will probably buttress corporations against losses that might otherwise take place during a depression; and I think we ought to recognize that factor as on the plus side in security values.

[Editor's Note: Lecture Number Three has been edited extensively. In the remainder of this lecture, Graham discussed LIFO in great detail, then talked about the effect of dividends on share price, and the impact of regional growth on the earnings of a railroad corporation. To read the complete lecture, log on the John Wiley & Sons website, www.wiley .com/bgraham.]

One very good reason why Southern Pacific sells so much higher than Northern Pacific is because it is paying dividends at the rate of $4 and Northern Pacific is paying dividends at the rate of $1. It is obvious that such a disparity in dividend policies would have a substantial effect on market prices.

A question that we shall have to consider from time to time in the future is how valid is the dividend rate as a determinant of proper market prices. That it actually has a great effect on market price cannot be denied—certainly in the field of securities that are bought by investors.

Two years ago, when we were giving a course here on appraisal of stocks, we had occasion to compare Reading and Pennsylvania [railroads]. There we found that Reading and Pennsylvania made practically the same showing with regard to earnings and financial strength. But Reading was satisfied to pay $1 to its stockholders, while Pennsylvania was paying about $2 to $2.50. The result was that you had prices averaging $20 for Pennsylvania in 1945, against $24 for Reading. Before that time, I think, the ratio of prices was about two-to-one, although the ratio of earnings was about the same.

I have also had occasion recently to see rather startling evidence of the effect of dividend policy on prices in a number of the insurance companies. If you take two companies like New Amsterdam Casualty Company and the United States Fidelity & Guaranty, you would find that these companies are almost identical in every respect, in the character of their business and their assets, except that one of them has twice the amount of stock and twice the assets and business. The earnings per share are about the same. But United States Fidelity pays $2 and New Amsterdam Casualty $1, and so you have a relationship in price of $42 for one and $26 for the other.

There is no doubt, therefore, that the dividend rates of Southern Pacific and Northern Pacific are sufficient to explain the market relationship, even by themselves, without reference to any other questions that the analyst might ask himself.

We must consider later—but I don't think we shall do it now— whether the analyst can take advantage of the fact that two companies would be worth, say, approximately the same amount from every stand-point other than dividends, and sell at considerable difference because of dividend policy. The question that would come up is whether you can expect in the normal course of events that the dividend policy will adjust itself to the earnings and that therefore eventually the market price will adjust itself to the earnings and will not be determined by an arbitrary dividend policy. That is a very difficult question to reach a conclusion about, and I prefer to talk about it at some other time.

STUDENT: One of the appraisals that I hear is that since Southern Pacific is so largely in the Southwest, Texas, in a territory that is growing much more rapidly that the Northwest territory, that some rail analysts are strong in their preference for Southern Pacific on that basis over Northern Pacific.

[Editor's Note: Graham replied in great detail, but his final state-ment, which follows, summarized his thoughts on the matter. For Graham's complete answer, log on to www.wiley.com/bgraham.]

MR. GRAHAM: The question that was asked about the general future prospects of one territory as compared with another is certainly very relevant to analysis of railroad securities. Yet I must say that I have found in my own work that you can count very much more dependably upon differences of value which can be established from the earnings and expense picture than you can on those which seem to be inherent in the possibilities of the different territories.

LECTURE NUMBER FOUR

I find one of the students presents me with a question which I shall be glad to answer for his benefit and for the benefit of the class. He quotes a statement made in *Security Analysis*, page 691, which says, "Judging from observations made over a number of years, it would seem that investment in apparently undervalued common stocks can be carried on with a fair degree of overall success, provided average alertness and good judgment are used in passing on the future prospect question, and provided also that commitments are avoided at the times when the general market is statistically too high."

That is our statement, and his question is: "That, after reading the article in the *Financial Chronicle* which we distributed, one reaches the conclusion that you consider 185 for the Dow Jones Average statistically very high. In general, above what Dow Jones Average price would you consider it high and between what ranges would you consider it normal?"

That certainly is a very direct and leading question, but I would like to start with a correction. If I recall the article of October, 1945, in the *Financial Chronicle*, in which we discussed the then level of stock prices, it was not our conclusion that the level of 185 was statistically very high. The conclusion, was that it was *historically* very high. That is quite a difference. We pointed out that in the past the market had not been able to go beyond that level without getting into dangerous territory.

As far as the statistical discussion was concerned, I think we found that 185 or thereabouts would appear to be a normal valuation for the Dow Jones Average as of last year, and that on a statistical basis there was no particular reason to be afraid of the stock market there. Our point was, though, that historically there was reason to be afraid of it, and we were inclined to advise caution for that reason. As near as we are able to determine a central value for the Dow Jones industrials, we are inclined to believe that somewhere around the present level or a little bit higher perhaps might be a central level in the future. The figure we gave provisionally in that article was 178 as so-called "appraisal value." For that reason there would be no special cautionary factor in the current general level, working against the purchase of undervalued securities.

The only caution we would want to add to that is this: If by any chance you are still going through the usual alternations of bull markets and bear markets—which is by no means unlikely—then there is no particular reason to believe that when the market has receded to about its average value it would necessarily have stopped going down.

Experience in former markets indicates that just as they are too high in bull markets, they get too low in bear markets. If we are going through a similar experience now, the historical analogies would point to lower prices, simply because in bear markets securities sell for less than they are worth, just as they sell for more than they are worth in bull markets.

Whether that means that a person should avoid a bargain security because he thinks the general market is going down still further is quite another question; and I think that is largely a personal matter. Our opinion is that for the investor it is better to have his money invested than it is to feel around for the bottom of the securities market. And if you can invest your money under fair conditions, in fact under attractive specific conditions, I think one certainly should do so even if the market should go down further and even if the securities you buy may also go down after you buy them. That is rather a long answer to this question, but it is an interesting one.

I might add another introductory statement: By a coincidence last week I noticed a news item with regard to the Taylorcraft Corporation, which was a company of which we gave a brief and unfavorable analysis at our first meeting. That company, you know, sold some stock on terms which we regarded as rather outrageous last summer. I find now they are in financial difficulties, and that trustees have been appointed. That is a rather extreme example of the value of security analysis. (Laughter.)

Our purpose tonight is to start our discussion of the factor of future earnings in the analysis of securities. In the past two lectures we spoke more or less exclusively about the analysis of the past earnings. Of course, volumes can be written on that question now before us. It is not our purpose to cover it in a comprehensive way, starting from scratch, but rather to assume that you are familiar with the general treatment of the future earnings component which we gave in *Security Analysis*, and to subject it to a further scrutiny, particularly with respect to what may have happened in the last few years in that sector.

I would like to start with something that would appeal to at least two members of this class, and that is with a *definition* of the term earning power. That term has been used so loosely that I am ready to start a movement for its official abolition in Wall Street. When somebody asserts that a stock has an earning power of so much, I am sure that the person who hears him doesn't know what he means, and there is a good chance that the man who uses it doesn't know what it means.

My suggestion is that we use two phrases: One is *past* earning power, and the other is *future* earning power. Past earning power is certainly definite enough and it should mean the average earnings over a stated period which would ordinarily be identified in the discussion. But if not so identified it would be some representative period such as 5 or 7 or perhaps 10 years in the past. That would be the meaning of past earning power.

When you are talking about future earning power, you should mean the *average expectable earnings* over some period in the future. I think most of us ought to think pretty much alike as to the period that we would talk about. My suggestion is that it would be a five-year period, and that when we speak of future earning power of a company, we should have in mind ordinarily the average earnings over the next five years. I say "ordinarily" because you have situations in which a company may be subject to abnormal conditions affecting earning power for some years to come; and there it may be desirable to make a further distinction. We shall talk later about the analysis of a building company stock, in which you might very well make some distinction between the earning power for a boom period, which is ahead perhaps for several years to come, and the earning power for a normal period, if there is such a thing in the building company industry. But apart from some special type of situation such as that, (and a war period such as we have gone through) I think the use of future earning power to mean earnings expected for the next five years would be useful as a general expression.

As far as the use of earning power or earning prospects in Wall Street is concerned, let me point out that in most of the current thinking earning power is not considered along the lines of an average over a period of time of medium duration. It is either considered as the earnings that are being realized just now, or those right around the corner, such as the next twelve months; or else the earnings are considered in terms of the long and almost endless future.

A company with good prospects, for example, is supposed to be a company which will go on and on, more or less indefinitely increasing its earnings; and therefore it is not necessary to be too precise about what earnings you are talking about when you are considering the company's future. Actually that idea of the long-term future of companies with good prospects shows itself, not in the use of any particular earnings, but in the use of the multiplier which is applied to the recent earnings or to the average earnings of the past.

I am reminded of an analysis that we used in this course in 1939, in the very first lecture, which I believe illustrates that pretty well. We put on the board three companies: A, B, and C. Two of them, which we did not name, showed earnings of practically identical amounts for the last five years—$3.50 a share in each case. The earnings year by year were closely similar. The only difference was that one stock was selling at $14 and the other was selling at $140. The stock that was selling at $140 was Dow Chemical; the one that was selling at $14 was Distillers Seagrams.

Obviously, the difference between $14 and $140 meant that the market believed that the prospects for Dow Chemical were very good and those for Distillers Seagrams were indifferent or worse than that. This judgment showed itself in the use of a multiplier of four in one case and a multiplier of 40 in the other.

I think that represents a very dangerous kind of thinking in Wall Street, and one which the security analyst should get as far away from as he can. For if you are going to project Dow's earnings practically to the year 2000 and determine values that way, then of course you can justify any price that you wish to. In fact, what actually happens is that you take the price first, which happens to be not only the present market but some higher price if you are bullish on the stock, and then you determine a multiplier which will justify that price. That procedure is the exact opposite of what a good security analyst should do.

I think if a person had tried to project the earnings of Dow Chemical for a five-year period and the earnings of Distillers Seagrams for a five-year period, and compared them, he could not have gotten values which would have justified the price differential as great as 10-to-1 in the two companies. It is always an advantage to give examples of this sort that have such a brilliant sequel; because I notice that this year Distillers Seagrams sold as high as $150 as compared with its earlier price of $14, and Dow Chemical sold as high as about $190, against $140—which is quite a difference in relative behavior.

We have been trying to point out that this concept of an indefinitely favorable future is dangerous, even if it is true; because even if it is true you can easily overvalue the security, since you make it worth anything you want it to be worth. Beyond this, it is particularly dangerous too, because sometimes your ideas of the future turn out to be wrong. Then you have paid an awful lot for a future that isn't there. Your position then is pretty bad. There will be other examples of that sort which we may take up as we go along.

Let me now get back a little more closely to the work of the security analyst, and ask the question, "What is the relationship of this concept of future earning power to the day-to-day, careful work of the security analyst, and his attitude toward security values?" That relationship has developed gradually over a period of years, and at a somewhat more significant rate in the last few years.

It is interesting to go back in one's thinking to the elements from which we started our ideas of the value of securities,—say, a generation ago or more than that. When I came down to the Street, the thing everybody started with in valuations was par value. That did not mean, of course, that a stock was worth its par value. It might be worth more or less. But it was considered as being worth a percentage of its par value. So much was this true—I don't know how many of you are aware of this—that prior to about 1916 stocks were regularly quoted on the stock value. Westinghouse and Pennsylvania would sell, say, at $150, which meant they were selling at $75 a share—because their par value was $50. I suppose we have gotten so far away from par values now that the only people who are interested in them are those who calculate transfer taxes on securities. Because of that tax reason, one-cent par values are regarded as a very smart procedure in Wall Street today.

I can imagine the attitude of the old-fashioned investor were he to buy a stock for $50 and looked at the certificate and found its par value was one cent. He would probably have fallen in a faint. Well, through many stages in a long period of development from that rather naive attitude toward the central point of value, you have come now to what might seem to be the ultimate stage where the central point of value is the future earnings power, something which you cannot read on any certificate. In fact, you cannot read it anywhere.

There is often a question in my mind whether we have really made so much progress in moving on from the physical to the almost metaphysical in this way; but be that as it may, we have. And now it is the law of the land that the values of securities, if they must be determined for the purpose of judging fairness of any kind of transaction, will be based primarily on the capitalization of expected future earnings. That is the burden of the famous Consolidated Rock Products case that you see referred to all the time in SEC proceedings, and in other cases of similar character.

When the Supreme Court says it is a fact that the value depends upon future earning power, that does not mean that the test of the value that the Supreme Court has laid down as the law on this subject has *therefore* become the proper test for us security analysts. I think rather that we have laid down the law to the Supreme Court. That is to say, the Supreme Court has said that the values are now to be determined primarily in relation to future earning power, because it has observed that values have actually been determined by buyers and sellers of securities more and more in relation to such expected earnings.

The Supreme Court had lagged behind the times for quite a while in that matter, and it just caught up. I think perhaps that it is still lagging behind the times in some other respects.

The concept that investment value is dependent upon expected future earnings is undoubtedly a more persuasive and a more logical one than thinking of value in relation to past earnings only, or in relation to the par value printed on the certificate, or any other stage in between. But I must emphasize to you that this concept does not make the job of the security analyst easier. On the contrary, it makes it a great deal harder, and it places him in a serious dilemma, for now the past earnings, with which he can become very closely familiar and which he can study with a great deal of skill and ingenuity—those past earnings unfortunately are not determinative of value. And the element which is determinative of value, the future earnings, is just the thing which he cannot analyze with any real feeling of assurance as to the correctness of his conclusions.

That would be a very sad dilemma indeed for us security analysts if it were not for that principle of continuity that I tried to emphasize in the first lecture. While it is true that it is the expected future earnings and not the past that determines value, it is also true that there tends to be a rough relationship or continuing connection between past earnings and future earnings. In the typical case, therefore, it is worthwhile for the analyst to pay a great deal of attention to the past earnings, as the beginning of his work, and to go on from those past earnings to such adjustments for the future as are indicated by his further study.

You all know, of course, that the dependability of past earnings as a guide to the future is sufficient to make it possible to rely almost exclusively on them in the selection of a high grade investment bond or preferred stock. We have said, in fact, that you cannot properly buy such an investment security on the basis of expected earnings, where these are very different from past earnings—and where you are relying on new developments, as it were, to make the security sound, when it would not have been sound on the basis of the past.

But you may say, conversely, that if you buy it on the basis of the past and the new developments turn out to be disappointing, you are running the risk of having made an unwise investment. We find from experience, though, that where the past margin of safety that you demand for your security is high enough, in practically every such case the future will measure up sufficiently close to the past to make your investment a sound one. This type of investment will not require any great gifts of prophesy, any great shrewdness with regard to anticipating the future. In fact, it would be a very unfortunate thing if you could not get 2.75 percent on your money without having to be something of a soothsayer as far as the future earnings of corporations is concerned.

When I make that statement, of course I do not mean to lay down the inflexible rule that any company that gives you a sufficiently great margin in its past earnings can be regarded as having sound securities for investment. If the investor has occasion to be fearful of the future of such a company, it is perfectly logical for him to obey his fears and pass on from that enterprise to some other security about which he is not so fearful. But the point I am making—and I hope you can understand it—is that in the selection of high-grade securities you start with a demand for an adequate coverage in past earnings; and in the typical case that is sufficient to justify the selection of the bond.

In the case of common stocks the technique of security analysis has made rather important progress from the rather hit-and-miss method of taking past earnings as a guide and then saying, "Well, I think the future is pretty good here, so I'll multiply the earnings by a higher than average multiplier." Or in the converse case: "I think the future is not so good, so I'll multiply these past earnings by a lower amount."

It is now becoming approved practice in any really good analysis to work out the future earning power along somewhat independent lines—by considering afresh the most important factors on which the earning power will depend. These factors in the ordinary case are not very numerous. They consist, first, of the physical output or volume of business that you expect from the company. Secondly, the price, or unit price, that it will get. Thirdly, its unit cost; and then, fourth, the tax rate. We now have a standard technique by which you go through these various motions and set up these successive figures—all of which are estimates, of course. By this operation you arrive at a conclusion as to future earning power. That is regarded, and should be regarded, as a better technique than the simple one of merely taking the past earnings over a period of time.

Consequently, when you undertake a full-scale analysis of a security and want to determine whether it should be bought or not—I should say, frankly, whether it should be bought or sold—your proper technique should consist of estimating the future earning power along the lines that I have mentioned, and then applying a multiplier to it which is influenced in part by your subjective ideas as to the security, but which has to be kept within a reasonable range of variation.

It is not, I assure you, admissible security-analysis technique to say, "I don't like this company, so I will multiply the future earnings by four; but I do like the other company so I will multiply the future earnings by 40." You will not get a passing grade on a security-analysis test if you do anything of that kind. But naturally there is room for some variation in your multiplier as applied to these earnings. When you use that multiplier, you arrive at a valuation which can be a guide to you in your attitude toward the stock.

I was going to go on with some other examples of that method, but I find that I have left out a little note that I put on one of my pages headed "The Digression." This was intended to contribute somewhat to your amusement and edification.

You may recall that I have been emphasizing the difficulty of peering into the future and coming through with some good ideas as to what will happen. Let me now indicate to you the position of somebody who really could have looked in the crystal ball and derived a good deal of dependable information about the future. Let us see how well he would have fared. I am assuming that each of you was one of these fortunate investors who really had a crystal ball, and could foretell in 1939 that different groups of stock would expand their business in the percentages that we show on the blackboard here.

Now, we say, suppose you were also told that in September 1946 the general level of industrial prices (as shown by the SEC calculations) would be 29 percent higher than they were in January 1939. That happens to be true. Consequently, the stocks in these groups would vary around a center of a 29 percent advance. Suppose, then, you were asked back in 1939, "What would be the change in the prices of these securities by 1946?" Here, for example, is aircraft manufacturing, which is expanding 31 times in volume, from 1939 to 1944. Here is aviation transport, which is expanding two and a half times. I could, for our amusement, ask you to make what you would regard as a reasonable estimate of the change in market prices from January 1939 to September 1946; but instead of going through that rigmarole I shall merely give you the results.

At September 16, 1946, the aviation transport securities were *up* 274 percent from January 1939—which was pretty good, I should say, compared with 240 percent increase in business. But the aircraft manufacturing companies were *down* 74 percent. I do not think you would have expected that if you had known the relative change in sales. Amusement stocks and tobacco products both benefitted just about the same in gross from the war conditions. But the difference was that the amusement stocks advanced 242 percent and the tobacco stocks declined 10.5 percent—which is quite a difference.

The tire and rubber companies did not do as well as electric manufacturing in sales, but in price they went up 85 percent while the electric machinery equipment went up only 2 percent.

Metal and metal mining did not do quite as well as paper in sales expansion. But the difference here is also rather surprising, because the paper and allied products stocks increased 107 percent in value, and the metal mining stocks declined 6 percent during that period.

You see that the discrepancies in market movement are so great that they should add an extra note of caution in our attitudes toward our future calculations. For even if we knew what was going to happen to a company, in terms of its business and its earning power, we might not be able to make too good a prediction as to what was going to happen to it in the market price, which interests us a good deal. That is just an added reason for being either as cautious as possible in regard to our own decisions on security purchases, or else protecting ourselves as much as we can in our own thinking and in our statements by qualifying comments, whenever we begin to make predictions as to the future.

Now I should like to go on and give you a detailed example of the kind of analysis which is now being made, that centers around an estimate of future earnings and works on from there to a valuation. I have two examples here. One of them relates to the Childs Company. That happens to be rather convenient because here we have our good friend, the Securities and Exchange Commission, sweating through a valuation of the Childs Company which is based primarily upon their estimate of future earnings. They do this because they have to. They are required to find out the comparative values of the preferred and common stocks in their report to the court on the fairness of the proposed reorganization plans. The only way they know of determining the *comparative* value is by getting the total value of the enterprise and then comparing that with the claim of the preferred stock. And so they go through an elaborate technique in order to value the Childs preferred and common shares.

It might be worthwhile to take a little time and see just how they have done it. Perhaps I should make the matter a little clearer to you. The Childs Company, most of you know, has been in trusteeship. The company is now evidently solvent, and can easily take care of its debts. So the problem of reorganization actually turns upon giving the proper amounts of new securities to the old preferred and common stock.

The SEC, in its wisdom, decided that the capitalization of the preferred and common stock should be changed from what it was before. It is thus necessary to determine what proportion of a new common stock issue, if that is to be the only stock, should go to the preferred and what to the common. The problem before the SEC, then, was to determine what the whole enterprise was worth. If the preferred stock claim was 75 percent of such value, for example, they would then allot 75 percent of the stock to the preferred and the balance to the common.

What they did was to start with a projection of the sales of Childs, which they took at $18 million, somewhat less than the figures for 1945, then assuming that business would not be as good in the long-term future as it was under war conditions. They then took a percentage of profit of 6 percent before taxes. That was based upon a study of profit margins both for this company and for other restaurant companies; and I do not believe that analysts would be likely to differ very much with them. So they got a net before taxes of $1.1 million.

Then they subtracted the expected average tax rates. Here the SEC decided to cut down the current rate of 38 percent to 35 percent—a very valiant gesture of guessing. The main question, in estimating the tax rate, was whether it was likely that the great pressure to eliminate double taxation on corporations would be effective in the future in such a way, perhaps, as to relieve corporations of either all or most of the tax. Their guess, and mine too, was that such was not likely to happen, desirable as it might be.

So the net after tax was estimated at $715,000. That is the future earning power, and you can see that is a relatively simple calculation. It represents smaller earnings than Childs had during the war period before taxes, but considerably more than in the pre-war period.

QUESTION: How do they estimate the future sales?

MR. GRAHAM: Well, here is sort of a summary of a rather long discussion about the effect of retaining some restaurants, closing others, and opening up others. They say, "Considering the record of the 53 units"—which includes some which would be closed—"and giving weight to the various factors that affect future sales to the chain, we believe that the management forecast of $20 million restaurant sales for the average future years is excessive. For such a figure to be achieved, the chain would have to average in good years and bad years sales which would be 10 percent higher than those achieved by the 53 restaurants in 1945, which in turn were higher than in any previous recent year for more than a decade. It is true that in 1946, with the first six months' results known, the management estimated that the sales will exceed $21.4 million. However, it must be recognized that the company is experiencing extraordinarily high retail sales and Childs' current high sales level cannot be considered to correspond to the level which may reasonably be forecast for a normal year in the future. We believe however, even giving consideration to normal retail business, that the chain can reasonably be anticipated to average sales of $18 million, which was the amount realized in 1945 by the 53 restaurants—"

The conclusion is a rather interesting point of technique. Rather than take a figure completely out of the air, you go back to the earnings of a past year which you think will correspond to a typical future year and arrive at the figures that way.

QUESTION: Wouldn't the common stock holders have a basis of argument about the sales and therefore throw out the whole business?

MR. GRAHAM: You mean can they argue against that?

QUESTION: Yes. Well, they can say it is higher; it should be $21 million, or whatever it was in 1946.

MR. GRAHAM: Well, your point is perfectly right. The common stock holders can say that, and so could the SEC have said it—but they didn't. And when you get down to the judicial question on which this matter turns, here is what the courts say on a matter of that kind: They would say that the SEC is competent and impartial; that their guess is probably a better guess than one advanced by an interested party such as a common-stock holder. But if the common-stock people could adduce very convincing evidence—not merely an insistent argument—which would show that the estimate is out of line with normal expectancy, then the SEC's figures could be reflected by the court.

QUESTION: Did the trustee represent the common stockholder's viewpoint here?

MR. GRAHAM: No, a trustee wouldn't normally represent just the common stock. The SEC assumed Child's trustee's views were too liberal. In other cases, the commission has considered the trustee's estimate as not liberal enough.

QUESTION: Didn't the SEC introduce the price level in their computations somewhere?

MR. GRAHAM: Not in any explicit calculation.

QUESTION: By using the 1945 level they might discount what they consider to be a bulge in food prices right now.

MR. GRAHAM: Perhaps they do refer to the fact, in their analysis of merchandise costs, that there has been a scarcity of supplies, and that the opportunities to purchase food and liquor at bargain prices have disappeared during war years.

QUESTION: Let me ask another question, then. From your observation isn't retail merchandising, whether it is a restaurant chain or anything else, strictly a matter of percentages? In other words, give them a price level, they work both their costs and selling prices up and down accordingly.

MR. GRAHAM: It generally works out that way. This 6 percent figure which they give for net before taxes is based pretty much upon average experience in the past. I presume that is the percentage you are referring to. We know, for example, that food in the typical restaurant represents anywhere between one-third and 40 percent of the total sales check. Once a stable price level has been established, that percentage tends to be established again, even if it was set aside for a while because of sudden changes in price level. For Child's merchandise costs have risen from 34.7 percent in 1938 to 38.5 percent in 1945.

QUESTION: No question that the prevailing prices that this chain has to deal with in 1946 would be higher than in 1945? No question in your mind, is there?

MR. GRAHAM: No.

QUESTION: And that automatically would govern in actual volume of sales, wouldn't it?

MR. GRAHAM: It would unless for some reason the customers were driven away from restaurants, which so far I don't think the figures show. But 1946, of course, is not regarded necessarily as a typical postwar year by the SEC, and probably correctly so.

These questions are really good questions, not so much as criticisms of what the SEC does, as they are indications of the necessary degree of uncertainty involved in any such procedure. The only thing you can say in favor of it is that something of this kind must be done. The SEC must do it as intelligently as they can; and you as security analysts must also do it intelligently. But don't ever think that because you go through some very careful operations and work things out to two or three decimal places, as I sometimes see it done, that you have got an accurate and precise idea as to what will happen in the future. You just don't have any such thing. It isn't there.

QUESTION: I would like to raise the question of working with post-tax margins rather than pre-tax margins to avoid the dilemma of estimating what the tax rate will be, on the theory that competition will drive the post-tax margin down to about what it was.

MR. GRAHAM: There has been a great deal of discussion in academic circles on the incidence of the corporation tax—as to whether it is really paid by the consumer or whether it is paid by the prosperous corporation as compared with a non-profitable corporation that couldn't have to pay any tax. That matter is still very controversial, and apparently the SEC prefers to follow the assumption that the margin should be calculated before tax. In practice, it didn't make much difference, since they use practically the current tax.

We are really going on further in the Childs' matter, than the mere matter of estimating future earnings; because I think we ought to follow it through to its conclusion by the SEC, and perhaps by ourselves as sitting in judgment on the SEC.

They next came to the multiplier and they said that their multiplier should be 12.5 That is to say, a capitalization rate of 8 percent, which gave them a value of about $9 million for the company on an earnings basis. I don't think much was said that would illuminate the question of why they selected a multiplier of 12.5 They reject the Trustees' multiplier of 10. That is the first thing they do. Then they add one of those precious clauses that you find in the tax court almost always, and in the SEC frequently. They say, "Giving consideration to all the factors, including rates of capitalization which have prevailed for other restaurant chains, it is our conclusion that estimated net earnings of $1.1 million before income taxes and $715,000 after income taxes can fairly be capitalized at rates approximately 12 percent and 8 percent, respectively, resulting in a capitalized earnings figure of about $9 million. That means that using their best judgment they will multiply the earnings after taxes by 12.5. I assure you that the alternative capitalization of earnings *before* taxes was figured out at a rate to correspond with their capitalization of the earnings *after* taxes. I think it was put in there, because in the McKesson and Robbins case they were led by the trustees' calculations there to do some valuation of earnings before taxes—something that had never been done before, as far as I know. Their capitalization rate, of course, is pretty much an arbitrary matter, and yet I assume that most analysts would not get very far away from their multiplier.

QUESTION: They use a lower times multiplier than the trustees. Is that the effect of that?

MR. GRAHAM: No, a higher multiplier. They cut down his earnings somewhat, and they increase his multiplier so I think they end up pretty near the same evaluation.

QUESTION: You said eight times, didn't you?

MR. GRAHAM: No, an 8 percent figure. That 9 percent is 12.5 times. The trustee had used a multiplier of 10.

QUESTION: And they were giving arguments against the use of the 10 percent by the trustee?

MR. GRAHAM: Yes, but the matter is too complicated to take up here. The trustee had used what he called a "segmental method," in which he considered that part of it was equivalent to bonds, another part to preferred stock, another part to common stock, and the SEC argues about it. Incidentally, you should know that the SEC goes at these things very seriously. I mean, their valuation isn't so much of a rule of thumb way as you may think from my description—though I have a little mental reservation on that, and believe that you might get pretty much the same results by rule of thumb method. But they certainly don't do it that way. When they start with analysis of estimates of earnings, they have a discussion of about three pages on the management factor. Then they have three pages on the sales, half a page on merchandise cost, half a page on labor costs, then paragraphs on other costs, on building operating profits, on depreciation and rentals, on overhead. Then, after all those discussions, they reach this calculation of 6 percent of the sales of $18 million. Evidently, a great deal of work of the staff went into this.

Thus they got a valuation of $9 million, based upon earning power. Then they went through some motions after that, on some of which I part company very definitely with the SEC. First they figure out some tax savings due to carry backs and things of that sort, and they say they will get $1.2 million from that. Then they say they have to spend $1.8 million for rehabilitation of the restaurants, so they subtract that. And therefore they reduce their $9 million by $600,000 net and get $8.4 million. That is their net value by the earnings method.

Then they add excess working capital and unneeded real estate to that figure. From their calculations these amount to $5.1 million, and so they get a final total of $13.5 million. They have to deduct from this $13.5 million, the funded debt of $3.2 million. So they get a net value for stock of $10.3 million. They value the preferred stocks' claim at par and back dividends, amounting to $7,649,000. Thus the balance left for common would be $2,656,000.

Consequently they reach the conclusion that, if one class of stock is to be issued, then somewhere between 70 percent and 75 percent of the total should be given to the preferred stock and somewhere between 25 percent and 30 percent should be given to the common.

That happens to be an unusually modest type of conclusion for the SEC. In the past they have generally come out with an elaborate calculation and said: "We believe that 72.45 percent of this company should go to the preferred and the balance of 27.55 percent to the common." But I think they are getting a little mellow and are realizing that their calculations are pretty much estimates and should be turned into round amounts.

As a practical matter it turned out that the reorganization is now being carried through on close to the SEC's basis, although the original plans which were proposed by the trustee and by a number of other people for the most part departed very substantially from these proportions. I won't take the time to tell you what the different plans were; but the trustee now allocates 76.66 percent of the new stock to the preferred.

LECTURE NUMBER FIVE

As a preliminary perhaps I might answer any questions that are in your mind growing out of the last lecture, which ended rather precipitously. Does anyone have anything on his mind? We were discussing the Childs' valuation by the Securities and Exchange Commission. At that time, you will recall, we had indicated that the SEC had valued the Childs Company primarily on the basis of its future earning power, which was the thing that interested us, but had added a certain amount for excess working capital—actually $1.3 million net after paying the bonds. Let me make the point here that a security analyst would not be inclined to add in the excess working capital to the valuation of the property unless he believed that the money was to be returned in some way or other to security holders. As a matter of fact, some part of the excess working capital was to be used to pay off the old debt of Childs, and that portion, of course, represented an addition to the earning-power value of the old company. Thus our own "practical" valuation would tend to be $9 million rather than the $10 million found by the SEC.

Since we discussed the matter two weeks ago, the Federal Court has approved the Childs plan, based upon the modified proposals of the trustee; and it has apparently placed the stock equity at $9.98 million, which is $300,000 less than the amount that the SEC found.

It may be interesting to look a bit at the prices of the securities, to see what they indicate as of now. The preferred and common together were selling for about $8.4 million yesterday, preferred at $155 and the common at $7.16. This is less than the valuations that we have been talking about. There is nothing surprising about that, of course; because it is a normal experience to have the securities of a company in trusteeship sell at less than the valuations that an analyst would find for the property on a reorganized basis. It would be expected that the value would normally increase over a period of time—such as one year or two years, following trusteeship—as the enterprise gains its proper position in the public's esteem. That is almost an invariable experience.

Here we have a five page discussion of American Radiator, in which a great deal of information is supplied on the industry—not only its past, but future calculations, based upon somebody else's estimates for the year 1947; and also some other estimates for the years running between 1946 and 1951, on the demand and supply of new houses.

Then they take up the earning power of American Radiator Company; and for the first time in this group of analyses that we are speaking of they actually endeavor to determine what the value of the company would be, based on assumptions as to earning power and as to multipliers. Their method is as follows: They project sales at the rate of $10 million; and this, you see, is our now familiar Childs Company method. Then they apply a profit margin, which they expect to be 15 percent. Then they say, "Net per stock: $1.40 per share." They do not give you the arithmetic of that, but here it is: Net before taxes would be $24 million, less taxes at about 40 percent, brings it down to about $14 million-odd, and that is about $1.40 on 10 million shares of stock. Then they add: "Foreign earnings, estimated 25 cents"—and that is a very rough estimate. So they get $1.60 to $1.70 per share, total. Further, they state that in the relatively near future—and because these favorable earnings should continue over a considerable period of time—the stock of this company should prove to be relatively attractive even at its present level, the "present level" being about $20, in February, 1946. That analysis was later used by a stock exchange house, which concluded, without needing quite as much courage, that the stock looks relatively attractive at $15, which was the price on October 23, 1946.

Now before I attempt a criticism, not necessarily unfavorable, of this analysis, I may as well go on to the last one that reached my desk, which is headed "Active Years Ahead for the Building Industry." It gives a great deal of information on the building industry, and information about the companies in the industry, including American Radiator, which is the first one. There they make a calculation of the earning power of the company in what they call year 194x, which they figure at $1.75 per share. They use an expected profit margin of 12 percent. There is a little discrepancy between the 12 percent and their final result. It can be explained, if you want to go to the trouble, partly because they take into account foreign earnings to a greater extent than did the research company analysis.

Now, the interesting thing about this analysis is two-fold: First they get earnings of about $1.75, which is not so different from the other projection. But they describe that estimate as follows: "A rough guess of potential earning power under optimum conditions over the next few years is shown by the line designated 194x." In the rest of the circular, while not too specific, they imply that these stocks are attractive, the ones that they have listed, because of the expected earnings in the 194x year. That is particularly true because the price of American Radiator was only $13.50 on that date, and the estimated earnings of $1.75 would make the price of $13.50 look quite reasonable if that represented future earning power.

My comment on these analyses—the last two, which are the only ones that seriously attempt a projection of future earnings—is this: They do not emphasize enough the fact that the earnings they are dealing with are earnings of a boom period; but the technique of analysis should take that carefully into account.

The earnings for the building boom should be evaluated pretty much in the same way as we were accustomed to evaluating war earnings, that is to say, by assuming that they were to last for a limited number of years. The excess earnings during that period should be added to what we would assume to be the normal valuation of the company based upon its average peacetime earnings. Thus, if you want to attempt a serious evaluation of a company like American Radiator, the only proper method is to take what you would assume to be its *normal* earning power, not its *optimum* earning power, evaluate that, and then add to it a fair allowance for the fact that it is facing some very good years.

I might say that if you want to be somewhat pessimistic you could criticize even that method; because you might argue that these boom years are simply part of a building cycle period. They are not really excess earnings. They are the good part of the normal earnings and will be offset by very low earnings when the building boom subsides. That comment may be justified; but in any event the method that I spoke of before seems to me to be as liberal a method as you could use.

QUESTION: What makes you say that in that estimate of $160 million of sales, those factors were not considered?

MR. GRAHAM: You mean the fact that they were boom period sales?

QUESTION: Possibly they did consider that.

MR. GRAHAM: I can give you a specific reason for that. They say that the earnings are related closely to the residential building totals that will be expected. And over the period 1946–1951 they have gone to the trouble of giving you a projection of the amount of buildings needed and the amount that will be supplied. During the years 1947–1951 they are expecting a million units of building annually. At the end of that time the deficiency will be completely remedied; and, on the basis of their statistics, demand would be reduced to somewhere around 550,000 buildings a year, that is to say, about half a million new families plus demolition. Following through this calculation to the year 1952, you would find that the expectation of new units would be not more than half of the one on which they had based their $160 million of sales.

Another reason, of course, is that the sales actually realized in 1939 were only $80 million, and in 1938, $68 million. Thus the volume of

$160 million, even allowing for some increase in prices, would obviously be on the high side.

Were there other questions about that? Questions of this kind are very good, because they help clarify the reasoning behind these evaluations.

It seems to me that the method of evaluation, then should be somewhat different for American Radiator than has been used. You ought to start, not with the optimum earnings, but what you would consider to be normal earnings for the company.

The company had been earning on the order of about 50 cents a share in the period before the war; and I would assume that if you take earnings of $1 a share after the war, you would be about as optimistic as you would have any right to be about this company's earnings after the building boom has subsided. I am inclined to think that is over-optimistic, as far as one can see now, for the very reason that when the building boom has subsided you are likely to go into a period of *subnormal* earnings if the building cycle behaves in the future as it has in the past. But if you accept the $1 earnings—and I really want to mark that as liberal—I think the multiplier would be somewhere between 12 and 15. That is higher than the company's past record would justify—but the American Radiator has some advantages in being a large and strong company, well thought of, and which many years ago was a very large earner. Consequently, I think you would get a valuation of $12 to $15 on a normal basis.

To that you would add an allowance for the boom time earnings, which are 75 cents a share over expected normal. If you multiply this by four you are again pretty liberal; that will give you $3 extra. The valuation, thus comes to about $15 to $18 a share for the stock, giving the company the benefit of certain doubts that I would have in my own mind. This valuation, I think, could properly have been made for American Radiator at any time during the past year, and would have justified caution with regard to a purchase of that stock for investment at the prices of early 1946.

But on that subject let me add that it is perfectly proper to buy stocks for speculation. There is no crime in that. When you buy stocks for speculation it is perfectly proper to take speculative factors into account, which are different from investment factors. The normal expectancy would be that if this company is to earn $1.75 a share for three or four years, the market will reflect those earnings in full on a speculative basis, without making allowance for the fact that they are temporary.

That hasn't always happened. For example, during the war the market certainly didn't reflect war earnings on the theory that they were permanent earnings. But the market does tend to do so with regard to cyclical earnings; it regards the boom time earnings as permanent earnings. For that reason it is quite possible that American Radiator could sell, under good general market conditions and during its own boom period, at a price very much above our value of $15 to $18.

We must not forget that American Radiator as recently as 1942 sold at $3.75. What we are saying is that American Radiator is a speculative type of security by the nature of its business, as well as by the fact that it is a common stock. Just as it can sell at $4 in bad year, it can easily sell at $30 in a good year, and both prices would be fundamentally justified. Our own valuation represents the type of investment approach which tends pretty much to bring you what you would consider to be a *central* value for the stock. This interests the investor primarily; but second it may interest the intelligent speculator too. For he could then see how far he is getting away from central value when he is following up the speculative aspects of the situation.

I welcome questions about that, because I think that is very important.

QUESTION: If we are to estimate future earnings for just a period of five years, when you speak of a normal period for this industry, wouldn't your analysis go beyond that five-year period? The boom years might be the next five years. Then if you are striking for a normal level, that would go beyond the next five years; so as a result your earnings in the coming five years would be on a higher level and your normal period lower.

MR. GRAHAM: Yes, you are right in making that point. If my recollection is correct, I did make that point too, in my third lecture. I said that normally the earnings that you are trying to estimate are those of the next five years—perhaps five to seven years—but that there

might be some exceptional cases. And I did have the building industry in mind, in which the next five years would not be regarded as a
normal expectancy. The analyst is under a special disadvantage,
then, because the normal earnings that you are thinking of lie so
much further ahead in the future that your chance of being wrong
in calculating what they are going to be is that much greater. But
there is no help for it. You cannot properly evaluate the boom earnings of the next few years as normal, so you must jump ahead to the
later earnings.

QUESTION: But when the market regards the earnings of a company, if
the company went along for five years at a high rate of earnings,
then wouldn't the market place a higher valuation on those earnings, considering the length of time the earnings would be at that
high level?

MR. GRAHAM: Yes; because the market would tend to multiply the
earnings by your standard multiplier of 15 or thereabouts, instead
of merely adding them in the way we suggest you do. (I am speaking, now, of the abnormal or excess component of those earnings.)
The investor would then be out of step with the market in his attitude toward a stock like American Radiator.

The investor is very often out of step with the market, incidentally,
and that would be no new experience for him. But I think it is useful
for the investor to have some idea of what would seem to be the reasonable value, even if the current market may not reflect it at all.

A thing I would like to warn you against is spending a lot of time on
over-detailed analyses of the company's and the industry's position,
including counting the last bathtub that has been or will be produced;
because you get yourself into the feeling that, since you have studied this
thing so long and gathered together so may figures, your estimates are
bound to be highly accurate. But they won't be. They are only very rough
estimates, and I think I could have given, and probably you could have
given me, these estimates in American Radiator in half an hour, without
spending perhaps the days, or even weeks, of studying the industry.

I want to say finally on this question that an elaborate forecasting technique has been developed in recent years on the amount of dollar business and physical volumes that would be done in various industries at certain levels of employment, or certain levels of gross national product. The Committee for Economic Development has gotten out studies of that kind which gives you estimates of the industry totals under full employment conditions, and the same has been done by the Department of Commerce. Those of you who want to go into that aspect of analysis should start pretty much with these forecasts, and accept them or reflect them as far as your own judgment is concerned. If you accept them, then build your forecast of the individual company's sales in relation to the industry totals which you are starting with. You may make three different estimates—as is now done sometimes—based upon full employment, moderate unemployment, and considerable [un]employment; and make your estimate of sales accordingly. That is the new technique, and I think you will find it interesting as applied to security analysis.

LECTURE NUMBER SIX

The first thing that I want to make clear in any attempt to obtain a view as to future earnings, either in general or in particular, is that the analyst is not really trying to look into the crystal ball and come out with the correct answer for the period of time that he is forecasting. What he is really trying to do is to determine how the analyst should act and think—that is, how far he can go in logical thinking with respect to the always enigmatic future.

I don't believe any of us have the pretension of believing that by being very good analysts, or by going through very elaborate computations, we can be pretty sure of the correctness of our results. The only thing that we can be pretty sure of, perhaps, is that we are acting reasonably and intelligently. And if we are wrong, as we are likely to be, at least we have been intelligently wrong and not unintelligently wrong. (Laughter.)

In a study of 14 companies which I made—mainly those that appeared in the Dow Jones Average, either before or after 1914—I found that seven of them showed larger earnings in the post-war period than before the war, six of them showed lower average earnings, and one of them was even. That one, incidentally was United States Steel, which had widely fluctuating earnings in the period after the war, but which averaged in those five years the same figure as it did in the preceding three.

Those results were not as satisfactory as they should have been, because in that period we had the very serious depression of 1920 to 1922; and the effect of depressed conditions was to reduce the average earnings well below what they would have been if we had had a level period of national income. You recall that the figure of $62 billion, which I gave you, was an average national income for the five years. But there were rather wide fluctuations from year to year, and the effect on earnings as a whole was bad. You do not gain as much from periods of unusual prosperity as you lose in periods of depression when you are in business. That is almost an axiom.

I am more and more impressed with the possibilities of history's repeating itself on many different counts. You don't get very far in Wall Street with the simple, convenient conclusion that a given level of prices is not too high. It may be that a great deal of water will have to go over the dam before a conclusion of that kind works itself out in terms of satisfactory experience. That is why in this course we have tried to emphasize as much as possible the obtaining of specific insurance against adverse developments by trying to buy securities that are *not* only *not too high* but that, on the basis of analysis, appear to be very much *too low*. If you do that, you always have the right to say to yourself that you are out of the security market, and you are an owner of part of a company on attractive terms. It is a great advantage to be able to put yourself in that psychological frame of mind when the market is not going the way you would like.

There are great advantages in dealing with a group valuation, because you are more likely to be nearly accurate, I am sure, when you are considering a number of components together—in which your errors are likely to cancel out—than when you are concentrating on an individual component and may go very wide of the mark in that one.

Furthermore, there is nothing to prevent the investor from dealing with his own investment problems on a group basis. There is nothing to prevent the investor from actually buying the Dow Jones Industrial Average, though I never heard of anybody doing it. It seems to me it would make a great deal of sense if he did.

When we talk about buying bargain issues, for example, the emphasis on group operation becomes even greater, because you then get into what could practically be known as an insurance type of operation. Here you have an edge, apparently, on each individual company. That advantage may conceivably disappear or not be realized in the individual case; but if you are any good at all as an analyst you ought to realize that advantage in the *group*. And so I have had a great partiality for group operations and group analysis. I must say, however, that you gentlemen, as functioning security analysts, advisers to the multitude, and so on, are unable to obtain that advantage in all the work you do. For I am sure you are compelled to reach rather definite conclusions about individual companies, and can't hide them in a group result.

LECTURE NUMBER SEVEN

Good evening. You have all had a month's rest since the last lecture. I hope you had a pleasant vacation during that period and you are now ready to absorb some more punishment.

If you recall as far back as the last lecture, we dealt there mainly with the prospective earning power of the Dow Jones list considered as a unit, and with its prospective central market value.

You might now ask the question: What about the earnings of the individual components of the Dow Jones list? How would one go about evaluating them, and what results would you get?

As it happens, that job was done—at least from the standpoint of expected earnings power—in an article that appeared in the *Analyst Journal* in July 1945. It is called "Estimating Earnings of an Active Post-War Year," and it is by Charles J. Collins. There he gives his estimate of the post-war earnings of all the companies in the Dow Jones unit, together with the sum of these earnings.

His total figure varies from $15.96 to $17.58 per unit. You may recall that my rather rough calculation gave a figure of $13.60, and it may thus appear that my figure is rather definitely lower than Collins'. Actually that may not be true, because Collins identifies his earnings as those of an active post-war year, whereas the earnings that I had used in the last lecture are supposed to represent the average future earning power of the Dow Jones unit—which would include some allowance for poor years as well as good ones.

It is interesting to note that Collins' estimates for individual companies show considerable variation from their pre-war earnings, say, their 1940 figures. I might read off a few to you to show how different are his expectations for different companies.

Here are four that show large expected increases, taking 1940 as against the future years: American Smelting, from $4.21 to $9.50; Chrysler, from $8.69 to $17.75; Johns Manville, from $6.34 to $14.75; Goodyear, from $3.44 to $8.60.

Here are four others that show very small increases, if any: (I am using here, the average of his range of figures) American Tel. and Tel., from $10.80 to $10.50; American Tobacco from $5.59 to $5.90; National Distillers, from $3.28 to $3.35; and Woolworth, from $2.48, in 1940, to $2.62 in the postwar year.

Collins does not give his method of calculation in detail, but he does give you a description which you can follow through fairly well.

He starts from industry sales projections which have been made by the Committee for Economic Development of the Department of Commerce, and he adjusts them to an expected national income of $112 billion. That happens to be quite a conservative figure, because the national income for the year 1946 was about $165 billion.

He does not apply the exact percentage increase in each industry to the particular company; but he allows for its better or poorer trend than that of the industry as a whole over the period from 1929 to 1940. He assumes, in other words, that a company which did better than its industry from 1929 to 1940 will do proportionately better in the increase that is to be seen from pre-war; and correspondingly for those that may have done worse.

From the estimated sales he then calculates net before taxes based on pre-war ratios; he takes taxes of 40 percent; and that gives him his figure, with a small range that he allows for possible adjustments.

You will recall that the profit margin that we used was distinctly lower than the pre-war; but on the other hand we took a considerably higher national income, and we also took a lower expected tax.

These variations in method suggest that there is no single way of dealing with a projection of future earnings and that individual judgment will have to play a considerable part. But the variations in this technique are not likely to be as great as the variations in the market's response to what it thinks are the possibilities of different companies.

I would not criticize the Collins method, except in one respect which I think it is rather significant to consider. He assumes that the trends shown from 1929 to 1940 will continue in the future, and that seems a natural assumption to make. But I would like to warn you against placing too much reliance on that supposition.

Some years ago we made a rather intensive study on the subject of whether earnings trends did or did not continue. We tried to find out what happened to companies showing an improvement in their earnings from 1926 to 1930, comparing them further with 1936 [results]; and also those that had failed to show improvement in the period. We found that there were at least as many cases of companies failing to maintain their trend as there were of those that did continue their trends. And that is a very vital consideration in all future projections.

As a matter of fact, Collins himself says that, when he accepts the trends, in some cases he finds he gets such large earnings that he felt constrained to reduce them in the interests of conservatism; and I imagine he was probably right.

Now I would like to return for a moment to the analyst's view of Wall Street as a whole—that is, the scope of his own activities in the securities markets and his approach to his function of analyzing securities and drawing conclusions from his analysis.

I suggest that there are two fundamentally different approaches that the analyst may take to securities as a whole.

The first I call the conventional one, and that is based primarily on quality and on prospects.

The second I call, in complimentary fashion, the penetrating one, and that is based upon value.

Let us first attempt a brief description of these different approaches as they relate themselves to actual activities of the analyst.

The conventional approach can be divided into three separate ways of dealing with securities. The first is the identification of "good stocks"—that is "strong stocks," "strong companies," "well-entrenched companies," or "high quality companies." Those companies presumably can be bought with safety at reasonable prices. That seems like a simple enough activity.

The second is the selection of companies which have better than average long-term prospects of growth in earnings. They are generally called "growth stocks."

The third is an intermediate activity, which involves the selection of companies which are expected to do better business in the near term than the average company. All three of those activities I call conventional.

The second approach divides itself into two sub-classes of action, namely, first, the purchase of securities generally whenever the market is at a low level, as the market level may be judged by analysts. The second is the purchase of special or individual securities at almost any time when their price appears to be well below the appraised or analyzed value.

Let me try to do a little appraising of the appraisers or the analysts themselves, and embark on a brief evaluation of these five lines of action which I have briefly described to you. Of course, I am expressing, basically, a personal opinion, which is derived from experience and observation and a great deal of thought; but it should not be taken as in any sense representing the standard view of the work of the security analyst.

The first division, you recall, was the simple identification of good companies and good stock; and one is inclined to be rather patronizing about a job as easy and elementary as that. My experience leads me to another conclusion. I think that it is the most useful of the three conventional approaches; provided only that a conscientious effort is made to be sure that the "good stock" is not selling above the range of conservative value.

Investors do not make mistakes, or bad mistakes, in buying good stocks at fair prices. They make their serious mistakes by buying poor stocks, particularly the ones that are pushed for various reasons. And sometimes—in fact, very frequently—they make mistakes by buying good stocks in the upper reaches of bull markets.

Therefore, the very simple kind of advice which keeps the investor in the paths of righteousness, or rather of rightness, I would say is very worthwhile advice—saying merely "These are good companies, and their prices are on the whole reasonable." I think also that is the key to the policy of the well-established investment-counsel firms; and it accounts for their ability to survive, in spite of the fact that they are not in a very easy kind of business.

When you move from that simple and yet valuable occupation, namely, telling an investor that General Motors and General Electric are safer things to buy than Barker Brothers at $25.75, for example—when you move from that into the next activity, you are getting into much more difficult ground, although it seems to be much more interesting. And that is the selection of growth stocks, which for a long while was the most popular or rather the best-regarded type of activity by analysts.

The successful purchase of growth stocks requires two rather obvious conditions: First, that their prospect of growth be realized; and, second, that the market has not already pretty well discounted these growth prospects.

These conditions do obtain with regard to some growth stocks, as they are identified by analysts; and highly satisfactory profits are made from that work. But the results vary a great deal with the skill of the selector, and perhaps with "the luck of the draw." It is quite questionable to my mind whether you can establish a technique of a communicable sort—that a good instructor can pass on to his pupil—by which you will be enabled to identify those stocks not only which have good prospects of growth but which have not already discounted pretty much those prospects in the market.

Let us put it in this way: I think at bottom success in the identification of growth stocks comes from being smart or shrewd, but I do not consider it a standard quality of good security analysis to be smart or shrewd. Not that I have any objection to that, but it just doesn't seem to me to fit into the general pattern or canon of security analysis to require those rather rare qualities.

I might say rather that a security analyst should be required to be *wise*, in the sense that he is technically competent, that he is experienced, and that he is prudent. And I don't know that wisdom of that sort is particularly well adapted to the successful selection of growth stocks in a market that is so full of surprises and disappointments in that field as in many others. I have in mind many examples. If you take the chemical companies, which have been the standard example of growth stocks for as long back as I can remember, you will find that for a long period of years their market behavior was quite unsatisfactory as compared with other companies, merely because they had previously had a great deal of popularity at a time when other companies were not so popular.

If you take the air transport stocks, the selection of those securities for investment, based upon the idea of growth, seems to me to have been an exceedingly speculative type of thing; and I don't know how it could have been properly handled under the techniques of well-established security analysis. As you know, there are many, many hazards which exist in that kind of industry, and in many others that have been regarded as having unusual growth prospects.

Now let me pass on to the third activity of the conventional sort, which I think is done most constantly in day-by-day Wall Street organizations—the trade investigation, which leads one to believe that this industry or this company is going to have unusually good results in the next 12 months, and therefore the stock should be bought.

Permit me to say that I am most skeptical of this Wall Street activity, probably because it is the most popular form of passing the time of the security analyst. I regard it as naive in the extreme. The thought that the security analyst, by determining that a certain business is going to do well next year has thereby found something really useful, judged by any serious standard of utility, and that he can translate his discovery into an unconditional suggestion that the stock be bought, seems to me to be only a parody of true security analysis.

Take a typical case. What reason is there to think that because U.S. Plywood, for example, is going to do better in 1947 than it did in 1946, and National Department Stores will probably do worse in 1947 than it did in 1946—what reason is there to believe that U.S. Plywood should be purchased at $34 rather than National Department Stores at $17? There is scarcely any serious relationship between these concepts of next year's operations and the purchase and sale of the securities at the going market price; because the price of $34 for U.S. Plywood might have discounted very good earnings for three years, and the price of National Department Stores might theoretically have discounted poor earnings for three years. And in many cases that is not only theoretically so, but is actually so.

I would suggest, and this is a practical suggestion—what I said before has been perhaps only a theoretical analysis in your eyes—that if you want to carry on the conventional lines of activity as analysts, that you impose some fairly obvious but nonetheless rigorous conditions on your own thinking, and perhaps on your own writing and recommending. In that way you can make sure that you are discharging your responsibilities as analysts. If you want to select good stocks—good, strong, respectable stocks—for your clients, that's fine, I'm all for it. But determine and specify that the price is within the range of fair value when you make such a recommendation. And when you select growth stocks for yourself and your clients, determine and specify the round amount which the buyer at the current price is already paying for the growth factor, as compared with its reasonable price if the growth prospect were only average. And then determine and state whether, in the analyst's judgment, the growth prospects are such as to warrant the payment of the current price by a prudent investor.

I would like to see statements of that kind made in the security analyses and in circulars. It seems to me that you would then be getting some kind of defensible approach to this process of handing out recommendations.

And finally, in recommending a stock because of good near-term prospects, you should determine and state whether or not, in the analyst's judgment, the market price and its fairly recent market action has already reflected the expectations of the analyst. After you have determined that it hasn't, and that the thing has possibilities that have not been shown in the market action, then it would be at least a reasonable action on your part to recommend the stock because of its near-term prospects.

Have you any questions about this evaluation, perhaps somewhat biased, of the conventional activities of the security analyst?

QUESTION: Do you confine your near-term valuation, your point three, to just one year?

MR. GRAHAM: I am thinking more or less of between one and two years. Most people seem satisfied to talk about the next 12 months in this particular field.

Let us spend the next five minutes on the unconventional or pene-trating type of security analysis, which emphasizes value.

The first division represents buying into the market as a whole at low levels; and that, of course, is a copybook procedure. Everybody knows that is theoretically the right thing to do. It requires no explanation or defense; though there must be some catch to it, because so few people seem to do it continuously and successfully.

The first question you ask is, of course: "How do you know that the market price is low?" That can be answered pretty well, I think. The ana-lyst identifies low market levels in relation to the past pattern of the mar-ket and by simple valuation methods such as those that we have been discussing. And bear in mind that the good analyst doesn't change his concept of what the earnings of the next five years are going to be just because the market happens to be pessimistic at one time, or optimistic at another. His views of average future earnings would change only because he is convinced that there has been some change of a very sig-nificant sort in the underlying factors.

Now he can also follow a mechanical system of operating in the market, if he wishes, like the Yale University method that many of you are familiar with. In this you sell a certain percentage of your stocks as they go up, or you convert a certain percentage of your bonds into stocks as they go down, from some median or average level.

I am sure that those policies are good policies, and they stand up in the light of experience. Of course, there is one very serious objection to them and that is that "it is a long time between drinks" in many cases.

You have to wait too long for recurrent opportunities. You get tired and restless—especially if you are an analyst on a payroll, for it is pretty hard to justify drawing your salary just by waiting for recurrent low markets to come around. And so obviously you want to do something else besides that.

The thing that you would naturally be led into, if you are value-minded, would be the purchase of individual securities that are undervalued at all stages of the security market. That can be done successfully, and should be done—with one proviso, which is that it is not wise to buy undervalued securities when the general market seems very *high*. That is a particularly difficult point to get across: For superficially it would seem that a high market is just the time to buy the undervalued securities, because their undervaluation seems most apparent then. If you could buy Mandel at $13, let us say, with a working capital so much larger when the general market is very high, it seems a better buy than when the general market is average or low. Peculiarly enough, experience shows that is not true. If the general market is very high and is going to have a serious decline, then your purchase of Mandel at $13 is not going to make you very happy or prosperous for the time being. In all probability the stock will also decline sharply in price in a break. Don't forget that if Mandel or some similar company sells at less than your idea of value, it sells so because it is not popular; and it is not going to get more popular during periods when the market as a whole is declining considerably. Its popularity tends to decrease along with the popularity of stocks generally.

QUESTION: Mr. Graham, isn't there what you might call a negative kind of popularity, such as the variations of Atchison? I mean, in a falling market, while it is perfectly true that an undervalued security will go down, would it go down as fast as some of the blue chips?

MR. GRAHAM: In terms of percentage I would say yes, on the whole. It will go down about as fast, because the undervalued security tends to be a lower-priced security; and the lower-priced securities tend to lose more percentagewise in any important recessions than the higher ones. Thus you have several technical reasons why it does not become really profitable to buy undervalued securities at statistically high levels of the securities market.

If you are pretty sure that the market is too high, it is a better policy to keep your money in cash or government bonds than it is to put it in bargain stocks. However, at other times—and that is most of the time, of course—the field of undervalued securities is profitable and suitable for analysts' activities. We are going to talk about that at our next lecture.

LECTURE NUMBER EIGHT

It follows that, in dealing with undervalued securities, the analyst is likely to become greatly interested in specific corporate developments, and therefore in proper corporate policies. And from being interested in corporate policies, he may pass over into being critical of wrong policies and actively agitating to bring about correct policies—all of which he considers to be in the stockholders' interests. For it is true that in a fairly large percentage of cases the undervaluation in the market can be removed by proper action by or in the corporation.

Consequently, by insensible stages of reasoning, the specialist in undervalued securities finds himself turning into that abomination of Wall Street known as a disgruntled stockholder.

I want to say a word about disgruntled stockholders. The trouble with stockholders, in my humble opinion, is that not enough of them are disgruntled. And one of the great troubles with Wall Street is that it cannot distinguish between a mere troublemaker or "strike-suitor" in corporation affairs and a stockholder with a legitimate complaint which deserves attention from his management and from his fellow stockholders.

QUESTION: In connection with investment income, isn't it possible that the method in which that is determined might be conservative? In other words, investment income, as I understand it, would probably be income from interest, dividends, and excluding capital appreciation.

MR. GRAHAM: Yes. I am glad you raised the question, because I omitted any reference to the question of capital appreciation or depreciation in insurance company investments.

Speaking about that I would like to go back to the reasons for the popularity of insurance company shares in the 1920s. The analyses that used to be made at that time indicated that the insurance stockholder was a very fortunate person, because he had three different and valuable sources of income. One was the insurance business, which was supposed to be a very good industry, although there was no analysis of how much it contributed in earnings in those days. It was taken for granted that it was a good business for the stockholder.

Then it was said that you got the interest on money, not only your own money, but you got interest and dividends also on a lot of money that the policyholders had left with you in the form of unearned premiums and unpaid losses, and so on. Thus, for every dollar of your own, you had a total of about $2 working for you, drawing investment income.

The third advantage was that you had extremely capable investment managements putting your money in securities and making a lot of profits for you.

Of course they made profits for you in the 1920s when the market was going up, and of course they lost a great deal of money in the early 1930s when the market was going down. The same thing happened in 1937–1938, when they made a lot of money up to March 1937, then they lost a great deal in the ensuing decline.

The net of all this history, I am pretty sure, is that today's sophisticated investors are not willing to pay very much for the ability of insurance managements to make capital gains for them over the years. It turns out that we do not have the type of check-ups and careful analysis of insurance company investment results that we have in the case of investment trusts, because the business does not lend itself so easily to that kind of thing. But it can be done. I am going to give you some figures on American Equitable Insurance Company over a 20 year period, to indicate how that company made out in that period of time with its investments as well as with its underwritings.

But on the whole, just answering the specific question asked, no investor today—and I don't think any analyst—is willing to give the insurance business any special credit for ability to make profits on the principal value of its securities. It will make profits in good years and it will lose money in bad years from that department. That may be doing it an injustice; but that I am sure is the general opinion of security analysts at the present time.

QUESTION: Would you care to take a minute to differentiate between premiums and underwriting profit? That is a little technical. What is underwriting profit?

MR. GRAHAM: Underwriting profit is the profit earned from the insurance business as such. It consists of the balance left after you pay the losses and the expenses of the underwriting business. It includes, moreover, a certain component known as the increase in the unearned premium reserve, which is a technicality. It is generally accepted that the liabilities shown on the balance sheet for "unearned premium reserves" include, to the extent of 40 percent ordinarily, an amount that is really the stockholders' equity. When that figure goes up, the insurance profits for the year are increased accordingly, and conversely. Thus you really have two parts to your underwriting results: One, the straight result, and the other the equity in the increase or decrease in the unearned premium reserve.

I do want to say something about the method of calculating liquidating values, or equities, in this business, but I will delay that for a while.

QUESTION: What of the possibilities of increasing the underwriting profits, rather of raising rates in underwriting business? You always get a lull after a war, when the insurance on property has to be marked up after the replacement value advance.

MR. GRAHAM: In answering that question now, I would like to distinguish very sharply between recent results and long-term average results. The recent results of the fire business have been bad. Most companies, I think, showed losses for 1946—the figures are not out yet—and about half of them, perhaps, showed losses for 1945.

The results that I have been dealing with have been 10-year average figures, and I think that they pretty fairly represent what you can expect over the years in the insurance business. It may be that the results will be a little better in the next 10 years than they were in the last 10 years, but I don't believe that an insurance analyst or an investor ought to count particularly upon that. He should count upon their being better in the next five years than they were in the last two or three, which is of course a different matter.

QUESTION: Why do companies like the American Reserve [Insurance Company] or even the North River [Insurance Company] stay in business, then?

MR. GRAHAM: The North River Company stays in business, of course, because it has been in existence for 126 years, and has built up a large business, which has increased over the years, which has been satisfactory to the people running the business, to its agents, and to its policyholders. Whether it is now satisfactory to the stockholders I don't think has ever been asked, and I don't think such questions are asked in any of these companies.

I have read a number of reports of fire insurance companies to their stockholders. They consist generally of a one-page balance sheet and a few pages listing the securities owned. The question of how profitable is the business, is just not discussed. I suppose it would be ungentlemanly to raise the point.

QUESTION: Do your figures here show underwriting profit as reported, or is some adjustment made such as the Best adjustments for unearned premiums?

MR. GRAHAM: These include the unearned premium adjustment, which is pretty standard. In fact, the companies themselves, in many cases, indicate what that amounts to in their discussions at their annual meetings. It is really standard procedure.

In the casualty business there is still another adjustment, which I will mention later on—the difference between one kind of reserve and another kind of reserve method.

QUESTION: Well, one of the reasons for stockholders not knowing anything about insurance companies is the fact, that I think, until recently they didn't publish any profit or loss statements. They just gave balance sheets on the statement, just like the bank did.

MR. GRAHAM: Yes. If I were a stockholder in an insurance company, I would like to know whether the business was profitable enough, and I would ask. But apparently the stockholders in the insurance companies don't ask that question, to the extent of requiring that the figures be analyzed or presented in the annual reports.

The casualty companies, interestingly enough, tend to publish rather elaborate reports, with a good deal of information. One reason, perhaps, is that the casualty business has been quite profitable in the last 10 years.

QUESTION: Don't you think the stockholders' complacency is caused by the fact that the early investor in insurance companies—such as Continental, or what is called the "Home Group"—has done very well over the last 20 years with his money. Whether he has been lulled to sleep is another thing, but I think that has been the cause of it.

MR. GRAHAM: I am not in a position to tell you what happened in the last 20 years to every one of these companies. But I do know that in the fire group some companies have done very badly for 20 years; and a company like North River, which I believe is pretty representative, has started off doing very well and is finishing up in a situation which does not permit it to do really well for its stockholders. I don't believe that this analysis would be subject to much change if you took other companies. You might find one or two exceptions, such as the St. Paul Fire and Marine. But they are extraordinarily few.

QUESTION: Is the competition of mutual [companies] a factor here?

MR. GRAHAM: I don't know whether that really is a factor. It might be. But the insurance companies endeavor to obtain higher rates when they need them by application to the various insurance boards, and there is always a lag in getting them.

QUESTION: The solicitors for the mutual [company] insistently cite expenses cheaper than the stock company. That is one of their big points. That is to say, in the form of commissions to agents. Net costs to the policyholder.

MR. GRAHAM: I shouldn't be surprised if that were so. There is reason to believe that the scale of commissions paid on fire insurance policies has been too high—the commissions paid to agents. It doesn't take a great deal of salesmanship in my opinion to sell a fire insurance policy. It does take quite a bit perhaps to sell a life insurance policy. The fire commissions have been pretty large, and I think that in some cases recently the state insurance departments have hesitated to permit premium raises on the ground that the commissions to agents have been too high. At least so I am informed, but I will not state that as a fact.

QUESTION: The casualty men always stress cost to the policyholders.

MR. GRAHAM: In the mutual, too? Well, in the casualty field, in spite of the competitions with the mutual companies, the stock companies have been able to earn a very considerable sum of money for their stockholders.

Are there any other questions about that?

QUESTION: To get back to a point that might be elementary. I am not at all familiar with these industries. You have 1927 and 1945 statistics on the board. I can see why there has been a decline in investment income; but even if it is repetitious, will you explain why there has been that sharp decline in underwriting profit, and whether that is a transitory situation or will it continue?

MR. GRAHAM: The decline in the underwriting profit of North River is due to two factors: One is the profit per dollar of insurance written, which went down from about 6 percent to 4 percent for those two years. It is difficult to say whether that is a permanent thing or not. I am inclined to think that there is a slight tendency for that rate to go down through the years.

The more important fact is that the amount of premiums written by this company, per dollar of stockholders' equity, has been cut in two. Therefore, with the same rate of profit you would only earn half as much on your stock.

That is just like saying you now have only 50 cents of sales per dollar of capital, instead of a dollar of sales.

The reason for that is very interesting, and I would like to comment on it a bit. What has happened is that these companies have built up their stockholders' equity in various ways in the period to a much greater extent than they built up their premiums. The result is that from the standpoint of good results for the stockholders, they seem to have much too much capital per dollar of business done in 1945.

Of course, the insurance companies will insist that is not true. They will say that the more capital they have the better the policyholders are, and therefore the better the stockholders are. They will also say that they expect to do very much more business in the future, and therefore they should have the capital available for the expanding business. But the fact remains that in dollars and cents you have the situation that the North River Company had $25 million of stockholders' capital and did about $9 million of business in 1945, which is a very small amount of business per dollar of capital. In 1927 they did a somewhat larger amount of business with less than half the amount of capital.

No attention has been paid to that matter by anyone, that is by any stockholder. As far as the management is concerned, the more capital they have, the better off they are. There isn't the slightest doubt about that.

QUESTION: Haven't they got more money to invest in stocks?

MR. GRAHAM: They have more money to invest in stocks, but that is no special advantage to the stockholder because he has more money of his own invested. The question is what about the rate of return, and that has gone down too, of course.

There is a better answer to your question. Because they have more capital, the amount of investment per dollar of capital goes down. The reason is that in addition to investing the stockholders' capital they invest other moneys that come out of the conduct of the business. The more capital there is in relation to the business, the less proportionate excess do they have. That is shown in this figure: In 1927 they had $1.45 of invested assets per dollar of stockholder's capital, and now they have only $1.18. So they lost out in that respect too.

Now, I might suggest that somebody should raise the question, "What can the stockholders do to get a decent return on their investment on the North River Insurance Company?" Let us assume it was a matter for the stockholders to decide, which would be a very extraordinary suggestion for anyone to make—elementary as it sounds in theory. Here is a possible answer: Suppose you reestablished the relationship between capital and premiums that existed in 1927, when things were quite satisfactory, by simply returning to the stockholders the excess capital in relation to the business done. If you did that, you would be able to get the earnings of about 6 percent on your capital and to pay the 4 percent dividend on your capital, which I suggested might be a definition of a reasonable return to the stockholder. That could happen because, when you take out $15 a share from the present $31—and you have left only $16 to earn money on for the stockholder—you are reducing your earnings only by the net investment income on the $15 withdrawn, which is on the order of, say, 40 cents at the most. Thus you would earn about 85 cents on the remaining investment of $16 and you would get reasonably close to the 6 percent which you need.
That is a method that will not recommend itself to insurance company managements, but which at least has some arithmetical validity as far as the stockholders are concerned.
Are there any other questions about this analysis with regard to the North River Company?

QUESTION: I don't quite understand. What is the reason for the decline in the volume, dollar volume, of premiums underwritten? Is it a question of growth and competition in the industry? Would you not expect the overall dollar amount of premiums to increase over a period of 20 odd years?

MR. GRAHAM: The situation is this: For the country as a whole net premiums written by fire companies grew in volume from $966 million in 1927 to $1,226,000 in 1945. That would represent an increase of about one-third.

The North River Company had $9.1 million in premiums in 1945, and $10.9 million in 1927. That was a reduction of about 16 percent. It is pretty clear that the North River Company individually went back in that period of time. Many of the other companies, which increased their premiums, however, increased them by absorbing other companies over the 20 year period. Also a good deal of the insurance written was taken by new fire subsidiaries of casualty companies, and so on. It may well be that the typical company which didn't go through corporate changes, but just stuck to its old setup, might have had a situation not so different from the North River Company, namely, a decline in premiums.

It is important to point out that the rate of premiums per $1,000 of insurance went down very much from 1927 to 1945. The companies gave more to the policyholder for their money. The result is that their premium income suffered, and does not reflect the true growth in the amount of coverage extended.

QUESTION: Did North River sell additional shares during that 18-year period?

MR. GRAHAM: Yes. I made an error in my previous statement that I want to correct. I said that the North River Company had retained its old position. That was not right. They took over another company, which represents about one-fifth of their total capitalization. That means they added about 25 percent, presumably, to their business by absorbing another company in that period of time, so they should have shown an increase in their business. Exactly why this company didn't do it, I don't know.

QUESTION: Isn't the North River one of a group of companies?

MR. GRAHAM: Yes, it is operated by the Crum and Forster organization.

QUESTION: They may have stuck the premiums in some of their other companies.

MR. GRAHAM: That might be the reason. That is another interesting question that arises in the treatment of stockholders' interest by insurance company managements. Many of the insurance companies are part of so-called "fleets" or groups of companies, and you find some very surprising things in those fleets. Some of the companies tend to be quite profitable, and others in the same group tend to be unprofitable. When you ask for an explanation, as I have done in one case, you may be a bit surprised at the kind of explanation you get. The thing that surprises me always is that the insurance people never talk in terms of what happens to the stockholder. They always talk in terms of what happens to the business as such. You can find many business reasons why Company A should be profitable and Company B should be unprofitable—but no reason that will satisfy the *stockholder* of Company B, in that case.

LECTURE NUMBER NINE

Now, we turn to the New Amsterdam Casualty case, which is interesting for a completely different set of reasons, as I pointed out in the previous lecture. Here you have a very large discount in price from break-up value, but instead of having an unprofitable company, you have one which, over the years, has shown very good results indeed. Instead of having the stockholders suffering from what might be called a certain waste of assets—in the sense of a business which is carried on for years on a relatively losing basis—you have exactly the opposite: The stockholder is suffering from an undue desire by management to gather together and retain all the assets possible and to give out as little as they decently can to the stockholders. I think the contrast in the two cases is very extraordinary, and it deserves some careful thinking on your side. For it shows that the stockholders' interests are affected by developments and policies of a very diverse nature, and that a stockholder can suffer from failure to pay out earnings, when they are realized, nearly as much as he suffers from the failure to realize earnings.

Now, that will be vigorously denied by corporate managements, who insist that as long as the money is made and is retained in the treasury the stockholder does not possibly suffer and he can only gain. I think you gentlemen are better qualified than anyone else to be the judge of that very question. Is it true that the outside stockholder invariably benefits from the retention of earnings in the business, as distinct from the payment of a fair return on the value of his equity in the form of dividends? I believe that Wall Street experience shows clearly that the best treatment for stockholders is the payment to them of fair and reasonable dividends in relation to the company's earnings and in relation to the true value of the security, as measured by any ordinary tests based on earning power or assets.

In my view the New Amsterdam Casualty case is a very vivid example of how security holders can suffer through failure to pay adequate dividends. This company, as I remarked two weeks ago, has been paying a dividend, which is the same amount as paid by the other two companies. Its average earnings have been very much higher. For the five years 1941–1945, the earnings are shown to have averaged $4.33, after taxes, as against which their maximum dividend has been $1 per annum.

You will recall that the North River Company during that period earned an average of $1.12, one-quarter as much, and paid the same dividend of $1. And the American Equitable, which earned an average of nine cents in those five years, also paid $1.

If the New Amsterdam Company had been paying a dividend commensurate with its earnings and its assets, both, there is no doubt in my mind but that the stockholders would have benefitted in two major ways: First, they would have received an adequate return on their money, which is a thing of very great moment in the case of the average stockholder, and, secondly, they would have enjoyed a better market price for their stock.

It turns out that we have an extraordinarily pat comparative example here in the form of another casualty company, called the U.S. Fidelity and Guaranty. This pursues an almost identical line of business, and has almost identical earnings and almost identical assets, per share, as has New Amsterdam. But it happens to pay $2 a share in dividends instead of $1 a share, and so it has been selling recently at about $45; whereas New Amsterdam stock has been selling at somewhere around $26 to $28.

The difference in results to the stockholder between paying a reasonable and fair dividend and paying a niggardly dividend is made as manifest as it can be by these contrasting examples.

You may ask: What is the reason advanced by the management for failure to pay a more substantial dividend, when it appears that the price of the stock and the stockholders' dividend return both suffer so much from the present policy?

You will find, if you talk to the management on the subject, that they will give you three reasons for their dividend policy; and if you have done similar missionary work over a period of time, the arguments will sound strangely familiar to you.

The first reason they give you is conservatism—that is, it is desirable, and in the interest of the stockholders, to be as conservative as possible. It is a good thing to be conservative, of course. The real question at issue is, can a company be too conservative? Would the stockholders be better off, for example, if they received no dividend at all, rather than $1—which would be carrying the conservatism to its complete extreme? I believe that experience shows that conservatism of this kind can be carried to the point of seriously harming the stockholders' interest.

The second reason that you will get from the company—and you will get it from every other company in the same position—is that theirs is a very special business and it has special hazards; and it is necessary to be much more careful in conducting this business than in conducting the average business or any other one that you might mention. In this particular case they would point out also that the results for the year 1946 have been unsatisfactory, and that the current situation is by no means good.

Since every business is a special business, it seems to me that the argument more or less answers itself. You would have to conclude that there would be no principles by which the stockholders can determine suitable treatment for themselves, if it is to be assumed that each business is so different from every other that no general principles can be applied to it.

With regard to the statement that the 1946 results have been poor, it happens that if you analyze them in the usual fashion you would find that even in a bad year like 1946 the New Amsterdam Casualty Company appeared to earn on the order of $2.50 a share. Therefore it could well have afforded a larger dividend than $1, even if you took the one-year results alone, which it is by no means the proper standard to follow. Dividend policy should be based upon *average* earnings in the past and upon expected *average* earnings in the future.

It will be pointed out that some companies have been having difficulties in the insurance business in the last two years, and for that reason it is very desirable that conservatism be followed. We all know there have been some very unprofitable insurance concerns, and some have been profitable. To say that stockholders of profitable businesses cannot get reasonable dividends because there are some unprofitable or some possibly shaky companies in the field, I would call rather irrelevant.

The third argument—and this is especially interesting, I believe, because it comes down to the essence of stockholders' procedures and rights—is that the stockholders do not understand the problems of the business as well as the management of a company. Therefore it is little short of impertinence for the stockholders to suggest that they know better than the management what is the proper policy to follow in their interest.

Of course, the trouble with that argument is that it proves too much. It would mean that regardless of what issue was raised, the stockholders should never express themselves, and should never dare to have an opinion contrary to the management's. I think you would all agree that the principle of stockholders' control over managements would be completely vitiated if you assume that managements *always* knew what was the best thing to do and always acted in the stockholders' interest on every point.

I want to say, with regard to the New Amsterdam Company—since in this course we have been mentioning names right along, for the sake of vividness—two things: First, I should have started by saying that my investment company has an interest in the New Amsterdam Casualty Company, and I have had a dispute with the management as to proper dividend policy. I want to say that, because you may believe that this presentation has been biased—and you are perfectly free to form that conclusion if you wish. You should be warned of the possibility of bias. My belief, of course, is that the statements made fairly represent the issues in the case.

The second point I want to make very emphatically is that the New Amsterdam Casualty Company is extremely well managed by very capable people of the highest character, and that the issue that arises here is not one of self-interest on the part of the management, or lack of ability, but solely the question of dividend policy, and its impact on the stockholders' interest.

The solution of this problem of the stockholders' interest in the New Amsterdam case, and many others, is not easy to predict. As I see it, after a good deal of thought, analysis, and argument on the subject, you need in these cases a long process of stockholders education, so that they will come to think for themselves and act for themselves. Whether that will ever be realized I don't know; but I am very hopeful that people in Wall Street might play a part in giving stockholders sound and impartial guidance in regard to the holdings that they have, as well as to the securities which they might think of buying or selling.

LECTURE NUMBER TEN

Ladies and gentlemen, this is the last of our series of lectures. I hope that you will have found it as enjoyable and stimulating to listen to them as I have found it in preparing them.

The final talk is going to be something of departure, for it will address itself to speculation—speculation in relation to security analysis.

Speculation, I imagine, is a theme almost as popular as love; but in both cases most of the comments made are rather trite and not particularly helpful. (Laughter.)

In discussing speculation in the context of this lecture it will be my effort to bring out some of the less obvious aspects of this important element in finance and in your own work.

There are three main points that I would like to make in this hour.

The first is that speculative elements are of some importance in nearly all the work of the security analyst, and of considerable importance in part of his work; and that the overall weight and significance of speculation has been growing over the past 30 years.

The second point is that there is a real difference between intelligent and unintelligent speculation, and that the methods of security analysis may often be of value in distinguishing between the two kinds of speculation.

My third point is that, despite the two foregoing statements, I believe that the present attitude of security analysts toward speculation is in the main unsound and unwholesome. The basic reason therefore is that our emphasis tends to be placed on the *rewards* of successful speculation rather than on our *capacity* to speculate successfully.

There is a great need, consequently, for a careful self-examining critique of the security analyst as speculator, and that means in turn a self-critique by the so-called typical investor, acting as speculator.

First, what do we mean by speculation? There is a chapter in our book on *Security Analysis* which is devoted to the distinctions between investment and speculation. I don't wish to repeat that material beyond recalling to you our concluding definition, which reads as follows: "An investment operation is one which, on thorough analysis, promises safety of principal and a satisfactory return. Operations not meeting these requirements are speculative." That is a very brief reference to speculation. We could amplify it a bit by saying that in speculative operations a successful result cannot be predicated on the processes of security analysis. That doesn't mean that speculation can't be successful, but it simply means you can't be a successful speculator in individual cases merely by following our methods of security analysis.

Speculative operations are all concerned with changes in price. In some cases the emphasis is on price changes alone, and in other cases the emphasis is on changes in value which are expected to give rise to changes in price. I think that is a rather important classification of speculative operations. It is easy to give examples.

If at the beginning of 1946 a person bought U.S. Steel at around 80, chiefly because he believed that in the latter part of bull markets the steel stocks tend to have a substantial move, that would clearly be a speculative operation grounded primarily on an opinion as to price changes, and without any particular reference to value.

On the other hand, a person who bought Standard Gas and Electric, four dollars preferred, sometime in 1945, at a low price—say at $4 a share—because he thought the plan which provided for its extinction was likely to be changed, was speculating undoubtedly. But there his motive was related to an analysis of value—or rather to an expected change of value—which, as it happened, was realized spectacularly in the case of the Standard Gas and Electric Preferred issue.

I think it is clear to you that in a converse sense nearly all security operations which are based essentially on expected changes, whether they are of price or of value, must be regarded as speculative, and distinguished from investment.

In our chapter on speculation and investment we discussed the concept of the speculative component in a price. You remember we pointed out that a security might sell at a price which reflected in part its investment value and in part an element which should be called speculative. The example we gave back in 1939–1940, with considerable trepidation, was that of General Electric. We intentionally picked out the highest-grade investment issue we could find to illustrate the element of speculation existing in it. Of the price of $38, which it averaged in 1939, we said the analyst might conclude that about $25 a share represented the investment component and as much as $13 a share represented the speculative component. Hence in this very high-grade issue about one-third of the average price in a more or less average market represents a speculative appraisal.

That example, which showed how considerable was the speculative component in investment securities, I think is pretty typical of security value developments since World War I. I believe it justifies and explains the first point that I wish to make, namely, that speculative elements have become more and more important in the work of the analyst. I think only people who have been in Wall Street for a great many years can appreciate the change in the status of investment common stocks that took place in the last generation, and the extent to which speculative considerations have obtruded themselves in all common stocks.

When I came down to the Street in 1914, an investment issue was not regarded as speculative, and it wasn't speculative. Its price was based primarily upon an established dividend. It fluctuated relatively little in ordinary years. And even in years of considerable market and business changes the price of investment issues did not go through very wide fluctuations. It was quite possible for the investor, if he wished, to disregard price changes completely, considering only the soundness and dependability of his dividend return, and let it go at that—perhaps every now and then subjecting his issue to a prudent scrutiny.

That fact is illustrated on the blackboard by taking the rather extreme case of the Consolidated Gas Company, now Consolidated Edison Company, during the years of the first postwar boom and depression—namely, 1919–1923. These vicissitudes really affected the company quite severely; for you will notice that its earnings suffered wide fluctuations, and got down in 1920 to only $1.40 a share for the $100 par value stock. Yet during that period it maintained its established dividend of $7 and its price fluctuation was comparatively small for a major market swing— that is, it covered a range of $106 down to $71.

If we go back to the years 1936–1938, which in the textbooks is now referred to as a mere "recession" that lasted for a year, we find that Consolidated Edison Company, with no changes in earnings to speak of, had extraordinarily wide changes in price. During the year 1937 alone, it declined from about $50 to $21, and the following year went down to $17. During that period it actually raised its dividend, and its earnings were very stable. (See comparative data in the following table [Table 8].)

The much wider fluctuations in investment common stocks that have come about since World War I have made it practically impossible for buyers of common stocks to disregard price changes. It would be extremely unwise—and hypocritical—for anybody to buy a list of common stocks and say that he was interested only in his dividend return and cared nothing at all about price changes.

The problem is not whether price changes should be disregarded— because clearly they should not be—but rather in what way can the

TABLE 8

Record of Consolidated Edison (Consolidated Gas)
in Selected Years (Per Share Figures)

Year	Earnings	Dividend	Price Range
1919	$ 4.10	$7	106–80
1920	1.40	7	94–71
1921	6.80	7	95–73
1922	10.16	7.50	146–86
	(New Stock)		
1936	2.33	1.75	48–27
1937	2.19	2.00	50–21
1938	2.09	2.00	34–17

investor and the security analyst deal intelligently with the price changes which take place.

I would like to go back for a moment to our statement that in the case of General Electric a considerable portion of the price in 1939 reflected a speculative component. That arises from the fact that investors have been willing to pay so much for so-called quality, and so much for so-called future prospects, on the average, that they have themselves introduced serious speculative elements into common stock valuations. These elements are bound to create fluctuations in their own attitude, because quality and prospects are psychological factors. The dividend, of course, is not a psychological factor; it is more or less of a fixed datum. Matters of the former kind—I am speaking now of prospects and quality—are subject to wide changes in the psychological attitude of the people who buy and sell stocks. Thus we find that General Electric will vary over a price range almost as wide as that of any secondary stock belonging in more or less the same price class.

Going ahead from 1939 to 1946, we find that General Electric declined from $44.50 down to $21.50 and came back again to $52 in 1946, and has since declined to $33, or thereabouts. These are wide fluctuations. I think they justify my statement that a very considerable part of the price of General Electric must be regarded as speculative and perhaps temporary.

I think also you might say that the pure investment valuation of $25 for General Electric could be said to be justified by the sequel, since there were opportunities both in 1941 and 1942 to buy the stock at those levels. It is also true that the price movement of General Electric was not as favorable between 1939 and 1946 as that of other stocks, and I think that reflects the rather over-emphasized speculative element that appeared in General Electric before World War II.

Speculative components may enter into bonds and preferred stocks as well as into common stocks. But a high-grade bond, almost by definition, has practically no speculative component. In fact, if you thought it had a large speculative component, you would not buy it for investment nor would you call it high grade. But there is one important factor to be borne in mind here. A rise in interest rates may cause a substantial decline in the price of a very good bond. But even in that event a high-grade bond may be valued on its amortized basis throughout the period that it runs, and the price fluctuations could therefore be ignored by a conventional treatment of value. As most of you know, that is exactly what is done in the insurance company valuation methods which we were discussing recently. High-grade bonds are valued from year to year on an amortized basis, without reference to price fluctuations.

It may be a pleasant thing for the security analyst to get away from the speculative components that are found chiefly in common stocks and which are so troublesome, and to concentrate on the more responsive and more controllable elements in *bond* analysis. Wall Street, I believe, has improved very greatly its technique of bond analysis since 1929. But it is one of the ironies of life that just when you have got something really under control it is no longer as important as it used to be. I think we must all admit that bond analysis plays a very much smaller part in the work of the analyst and in the activities of the investor than it used to. The reason is perfectly obvious: The greater portion of bond investments now consist of U.S. government bonds, which do not require or lend themselves to a formal bond analysis.

While it is true that for the minor portion of corporate bonds that remain you can go through all the motions of careful bond analysis, even that is likely to be somewhat frustrating. For I am sure that a really competent bond analyst is almost certain to come up with the conclusion in nearly every case that the typical buyer would be better off with a government bond than with a well-entrenched corporate security. The purchase of these corporate securities in the present market is a kind of *pro forma* affair by the large institutions who, for semi-political reasons, desire to have corporate bonds in their portfolios as well as government bonds. The result is that the wide field of bond analysis, which used to be so important to and so rewarding to the bond investor, must now, I think, be written down pretty far in terms of practical interest.

So much, then, for my first point: That willy-nilly we security analysts find that more and more significance attaches to speculative elements in the securities that we are turning our attention to.

On the second point, which relates to the analyst's role in distinguishing intelligent from unintelligent speculation, I would like to treat that matter chiefly by some examples.

I have picked out four low-price securities, which I think would illustrate the different kinds of results which an analyst may get from dealing with primarily speculative securities. These are, on the one hand, Allegheny Corp. common, which sold at the end of the month at $5, and Graham-Paige common, which sold at $5; and, on the other hand, General Shareholdings, which sold at $4, and Electric Bond and Share $6 preferred "stubs," which could be bought yesterday at the equivalent of $3.

When we first look at these securities, they all seem pretty much the same—namely, four speculative issues, which they certainly are. But a deeper examination by a security analyst would reveal a quite different picture in the two pairs of cases.

In the case of General Shareholdings we have the following: This is the common stock of an investment company, which has $21.5 million of total assets, with senior claims of $12 million, and a balance of about $9.5 million for the common. The common is selling for $6.4 million in the market. That means that in General Shareholdings you have both a market discount from the apparent present value of the stock and an opportunity to participate in a highly leveraged situation. For if you pay $6.4 million of the gross asset value; and consequently every 10 percent of increase in total asset value would mean a 30 percent increase in the book value of the common.

Furthermore, you are practically immune from any danger of serious corporate trouble; because the greater portion of the senior securities—in fact, five-sixths of it—is represented by a preferred stock on which dividends do not have to be paid and on which there is no maturity date.

Consequently, in the General Shareholdings case, you have that typically attractive speculative combination of (a) a low-price "ticket of entry" into a fairly large situation; and (b) instead of paying more than the mathematical value of your ticket, you are paying less; and (c) if you assume that wide fluctuations are likely to occur in both directions over the years, you stand to gain more than you can lose from these fluctuations.

So much for General Shareholdings, viewed analytically.

By contrast, if you go to Allegheny Corporation at $5, although it seems at first to be a somewhat similar situation—namely, an interest in an investment company portfolio—you find the mathematical picture completely different. At the end of 1945 the company had about $85 million of assets, and against it there were $125 million claims in the form of bonds and preferred stocks, including unpaid dividends. Thus the common stock was about $40 million "under water." Yet at $5 you would be paying $22 million for your right to participate in any improved value for the $85 million of assets—*after* the prior claims were satisfied.

The security analyst would say that there is plenty of leverage in that situation, of course; but you are paying so much for it, and you are so far removed from an actual realizable profit, that it would be an unintelligent speculation.

The fact of the matter is you would need a 70 percent increase in the value of the Allegheny portfolio merely to be even with the market price of the common as far as asset value coverage is concerned. In the case of General Shareholdings, if you had a 70 percent increase in the value of its portfolio, you would have an asset value of about $15 a share for the common, as against a market price of around $4.

Thus, from the analytical standpoint, while Allegheny and General Shareholdings represent approximately the same general picture, there is a very wide quantitative disparity between the two. One turns out to be an intelligent and the other an unintelligent speculation.

Passing now to Graham-Paige at $5, we find another type of situation. Here the public is paying about $24 million for a common stock which represents about $8 million of asset value, most of which is in Kaiser-Fraser stock. This you can buy if you want in the open market, instead of having to pay three times as much for it. The rest of the price represents an interest in $3 million of assets in the farm equipment business—which may prove profitable, as any business may be profitable. The only weakness to that is that there is no record of profitable operations here, and you are paying a great many millions of dollars merely for some possibilities. That, in turn, would be regarded as an unintelligent speculation by the security analyst.

Let us move on now to the Electric Bond and Share stubs, which I shall describe briefly. They represent what you would have left if you had bought Electric Bond and Share preferred at $73 yesterday and had then received $70 a share that is now to be distributed. What remains is an interest in a possible $10 payment, your claim to which is to be adjudicated by the SEC and the courts. That $10 represents the premium above par to which Electric Bond and Share preferred would be entitled if it were called for redemption. The question to be decided is whether the call price, the par value, or some figure in between should govern in this case.

It should be obvious, I think, that that is a speculative situation. You may get $10 a share out of it for your $3, and you may get nothing at all, or you may get something in between. But it is not a speculative operation that eludes the techniques of the security analyst. He has means of examining into the merits of the case and forming an opinion based upon his skill, his experience, and the analogies which he can find in other public utility dissolutions.

If we were to assume that the Electric Bond and Share stubs have a 50–50 chance of getting the $10 premium, then he would conclude that at $3 a share they are an intelligent speculation. For the mathematics indicates that, in several such operations, you would make more than you would lose in the aggregate. These examples lead us, therefore, to what I would call a mathematical or statistical formulation of the relationship between intelligent speculation and investment. The two, actually, are rather closely allied.

Intelligent speculation presupposes at least that the mathematical possibilities are not against the speculation, basing the measurement of these odds on experience and the careful weighing of relevant facts.

This would apply, for example, to the purchase of common stocks at anywhere within the range of value that we find by our appraisal method. If you go back for a moment to our appraisal of American Radiator, you may recall that in our fifth lecture we went through a lot of calculations and came out with the conclusion that American Radiator was apparently worth between $15 and $18 a share. If we assume that that job was well done, we could draw these conclusions. The *investment* value of American Radiator is about $15; between $15 and $18 you would be embarking on what might be called an intelligent speculation, because it would be justified by your appraisal of the speculative factors in the case. If you went beyond the top range of $18, you would be going over into the field of unintelligent speculation.

If the probabilities, as measured by our mathematical test, are definitely in favor of the speculation, then we can transform these separate

intelligent speculations into investment by the simple device of diversification. That, I think, is a clue to the most successful and rewarding
treatment of speculation in Wall Street. The idea, in fine, is simply to get
the odds on your side by processes of skillful, experienced calculation.
Going back to our Electric Bond and Share example, if we really are
skillful in our evaluation of the possibilities here, and reach this conclusion of a 50–50 possibility, then we could consider Electric Bond
and Share stubs as part of an investment operation consisting of, say, 10
such ventures of a diversified character. For in 10 such operations you
would get $50 back for an investment of $30, if you have average luck.
That is, you would get $10 each on five of them and you would get
nothing on another five, and your aggregate return would be $50.

Very little has been done in Wall Street to work out these arithmetical aspects of intelligent speculation based on favorable odds. In
fact, the very language may be strange to most of you. Yet it oughtn't to
be. If we are allowed to commit some misdemeanor by making some
mild comparisons between Wall Street and horse racing, the thought
might occur to some of us that the intelligent operator in Wall Street
would try to follow the technique of the bookmaker rather than the
technique of the man who bets on the horses. Further, if we assume that
a very considerable amount of Wall Street activity must inevitably have
elements of chance in it, then the sound idea would be to measure these
chances as accurately as you can, and play the game in the direction of
having the odds on your side.

Therefore, quite seriously, I would recommend to this group, and
to any other, that the mathematical odds of speculation in various types
of Wall Street operations would provide a full and perhaps a profitable
field of research for students.

Let us return for a moment to Allegheny common and Graham-
Paige common, which we characterized as unintelligent speculation
from the analyst's viewpoint. Is not this a dangerous kind of statement
for us to make? Last year Graham-Paige sold as high as $16, and
Allegheny as high as $8.25, against the current figure of five. It must be
at least conceivable that their purchase today might turn out very well,
either because (a) the abilities of Mr. Young or Mr. Fraser will create
real value where none or little now exists, or (b) the stocks will have a
good speculative move, regardless of value.

Both of these possibilities exist, and the analyst cannot afford to ignore them. Yet he may stick to his guns in characterizing both stocks as unintelligent speculations, because his experience teaches him that this type of speculation does not work out well *on the average.* One reason is that the people who buy this kind of stock at $5 are more likely to buy more at $10 than to sell it. Consequently, they usually show losses in the end, even though there may have been a chance in the interim to sell out to even less intelligent buyers. Thus, in the end, the criterion of both intelligent and unintelligent speculation rests on the results of diversified experience.

When I come to my third point I am going to indicate how very different are the ordinary and customary attitudes toward speculative risk in Wall Street than those we have been discussing. But I think I ought to pause here for a minute, since I finished my second point, and see if there are some questions to be asked on this exposition.

QUESTION: By diversification, as in the case of Electric Bond and Share stubs—you wouldn't concentrate on 10 situations similar in the way of redemption of preferred. You would want to diversify with Electric Bond and Share stocks and General Shareholdings, and some others; entirely different situations?

MR. GRAHAM: Yes, the approach is not based on the character of the operation, but only on the mathematical odds which you have been able to determine to your own satisfaction. It doesn't make any difference what you are buying, whether a bond or a stock or in what field, if you are reasonably well satisfied that the odds are in your favor. They are all of equal attractiveness, and they all belong equally in your diversification. You make a further sound point, and that is that you are not really diversifying if you went into 10 Electric Bond and Share situations—all substantially the same. You would not really be diversifying, because that is practically the same thing as buying 10 shares of Electric Bond and Share instead of buying one share of each; since the same factors would apply to all of them. That point is well taken. For real diversification; you must be sure that the factors that make for success or failure differ in one case from another.

QUESTION: As for that 50–50 chance, why didn't you come up with 60–40—in Bond and Share? I don't see how you can be so mathematically precise.

MR. GRAHAM: Of course you are right in saying that, and I am glad you raised the point. This is not something that admits of a Euclidean demonstration. But you can reach the conclusion that the chances are considerably better than seven to three, let us say—which are the odds that are involved in your purchase—without being exactly sure whether they are 50–50 or 60–40. Broadly speaking, you simply say you think the chances are at least even in your favor, and you let it go at that. But that is enough for the purpose. You don't have to be any more accurate for practical action.

Now, bear in mind I am not trying to imply here that the figure given is necessarily my conclusion as to what the odds in the Bond and Share are. Any of you are perfectly competent to study that situation and draw a conclusion based upon what has taken place in other utility redemptions. I am only using the stubs for purposes of illustration. I should point out that the market does not seem to be very intelligent in paying the same price for the $5 preferred stubs as for the $6 preferred stubs.

The final subject that I have is the current attitude of security analysts toward speculation. It seems to me that Wall Street analysts show an extraordinary combination of sophistication and naivete in their attitude toward speculation. They recognize, and properly so, that speculation is an important part of their environment. We all know that if we follow the speculative crowd we are going to lose money in the long run. Yet, somehow or other, we find ourselves very often doing just that. It is extraordinary how frequently security analysts and the crowd are doing the same thing. In fact, I must say I can't remember any case in which they weren't. (Laughter.)

It reminds me of the story you all know of the oil man who went to heaven and asked St. Peter to let him in. St. Peter said, "Sorry, the oil men's area here is all filled up, as you can see by looking through the gate." The man said, "That's too bad, but do you mind if I just say four words to them?" And St. Peter said, "Sure." So the man shouts good and loud, "Oil discovered in hell!" Whereupon all the oil men begin trooping out of Heaven and making a beeline for the nether regions. Then St. Peter said, "That was an awfully good stunt. Now there's plenty of room, come right in." The oil man scratches his head and says, "I think I'll go with the rest of the boys. There may be some truth in that rumor after all." (Laughter.)

I think that is the way we behave, very often, in the movements of the stock market. We know from experience that we are going to end up badly, but somehow "there may be some truth in the rumor," so we go along with the boys.

For some reason or other, all security analysts in Wall Street are supposed to have an opinion on the future of the market. Many of our best analytical brains are constantly engaged in the effort to forecast the movement of prices. I don't want to fight out the battle over again here, as to whether their activity is sound or not. But I would like to make one observation on this subject.

The trouble with market forecasting is not that it is done by unintelligent and unskillful people. Quite to the contrary, the trouble is that it is done by so many really expert people that their efforts constantly neutralize each other, and end up almost exactly in zero.

The market already reflects, almost at every time, everything that the experts can reliably say about its future. Everything in addition which they say is therefore unreliable, and it tends to be right just about half the time. If people analyzing the market would engage in the proper kind of self-criticism, I am sure they would realize that they are chasing a will-o'-the-wisp.

Reading recently the biography of Balzac, I recalled that novel of his called *The Search for the Absolute*, which some of you may have read. In it a very intelligent doctor spends all his time looking for something which would be wonderful if he found it, but which he never finds. The reward for being consistently right on the market is enormous, of course, and that is why we are all tempted. But I think you must agree with me that there is no sound basis for believing that *anyone* can be constantly right in forecasting the stock market. In my view it is a great logical and practical mistake for security analysts to waste their time on this pursuit.

Market forecasting, of course, is essentially the same as market "timing." On that subject let me say that the only principle of timing that has ever worked well consistently is to buy common stocks at such times as they are cheap by analysis, and to sell them at such times as they are dear, or at least no longer cheap, by analysis.

That sounds like timing; but when you consider it you will see that it is not really timing at all but rather the purchase and sale of securities by the method of valuation. Essentially, it requires no opinion as to the future of the market; because if you buy securities cheap enough, your position is sound, even if the market should continue to go down. And if you sell the securities at a fairly high price you have done the smart thing, even if the market should continue to go up.

Therefore, at the conclusion of this course, I hope you will permit me to make as strong a plea as I can to you security analysts to divorce yourselves from stock market analysis. Don't try to combine the two—security analysis and market analysis—plausible as this effort appears to many of us; because the end-product of that combination is almost certain to be contradiction and confusion.

On the other hand, I should greatly welcome an effort by security analysts to deal intelligently with speculative operations. To my mind the prerequisite here is for the quantitative approach, which is based on the calculation of the probabilities in each case, and a conclusion that the odds are strongly in favor of the operation's success. It is not necessary that this calculation be completely dependable in each instance, and certainly not mathematically precise, but only that it be made with a fair degree of knowledge and skill. The law of averages will take care of minor errors and of the many individual disappointments which are inherent in speculation by its very definition.

It is a great mistake to believe that a speculation has been unwise if you lose money at it. That sounds like an obvious conclusion, but actually it is not true at all. A speculation is unwise only if it is made on insufficient study and by poor judgment. I recall to those of you who are bridge players the emphasis that the bridge experts place on playing a hand right rather than on playing it successfully. Because, as you know, if you play it right you are going to make money and if you play it wrong you lose money—in the long run.

There is a beautiful little story, that I suppose most of you have heard, about the man who was the weaker bridge player of the husband-and-wife team. It seems he bid a grand slam, and at the end he said very triumphantly to his wife, "I saw you making faces at me all the time, but you notice I not only bid this grand slam but I made it. What can you say about that?" And his wife replied very dourly, "If you had played it right you would have lost it." (Laughter.)

There is a great deal of that in Wall Street, particularly in the field of speculation, when you are trying to do it by careful calculation. In some cases the thing will work out badly. But that is simply part of the game. If it was bound to work out rightly, it wouldn't be a speculation at all, and there wouldn't be the opportunities of profit that [are inherent] in sound speculation. It seems to me that is axiomatic.

I know something of the practical problems that confront the security analyst who wants to act logically all the time, and who wants to confine himself only to that area of financial work in which he can say with confidence that his work and his conclusions are reasonably dependable. The analysts all complain to me that they can't do that because they are expected by their customers and their employers to do something else, to give them off-the-cuff speculative judgments and market opinions. One of these days I am sure the security analysts will divide themselves completely from the market analysts.

It would be very nice to have a two-year trial period in which the market analysts would keep track of what they have accomplished through the period and security analysts would keep track of what they have accomplished. I think it would be rather easy to tell in advance who would turn in the better score. That is really the pay off. I think that eventually the employers and the customer will come to the conclusion that it is better to let the security analysts be security analysts—which they know how to do—and not other kinds of things, particularly market analysts, which they don't know how to do and they will never know how to do.

I would like to make some final observations, relating to a long period of time, as to what has happened to the conduct of business in Wall Street.

If you can throw your mind, as I can, as far back as 1914, you would be struck by some extraordinary differences in Wall Street then and today. In a great number of things, the improvement has been tremendous. The ethics of Wall Street are very much better. The sources of information are much greater, and the information itself is much more dependable. There have been many advances in the art of security analysis. In all those respects we are very far ahead of the past.

In one important respect we have made practically no progress at all, and that is in human nature. Regardless of all the apparatus and all the improvements in techniques, people still want to make money very fast. They still want to be on the right side of the market. And what is most important and most dangerous, we all want to get more out of Wall Street than we deserve for the work we put in.

There is one final area in which I think there has been a very definite retrogression in Wall Street thinking. That is in the distinctions between investment and speculation, which I spoke about at the beginning of this lecture. I am sure that back in 1914 the typical person had a much clearer idea of what he meant by investing his money, and what he meant by speculating with his money. He had no exaggerated ideas of what an investment operation should bring him, and nearly all the people who speculated knew approximately what kind of risks they were taking.

PART FIVE

THE COMMODITY
RESERVE PLAN

The post-World War II world has been characterized as
"brave" and "new." Brave it is, indeed, but we are not
positive that it is equally new. We can be skeptical about
a complete break with the past.

Security Analysis
Fourth Edition, 1962

The early part of the twentieth century was characterized by booms
and busts, episodes of rising prices and stagnant productivity, by
the global Great Depression of the 1930s, and finally by World War II.
Everyone, from political leaders to businessmen to ordinary citizens,
worried that economic chaos would reign following the armistice. But
people also knew that the break-down in economic systems during the
war presented an opportunity to improve upon the old ways.

Ben Graham focused his own thinking on this subject, and in 1937
published his ideas in a book called *Storage and Stability* (McGraw-
Hill). *Storage and Stability* was reissued in 1998. When the book was
first issued, Graham's concepts were promoted and put forward to
national and international leaders by an organization to which Graham
belonged, The Committee for Economic Stability. Graham's ideas were
taken seriously and led to correspondence with the renowned British
economist, Lord John Maynard Keynes. An article published by Graham and a friend, Professor Frank Graham, on "buffer stocks," or commodity reserves, led to a misunderstanding with Keynes, which Keynes
himself corrected.

"On the use of buffer stocks as a means of stabilizing short-term commodity prices," Keynes wrote to Ben Graham, "you and I are ardent crusaders on the same side, so do not let a falsely conceived controversy arise between us."

The new policies for international currencies, balance of payments, inflation control, and other economic factors were to be decided at the historic Bretton Woods Conference held in 1944 in the White Mountains of New Hampshire. Graham's friends enthusiastically put his ideas before President Franklin D. Roosevelt and the Congress, with the idea that they would be presented at Bretton Woods, but to no avail. Instead, the 44 nations that attended the conference (the USSR was invited but did not participate) adopted the "adjustable peg" or modified gold-standard monetary system to be managed by the International Monetary Fund. However, some champions of Graham's commodity plan remain and every few years economists dust off Graham's concepts and discuss them again. There are still those who believe world economies would be vastly more stable and inclined to peaceful cooperation had Graham's commodity reserve plan been adopted.

Proposals for an International Commodity-Reserve Currency

Submitted to the International Monetary
and Financial Conference at Bretton Woods, N.H.,
by The Committee for Economic Stability
June 21, 1944

I. The Background of the Proposals

An International Monetary Conference is about to consider methods of stabilizing the exchange value of currencies. Attainment of this objective would be greatly aided by according an international monetary status to basic commodities, similar to and in addition to that enjoyed by gold. Such an arrangement would place nations producing raw materials in the same general position as those producing gold. It would enable many countries to pay for their imports of finished goods by expanding their production of primary materials, being assured of a fair price for this output. It would thus reduce greatly the need for extension of credits in order to maintain stability of exchange rates.

Our proposal has other aspects which are even more important than its contribution to the stabilization of exchange rates. Its operation will stabilize also the underlying price structure of the world, and thus permit an unlimited, balanced expansion of global production and consumption. It will establish buffer stocks of basic commodities, which will

From Benjamin Graham's personal papers.

even out inequalities in supply and demand, and create non-commercial reserve supplies for emergency uses and to raise living standards. By functioning as monetary reserves, these buffer stocks become self-financing, self-liquidating to any extent called for by demand, and creators of increased purchasing power.

The combination of the buffer-stock device with the monetary-reserve device is intended to provide a single rational solution to a double challenge—that of alternate surplus and shortage on the one hand, and that of insufficient purchasing power on the other. The problems involved in the monetary use of basic commodities have been essentially those of technique. We believe that the composite or commodity-unit method is a workable means of according a monetary function to commodity reserves. It avoids the many pitfalls that beset the valorization of single commodities. The serious technical defects inherent in schemes to stabilize or monetize single commodities are largely overcome by permitting the individual prices to fluctuate within the framework of a stable composite value.

The commodity-reserve proposal will contribute to the successful operation of the projected International Monetary Fund by remedying elements of weakness which have inspired doubt and criticism. Since it will stabilize the world price-level of basic commodities, as well as that of gold, the plan will prevent the rigid gold standard from acting, as some nations fear, to spread deflation and depression from one part of the world to another. And since it will increase greatly the ability of primary producing nations to pay for goods with goods, it will hold down the credit operations of the Fund within a compass which the export-balance nations should readily accept.

II. SUMMARY OF THE PROPOSALS

The plan is designed to function within the framework of the International Monetary Fund, as described in the Experts' Statement of April 21, 1944. No provision in the statement needs to be changed because of the plan. An international commodity-unit currency would be established by the introduction of an additional section, to provide in substance for the following:

1. The Fund will define a suitable commodity unit, to which a base or par value will be given, expressed in gold or in (gold) dollars. The Fund will at any time acquire complete commodity units from member countries upon tender of warehouse receipts therefor, at a price of, say, 95 percent of their par value. It will sell complete commodity units to member countries, at, say, 105 percent of their par value, to the extent that it has units available.

2. Transactions in commodity units between the Fund and member countries will be settled, in general, in the same way as transactions in gold. By selling either gold or commodity units to the Fund, member countries may establish credit balances on the books of the Fund in addition to their quota contribution.

3. Suitable arrangements will be made for the physical custody of the commodity units either by vendor nations or by other nations desiring—for reasons of security, etc.—to hold complete units as agents of the Fund. Storage costs will be defrayed in the following ways: (a) By required assumption thereof for a limited period by vendor countries; (b) By assumption thereof by other nations desiring custody of units; (c) By profit derived from the difference between the buying and selling points, (d) By profit derived from the sale of spot commodities and their replacement by futures contracts at a lower price, during periods of temporary shortage in individual commodities, (e) By assessment against member nations.

4. The composition of the commodity unit can be modified from time to time in accordance with suitable statistical techniques. Annual corrections, based upon 10-year moving averages of world production and exports, can maintain the statistical soundness of the commodity unit without difficulty.

III. Normal Operation and Effect of the Proposals

Under the proposal the international value of the commodity unit will be fixed and maintained, in the same way as that of gold and of the several national currencies, subject to such spread between the buying and selling points as may seem most desirable. The price of the individual components will not be fixed but will be free to fluctuate in the open market to reflect normal changes in the relative supply-demand situations. But since the overall price level will remain constant, within narrow limits, the variations in individual prices will be much less severe than heretofore.

The actual accumulation of commodity units would be done by commodity brokers operating at a small competitive dealer's profit or it can be handled by an agency of the Fund. In either event commodities will flow automatically into the Fund when the world price-level falls slightly below the buying point, and will flow out of the fund when the selling point is passed.

It is not necessary that a member nation produce all the component commodities in order to benefit from the market demand supplied by the Fund. Units will be accumulated by the usual processes of world trade operating in the principal export markets for each component. Each raw-materials producing nation will benefit by supplying portions of the unit, in the same way as if it had provided an equivalent value of complete units.

IV. ADVANTAGES OF AN INTERNATIONAL COMMODITY RESERVE CURRENCY

1. In the Field of Exchange Stability

Commodity reserve currency will add to the world's physical money. It will enlarge the means of payment in the hands of many raw materials producing nations, and make it easier for them to pay cash for imports of fabricated goods and services. As previously stated, it should greatly reduce the need for direct or indirect granting of credit by financially strong and export-balance nations to financially weak or import-balance nations. It should permit the proposed International Monetary Fund to achieve its objectives by the use of a moderate amount of international credit.

2. In the Field of Price Stability

By directly stabilizing the price level of basic raw materials the proposed mechanism will remove a major cause of economic dislocation throughout the world. As a consequence, a sufficient degree of stability should be maintained in the price level of finished goods and services.

3. As the Creator of Buffer Stocks

The proposal will provide the nations of the world with interest-free buffer stocks which do not threaten their commercial markets. It will implement the conclusions of the Food Conference with respect to the need for a buffer-stock technique. The non-commercial stockpiles created by this plan will provide three major advantages—protective reserves, price-level stability, and encouragement of expanding output.

Although the benefits resident in buffer stocks are universally recognized, they are still greatly feared by businessmen because of the threat they carry to the price structure. The monetary technique will insulate buffer stocks from the commercial markets and permit the fullest development of their inherent advantages.

The provision for replacement of spot commodities in the unit by futures contracts, when the former sell at a premium, will permit the commodity reserves to be utilized advantageously under conditions of temporary shortage in individual products.

4. As the Key to an Expanding World Economy

No more direct stimulus to full production can be found than in the assurance of an unfailing demand at a stable price. The monetary system has heretofore provided this demand for gold, with the result that the gold-mining industry has been immune from depression and unemployment. The commodity-reserve proposal will provide a similar demand for basic commodities as a whole, and thus place the world in a position to proceed confidently to the balanced expansion of its primary production—with corresponding benefits to all factors of the global economy.

Without such a positive stimulus to production there is grave danger that the postwar world will be ruled by the cartel principle, and that output and exports of both finished goods and raw materials will be held down, by various restrictions, to the level of pre-existing commercial demand.

Summarization of the Multiple Commodity Reserve Plan

Committee for Economic Stability
March 1941

ORGANIZED: TO FURTHER ECONOMIC STABILITY, through research and education, and, as a first step to that end, TO ADVOCATE A MULTIPLE COMMODITY RESERVE, as an adjunct and supplement to our gold and silver redemption fund, thus: (1) establishing a store of basic, essential commodities that might be availed of in some period of scarcity; (2) effecting a long-needed separation between the problems of bank management and the control of monetary and credit volume; (3) setting up an automatic, impersonal, and effective mechanism for the prevention of inflation and deflation and their multifarious evil consequences, and; (4) providing our economy with a stable unit of value and a sound dollar, with a solid backing, limited issue, and a substantially constant purchasing power.

THE GENERAL PLAN: Provide a monetary base of essential, storable, raw commodities in common use, against which currency would be issued, by which it would be secured, and in which it would be redeemable, thus according exactly the same monetary treatment to a composite group of specified commodities as was formerly accorded to the signal commodity, gold.

DETAILS: Commodity units would be set up by law. These would consist of a composite of, say, 25 or more basic, storable, raw commodities. The relative amounts of the several commodities in the composite

---

From Benjamin Graham's personal papers.

group would be determined by their relative importance in commerce. The size of a commodity unit would be such as to make it convenient for purposes of deposit and redemption. The fraction of a commodity unit that would be equivalent to a dollar would be fixed at the time of the enactment of the plan by the Congress, in compliance with the constitutional provision authorizing the Congress to regulate the value of money (Article 1, Sec. 8, Clause 5), and might be determined by the average of the market prices of the group of commodities composing the unit over a period of years, say 1921–1940. These are matters of not very difficult statistical calculation.

The Treasury would issue legal tender currency against the deposit of warehouse receipts such as are currently dealt in on our commodity exchanges constituting one or more complete commodity units, or, per contra, the Treasury would surrender such warehouse receipts in exchange for an equivalent amount of currency, just as formerly anyone could deposit or withdraw gold in exchange for currency. So, under this plan, anyone could make such deposits or withdrawals of commodity units or of currency at any time.

Thus the dollar would in effect be a "commodity unit certificate" having all the desirable characteristics of a gold certificate and gold-secured money—solid backing, redeemability, limitation of issue—plus certain important qualities now lacking in our money.

There would be suitable provisions: (a) for periodic but infrequent changes in the composition of the commodity units, in accordance with shifts in the relative commercial importance of the various commodities comprising the units; (b) for methods of defraying the expense of storage; (c) for substitution, under stated conditions, of "futures" contracts for the actual warehouse receipts; and (d) possibly, for the inclusion of substantial components of gold and silver in the commodity units, or the redemption of the certificates in commodities units or gold or silver, at the option of the holder. These and other matters of detail, which do not affect the fundamental principles involved, will, no doubt, be the subject of official studies when the plan is considered by the Congress.

OPERATION: Let us now consider the plan in operation and try to visualize how it would function in practice, and what would be the results:

If, from whatever cause, the aggregate market price of the group of commodities composing the commodity units should begin to fall below their total minting (reserve) value, anyone could buy those commodities on the exchanges, deliver to the Treasury a group of warehouse receipts covering the appropriate amount of each of the commodities, and take out their equivalent in currency. This would have the effect of supporting the market price of the reserve commodities, taken as a group, and since it would increase the supply of money, would tend to support the general level of prices.

If, on the other hand, the aggregate market price of the group of commodities composing the commodity units should, for any reason, begin to rise above their total redemption value, anyone could withdraw commodity units from the Treasury at the fixed currency value and sell the commodities on the market. The currency thus redeemed would be retired and destroyed. This would have the effect of lowering the prices of these specific commodities, and, since it would reduce the supply of money, would tend to prevent a rise in the general price level.

The limits of fluctuation of the aggregate market price of the group of commodities in the unit would be narrow, depending upon what (if any) *seigniorage* charge was adopted and the commission and other costs of withdrawing and selling units or of assembling them for deposit in the reserve—all together probably not exceeding 1 or 2 percent. The reasons impelling exchanges of commodity units for currency, or vice versa, would be the same as formerly led to deposits of gold in the reserve banks or the Treasury or to its withdrawal therefrom.

RESULTS: The proponents of this plan believe that it would:

A. Stabilize within narrow limits the average price of the group of commodities composing the commodity unit.

B. Provide our economy with a sound (that is, a solidly backed) dollar of substantially constant purchasing power—thus preventing the far-reaching and serious political and social consequences of monetary inflation and deflation.

C. Promote equity as between debtors and creditors, employers and employees, and the parties to all contracts involving the two elements of time and money.

D. Assist in stabilizing business and economic conditions generally, as more fully developed below.

E. Offer a superior alternative to public works expenditures and other such means of providing employment in times of depression.

F. Go a long way toward eliminating the paradox of "poverty in the midst of plenty" in that it would prevent general surpluses of raw materials from demoralizing the price structure and intensifying depressions. It would remove two depression-accelerating factors: Destruction of the purchasing power of primary producers (farmers especially) and reduction of the volume of bank credit consequent upon the falling value of collateral of all sorts—the "vicious spiral".

G. Create a reserve store of primary commodities which might be of vital importance in some great emergency such as drought, pestilence, or war, and, for the reasons given in the following paragraph, would greatly facilitate the readjustment of our economy to a peacetime basis after the current phase of war expenditure has passed.

H. Tend to raise the scale of living, since it would promote production at maximum levels of consumption, with maximum employment, and would facilitate the adjustments necessitated by technological progress. Unemployment, labor, and business disturbances, in so far as they are caused by instability in the level of prices of basic commodities, would be prevented. Since there would be an unlimited market, at the fixed (minting) price, for the composite of commodities in the unit, a large sector of the economy would be sustained, or even stimulated, in any incipient depression, just as gold mining is now stimulated under similar circumstances.

I. Check inflationary booms by the withdrawal from the reserve of important raw materials, and the consequent redemption and cancellation of the equivalent currency.

J. Operate to protect the banking system and the price-structure as a whole against extreme deflations and inflations of bank credit, which have been such powerful factors in price-level gyrations and in resulting banking difficulties during recent decades.

K. Improve facilities for foreign trade and finance because the payment to us, in tangible goods, of sums due us on foreign debts, or for our exports, need not depress our markets but could be added to our store of usable commodities. There could be no competitive depreciation of exchange since the dollar value of foreign currencies would be automatically correlated with the foreign currency price of the composite of commodities in the unit.

COMMENT: This plan does not involve the fixing of the prices of individual commodities, which would be left entirely free to fluctuate with changing demand and supply. What would be fixed, directly and within narrow limits, is the aggregate price of the commodities in the unit, but the relationship between the prices of the individual commodities would be as free to vary as it ever has been. Indirectly, the level of the prices of all commodities would be substantially stabilized, since the play of competition would prevent any large discrepancy between the different classes of commodities.

The plan is automatic, impersonal, non-political, and self-controlling, involving no use of an index number, no curtailment of production or regimentation of any sort, no modification of banking or market procedures, no vesting of discretionary powers in anyone for managing the currency or regulating prices or production or consumption.

Many economists feel that the plan would relieve our bankers and banking authorities of responsibility for the purchasing power of the dollar, enabling them to concentrate on the problems of qualitative (rather than quantitative) credit and on other purely banking matters.

While it is not a panacea, the friends of this plan believe it would facilitate the solution of serious problems that are now presented by the fluctuating dollar.

To those who have not given this plan careful and objective study, it may seem that the claims of its adherents as to its beneficent results are exaggerated, but the committee welcomes concrete criticisms of its analysis of the effects of the plan, as above presented.

The committee also welcomes offers of assistance—moral, intellectual, financial—from anyone who has an interest in its objectives.

PERTINENT QUOTATIONS

DAVID RICARDO (1816): The introduction of the precious metals for the purpose of money may with truth be considered one of the most important steps toward the improvement of commerce and the arts of civilized life; but it is not less true that, with the advancement of knowledge and science, we (may) discover that it would be another improvement to banish them again from the employment to which, during a less enlightened period, they had been so advantageously applied.

HERBERT HOOVER (1925): What we all want from this economic system is greater stability, that men may be secure in their employment and their business.

OWEN D. YOUNG (1929): . . . when any sudden change affects the purchasing power of money, it touches every kind of moral question and every kind of obligation.

LORD STAMP (1928): . . . the problem of the price level is the most important single problem of our age . . . it is the most bitterly practical of all questions . . . the first necessity of thinking today on social questions.

LIONEL E. EDIE (1931): Central banks should aim at so regulating reserves of the banking system that the outstanding credit built upon those reserves will expand at the same rate as the long-term growth of production.

FRANKLIN D. ROOSEVELT (March 4, 1933): . . . there must be provision for an adequate but sound currency.

FRANKLIN D. ROOSEVELT (July 3, 1933): Let me be frank in saying that the United States seeks the kind of dollar which a generation hence will have the same purchasing power and debt-paying power as the dollar value we hope to attain in the near future.

KING GEORGE V (1933): It cannot be beyond the power of man so to use the vast resources of the world as to ensure the material progress of civilization.

HENRY FORD (1936): What we need is some financial engineers.

SIMEON STRUNSKY (1936): We know that depression is the enemy of democracy.

PAUL EINZIG (1936): The admission of the principle that non-perishable staple commodities can be included in currency reserves to a limited extent would go a long way toward solving the world's monetary problems and also the present problem of surplus stocks.

ALVIN JOHNSON (1937): We are all fairly agreed as to the qualities we wish to see realized in our standard money. We want it to be as nearly as possible stable in value. We want this stability to be maintained by impersonal forces. Mr. Graham's invention (the Multiple Commodity Reserve Plan) is designed to meet both requirements. The invention is of such startling simplicity that everyone who examines it must feel that he once had the idea himself.

HENRY A. WALLACE (1937): From the standpoint of the national interest, the consuming interest, and the agricultural interest, the increased stability of supply and price that would come with the ever-normal granary is essential.

BOARD OF GOVERNORS OF THE FEDERAL RESERVE SYSTEM (1939): The Board of Governors is in complete sympathy with the desire to prevent booms and depressions, and has always considered it its duty to do what it could to help accomplish these results.

BENJAMIN H. BECKHART (1940): There is general agreement among monetary theorists that the objectives of monetary policy should include a reduction of cyclical amplitudes and a furthering of continuous maximum production at minimum real cost.

W. RANDOLPH BURGESS (1940): . . . confidence in our money is the basis of our system of free enterprise.

MALCOLM A. MUIR (1940): Mismanagement of credit and money . . . is a principal factor leading to the danger of the destruction of the system of private enterprise.

PART SIX

INTERVIEWS WITH BENJAMIN GRAHAM

I want to say that at least half of all the pleasures that I have enjoyed in life have come from the world of the mind, from things of beauty and culture in literature and in art. All this is offered to everybody, virtually free of charge, except for the interest to start and the relatively slight effort to appreciate the riches spread out before you . . . take that initial interest, if possible: make that continued effort. Once you have found it—the life of culture—never let it go.

> Benjamin Graham
> At his 80th birthday party,
> La Jolla, California

A fter studying the practices and teachings of Benjamin Graham, many readers will regret never having had the opportunity to sit down and talk with him. The following interviews may ease that disappointment somewhat. Because all of these interviews were conducted near the end of Graham's life, they summarize both his life and his ideas.

Benjamin Graham: The Grandfather of Investment Value Is Still Concerned

John Quirt

In a television talk show back in the 1960s, one of the young gun-slingers of the day was chattering on about aggressive investing when someone brought up the name of Ben Graham. Although he knew Graham only by reputation, the go-go fund manager remarked brashly that "the trouble with old Ben is that he just does not understand this market." Today, more than half a decade later, the question is: Who didn't understand what? That gunslinger, along with his once-exuberant peers, has long since been ambushed by the excesses of the performance cult he represented. But "old Ben" Graham is still very much around, preaching the gospel of true investment value, of margin-of-safety, and saying unnervingly critical things about institutional investing that all of a sudden many people seem to be hearing once again.

Benjamin Graham, now a vigorous 79, can be found these days at his La Jolla condominium overlooking the California shoreline, busily putting the finishing touches on the soon-to-be-published Fifth Edition of his perennial best seller, *Security Analysis* (by Benjamin Graham and David L. Dodd, McGraw-Hill, 778 pages, in cooperation with Sidney Cottle). A classical scholar and translator—he's brought into English works ranging from Ovid to a relatively recent Spanish novel—Graham is still widely acknowledged as the dean of the investment profession. Indeed, before Graham, security analysis wasn't a profession at all; he

From *Institutional Investor*, April 1974. This copyrighted material reprinted with permission from Institutional Investor, Inc., 488 Madison Avenue, New York, New York 10022.

called for it to be made so in a speech during the mid-1940s, which eventually led to the designation of Chartered Financial Analyst. Meanwhile, he also put his ideas into practice, amassing a substantial fortune, and translated them for the layman, in *The Intelligent Investor*, another best seller that has gone through several editions. "Roughly speaking," says one usually cynical member of the investment fraternity, "Ben Graham has written half the good stuff that's ever been written about investment management."

AN ACCOUNTING

"Just call me Ben," he tells a visitor, setting aside a sheaf of papers that represents a day's work on the update of his book—at an age when most people prefer reminiscing, he's still revising his thinking. Then, he asks in a courtly, soft-spoken manner: "Would you care for some afternoon tea?" It is a cool, clear winter afternoon and Graham is attired in a plaid shirt, dark suit, and red bow tie. He moves slowly now, sometimes with the help of a cane, but speaks surely and irrefragably about developments in the investment business.

"In the past 10 years Wall Street has given a poorer account of itself than at any time in its history," he asserts, adding parenthetically that "perhaps I shouldn't say anything like that, but, hell, if I am going to be 80 I guess I can say what I want to. You can almost despair of expecting any rationality if you look back over what has happened. First, a virtual collapse of the whole Wall Street system following a period of irrationality, but with extra factors added in that I've never heard of in my lifetime, including brokerage firms going broke for having *too much* business to handle. That's important to mention because it's an indication that the desire to make a lot of money fast took precedence over the most ordinary, elementary business considerations."

After new highs were made for the indexes at the end of 1972 and the beginning of 1973, he continues, we saw "another kind of collapse very similar in terms of the figures to what we saw in 1970. How people could have had the lack of prudence to reestablish those late 1972 and early 1973 values is something I don't think I'll ever understand."

When Graham refers to "people," he is, of course, directing his dis-approbation largely at the institutional investors who led the ill-fated 1972 upsurge, including large pension funds that eschewed their usual conservatism to swing more aggressively into equities. He doubts the wisdom of any large fund striving for 12 percent compounded returns at a time when bonds yield 8 percent. And he continues to have grave misgivings about consanguine practices still in use, albeit less exten-sively, since the toppling of the two-tier market: The reliance on pro-jected future earnings to buy relatively high multiples, measurements of short-term and comparative performance, employment of standard rates of turnover to give the appearance of trying for better results, and weighing of risk through beta or price fluctuation analysis.

SOCRATIC DIALOGUE

Graham's views, which have been variously summarized as "the first step in making money is not losing money" and "you have to protect yourself against great adversity," got an unusual airing last year at a conference of money managers organized by Donaldson, Lufkin and Jenrette in Rancho la Costa. It was a meeting called to discuss some of the critical issues confronting the industry, and one of the participants, Charles D. Ellis, a frequent contributor to these pages, has since likened Graham's contribution there to that of Socrates addressing the Athenian youth.

The analogy is an extremely apt one. First of all, it's fitting that it's Greek; Graham is fluent in the language and actually called Adam Smith's attention to an error in a Greek quotation in Smith's book, *The Money Game.* But more important, as Ellis points out, Graham's co-discussants were mostly fourth generation investment managers who have long since considered Graham and Dodd, which was first published in 1934, as out of date as Currier and Ives. For them, the confrontation with the grandfather of their profession was undoubtedly an unnerving experience; some of them didn't even seem to understand his message. And it was also pretty unnerving for Graham.

"I was shocked by what I heard at that meeting," he says. "I could not comprehend how the management of money by institutions has degenerated from the standpoint of sound investment to this rat race of trying to get the highest possible return in the shortest period of time. Those men gave me the impression of being prisoners of their own operations rather than controlling them. I say 'prisoners' in the sense that they have held themselves out as being able to do what their employers or contractors want them to do—which is to obtain a better-than-average return on the enormous amounts of money they handle. By definition, that's practically impossible to do. They are promising performance both on the upside and on the downside that is not practical to achieve."

Their efforts to do so, Graham continues, "have required adopting an essentially speculative approach to the handling of the funds. As I listened to those fellows talk, I couldn't imagine how their approach could in the end ever produce anything but regrets, perhaps some very serious lawsuits, and a general discrediting of the whole idea of money management."

At one point during the Rancho La Costa meeting, Graham asked one of the money managers if he were convinced that the market was due to drop severely, what effect would it have on his operations? "None," came the reply. "Relative performance is all that matters to me. If the market collapses and my funds collapse less, that's okay with me. I've done my job."

"That concerns me," Graham admonished him. "Doesn't it concern you?'

On another occasion a participant pleaded that he really couldn't distinguish between an investor and a speculator. Graham responded, almost inaudibly, "That's the sickness of the time."

At still another juncture he asked, "is there a standard rate of turnover for the kind of money you manage?"

"Yes," a participant replied, "about 25 percent to 30 percent."

"Have you ever investigated to see what would happen if your turnover was less?" Graham inquired. Most of the participants conceded that they had not investigated. One who had, said "turnover seems to hurt performance most of the time."

"Then is there perhaps some self-interest reason for the high turnover?" Graham persisted.

"Well, we do get paid to manage the money," said a participant. "And our employers and clients expect us to be active managers. We're paid to try."

BURSTING BUBBLES

Toward the close of the meeting the conversation turned to growth stocks and rate of return, and Graham raised his voice to challenge the group: "How can you talk seriously about a 7.3 percent average annual rate of return that is based on stock prices that shoot up 40 percent one year and go down 20 percent the next?" he asked. "And how can the market be expected to outperform the underlying profits growth of publicly held corporations?"

Receiving no satisfactory answers to embarrassingly fundamental questions such as these, he drove home his feelings about growth stocks with a simple illustration. "Take a stock that has earnings growth of 15 percent per year," Graham said. "That's rather remarkable, but let's take it as an example. So long as the P/E just stays at its present level, the buyer will get 15 percent returns—plus dividends if any—which will be so attractive to other investors that they will want to own that stock too. So they will buy it and in doing so they will bid up the price and hence the P/E. This makes the price rise faster than 15 percent so the security seems even more attractive. As more and more 'investors' become enamored with the promised rate of return, the price lifts free from underlying value and is enabled to float freely upward creating a bubble that will expand quite beautifully until finally and inevitable it *must* burst. In other words, if you start low, you'll have a rise, and if you have a rise you'll have satisfaction and that will bring a further rise, and so on. But it won't go on forever. It may go too far, but never forever."

Some time later, Graham was asked whether the participants at Rancho La Costa had given any evidence of having learned something from the discussion. "Not in any worthwhile way," he concluded, rue-fully. Could he at least take some solace in the fact that his admonitions had proven on target twice in four years? "In a way that's an unfair question," he replied. "Human nature is human nature and naturally you can't help but feel vindicated to some degree after you've gone through a period where people say 'Graham was all right in his day, however' . . . ."

Why then, when investment managers have seen overvalued bubbles burst twice since 1970, can't more of them—indeed, why can't all of them—manage somehow to get back to something more closely approximating Graham and Dodd basics?

Graham smiled and adjusted his glasses. It was a question he had weighed many times before. "I myself think it's the consequence of the greater magnetism of the stock ticker," he said reproachfully. "These chaps start out reading Graham and Dodd and I'm sure most of them are quite impressed by it in business school. I take some malicious pleasure in saying it's the book on finance that's been read by more people and disregarded by more people than any other that I know of."

But after that, he continued, "when they come down to Wall Street, the principles and concepts they have learned seem only theoretical ones. My guess is that as they get into the work of finance where results are measured by what the stock ticker says rather than by the soundness of what's being done, they lose rather rapidly their theoretical viewpoint. They move over to what they would call a practical viewpoint and virtually turn their backs on what I consider sound approaches."

WHAT'S SOUND?

As anyone who has ever read *Security Analysis* knows, Graham's conception of a sound investment approach stresses net asset value and low multiples as criteria, and evaluates prices in relation to interest rates. His detractors frequently criticize this approach as a couple of decades out of date and hopelessly cast in stone. But in reality it *has* been modified in an attempt to keep up with the times. In the Fourth Edition published 12 years ago, he added a full 50 percent to the valuations in previous editions and justified the liberalization on the grounds of basic improvements in business plus the government's commitment to avert deep depressions. That line of reasoning, says Graham, "would have shown itself to be justified in practice except for the rise in interest rates in the late 1960s, which is something we had no fore-suspicion of."

Now, he says, assuming 7.5 percent or 8 percent instead of 4.5 percent as the going interest rate and using four-thirds of that as a divisor, (reflecting his view that one ought to get at least a third more from equity investments than debt ones, "in view of the troubles they go through with them") "we're back pretty much to the multiples that we were accustomed to prior to World War II." And the market in 1973, he adds, was "making a belated adjustment" to the higher rate.

What do the numbers point to today? Assuming 60 as the DJI's 10-year average earnings and taking four-thirds times 7.5 percent, says Graham, "you get only about 600 for the Dow. And if you substitute the last 12 months' earnings for the 10-year average you arrive at somewhere around 750. So you can't get very enthusiastic on either basis," he cautions.

What Graham can and does get a little enthusiastic about these days is the preponderance of *undervalued* situations around. On a straight Graham and Dodd basis the market is, in his words, "filled with bargains." Are they concentrated in certain industries? Graham says no, that they cut across industry lines, and he adds that he has very little regard any longer for research that purports to single out attractive opportunities on the basis of judgments of an industry's past performance, subjunctive evaluations of management, or any other factors that cannot be measured quantitatively. "The older and more experienced I get," he says, "the less confidence I have in judgmental choice as distinct from the figures themselves."

NEW COMBINATIONS

To help identify the soundest buys among the undervalued situations around, Graham has been experimenting with new combinations of the figures. But his experiments do not entail any further liberalization of what constitutes sound value. In fact, as he prepares the upcoming Fifth Edition, Graham says he finds himself "going back to earlier notions of investment," and specifically to the notion that "if you want to be sure of your ground you probably should start with and stick to the net asset value area as a point of departure. That doesn't mean you should not pay attention to other considerations," he adds, "but it does mean that whatever other factors you include should be justified by conservative viewpoints."

This, he continues, "is a very important thing to me, and it should be important for investment generally. What it really means is that the typical good company today often fails to offer a *feasible* basis for sound investment. The very fact that it is a good company introduces a speculative element in the area of price."

The newest approach Graham has experimented with in his efforts to develop a system for locating mathematically justifiable investments in the post-1968 market is a formula which he says may or may not be introduced in the Fifth Edition. Basically an adaption of his central value method but geared to individual companies rather than the DJI, it calls for buying at the lowest of three criteria:

- A low multiple (e.g., 10) of the preceding year's earnings;
- A price equal to half the previous market high ("to indicate that there has been considerable shrinkage");
- Net asset value.

Under this formula, stocks would be sold after a 50 percent profit and otherwise the operation would be closed out after a period of, say, three years.

Graham has been testing the formula and the results so far, he says, have been "quite satisfactory. If you look at the market since 1968—and I've actually done some tests back to 1961—you find that there were considerable buying opportunities along these lines. One study I made using 100 company samples in 1970 showed about 50 that could have been bought under these criteria with very good results." But actually, he confesses, "the results fascinate me a little too much right now, and of course I am going to have to study this a great deal more. But at least it is an example of the kind of approach that seems logical to look at today."

Investment managers who have begun to adopt longer perspectives and turn their attention more toward assets may take fairly kindly to Graham's latest approach. But those who are still under the gun to improve performance now or be fired are unlikely to embrace it any more eagerly than they have subscribed to his other conservative advice in the past. For one thing, it is a purely mechanical formula that gives no weight to fundamental research on a company or industry. Moreover, the investment opportunities it points to are largely unpopular companies with plenty of assets but little charisma—the kind of commitments that are not always easily explained to growth-minded clients. In addition, the considerable patience the system calls for obviously will not have very much appeal to customers who still believe results ought to be measured quarterly.

Finally, it perhaps is worth noting that issues depressed 50 percent below their market highs often tend to get less than the best risk ratings when subjected to beta analysis, no matter how low their multiples or how substantial their assets. Not surprisingly, Graham says he finds beta analysis "absurd," arguing that "the investment manager's job is to *take advantage* of price fluctuations."

PROMISES, PROMISES

What is needed to put the climate right for the kind of "sound value" investing Graham advocates, is, of course, a change in both client and investment management thinking. In Graham's view, one thing that is needed is a fundamental reform of the method by which money managers promote their wares. He would put an end to the practice of firms out-promising each other, even implicitly, and he would confine all promotion to "what can realistically be accomplished."

"The only way out of this mess is through some kind of joint or group action," Graham contends. "And investment managers will probably have to go through a wringer before they reach the point where they agree on limiting their promises to what is practical to achieve." That naturally raises a serious question, he admits. "Namely, if all that can be promised is an average result, how can managers expect to be paid large fees for providing that average result? I have not been able to figure out a solution or a new system of compensation though I've given it a great deal of thought," he admits. "But the whole issue is something that is going to have to be faced."

Graham's prescription for a radical change in the system of promoting competitive performance may very well draw a few guffaws along the Street. But that will be nothing new to a man who has been preaching more or less to deaf ears and going pretty much his own way in the investment world ever since his early days with Newburger Henderson and Loeb, starting 60 years ago. Graham then ran his own fund with Jerome Newman until he retired in 1956. One of his contemporaries recalls him as a "tough-minded guy who usually said and did what he felt was sound no matter which way the rest of the Wall Street mob was drifting." It is the sort of encomium that nearly everyone who has worked with Graham accords him today.

Younger critics who tend to dismiss Graham as too theoretical often overlook the fact that he *did* manage funds—and survived and prospered in the real world for three decades by putting his own theories to practice. That they should overlook this is probably unfortunate, though understandable enough, since it did not exactly happen yesterday. After all, it has been nearly two decades since Graham left his post as chairman of GEICO (which actually was one of his truly big winners) and ended his management of investment funds.

In fact, for quite a few years, Graham has been content to live a relatively quiet and private life, wintering in La Jolla and spending the summers at Aix-en-Provence in the south of France. He no longer invests in the market. ("Why should I try to get any richer?") And, other than updating *Security Analysis*, his only professional activity of late has been a rewrite of *The Intelligent Investor*. "It expresses what I feel about the period up to 1970," he says, "and I'm glad to hear that it's selling quite well."

Like this interview, Ben Graham's foray to the Rancho La Costa summit with the fourth generation last year was something of a rarity. But he remains sensitive to criticism that his comparative isolation of late has left him out of touch with the realities of modern institutional investing or made him unnecessarily critical of younger money managers. "I have the disadvantage of having a very good memory," he says. "And I try to distinguish between two aspects of being 80 next May— the subjective pessimism of an older individual, you know, and my objective pessimism from having observed stock market operations for many years. I'm not sanguine," the soon-to-be octogenarian says finally. "I am *concerned*."

The Simplest Way
to Select Bargain Stocks

Y ou'd be hard pressed to find anyone more knowledgeable about the stock market and the secrets of latching on to real stock values than Benjamin Graham, a man generally regarded as the dean of security analysts. Not only did Graham co-author a book, *Security Analysis*, that's become the bible of the business, but his record of picking winning stocks is legendary on Wall Street.

A millionaire at 35, Graham retired to California some time ago. In recent years he's devoted himself to distilling the methods of stock selection he used successfully for nearly half a century into a few easily followed principles. Now 82, Graham has lately gone into association with investment counselor James B. Rea to establish a fund whose investment policy will be based on those principles. Graham believes that a doctor handling his own investments should be able to utilize those same principles to achieve an average return of 15 percent a year or better.

Sitting in the study of his La Jolla oceanfront apartment, Graham outlined the fundamentals of his approach for *Medical Economics* West Coast Editor Bart Sheridan. Here Senior Associate Editor Laton McCartney gives the highlights of their conversation:

Q. Would you start by telling us how you arrived at the simplified Graham technique?

A. Well, for the past few years I've been testing the results of selecting undervalued stocks according to a few simple criteria. My research shows that a portfolio put together using such an approach would have gained twice as much as the Dow Jones Industrial Average over the long run. The research period goes back 50 years, but the approach has proven successful when carried out over far shorter periods. I was so impressed by it, I felt it should be put into practice.

Q. Are you seeking out growth issues with this technique of yours?

A. No. To my mind the so-called growth-stock investor—or the average security analyst for that matter—has no idea of how much to pay for a growth stock, how many stocks to buy to obtain the desired return, or how their prices will behave. Yet these are basic questions. That's why I feel the growth-stock philosophy can't be applied with reasonably dependable results.

Q. What about the conventional yardsticks like a company's projected earnings or market share for evaluating stocks?

A. Those factors are significant in theory, but they turn out to be of little practical use in deciding what price to pay for particular stocks or when to sell them. The only thing you can be sure of is that there are times when large numbers of stocks are priced too high and other times when they're priced too low. My investigations have convinced me you can predetermine these logical "buy" and "sell" levels for a widely diversified portfolio without getting involved in weighing the fundamental factors affecting the prospects of specific companies or industries.

Q. That kind of thinking—ignoring fundamentals—would be branded as heresy by many analysts today . . .

A. Maybe so, but my research shows it works. What's needed is, first, a definite rule for purchasing which indicates *a priori* that you're acquiring stocks for less than they're worth. Second, you have to operate with a large enough number of stocks to make the approach effective. And finally you need a very definite guideline for selling.

Q. Can a doctor or any investor, like me, do all that?

A. Absolutely.

Q. How should I start?

A. By making as large a list as possible of common stocks currently selling at no more than seven times their latest—not projected—

12-month earnings. Just look up the price-earnings ratios listed in the stock quotation columns of *The Wall Street Journal* or other major daily newspapers.

Q. Why a P-E ratio of seven instead of, say, nine or five?

A. One of the ways to determine what you should pay for stocks at any given time is to look at what quality bonds are yielding. If bond yields are high, you want to buy stocks cheaply, meaning you will look for relatively low P-Es. And if bond yields drop, then you can pay more for the stock and accept a higher P-E. As a rule of thumb in pricing stocks this way, I select only those issues whose earnings-to-price ratio—simply the P-E in reverse—is at least twice the average current yield on top-quality (triple-A) corporate bonds.

Q. Give me an example.

A. Sure. Just double the bond yield and divide the result into 100. Right now the average current yield of AAA bonds is something over 7 percent. Doubling that you get 14, and 14 goes into 100 roughly seven times. So in building a portfolio using my system, the top price you should be willing to pay for a stock today is seven times earnings. If a stock's P-E is higher than seven, you wouldn't include it.

Q. What if AAA bond yields go down to, say, 6 percent?

A. Then the acceptable P-E goes up. Twice six is 12; divide 12 into 100 and you get a maximum P-E of eight. However, in my opinion, you should never buy a stock with a P-E ratio over 10 no matter how low bond yields get. Conversely, in my system, a P-E of seven is always allowable no matter how high bond yields go.

Q. Okay. So, as of today, your formula says to consider only stocks with a P-E of seven or less. Is that all there is to it?

A. Well, that group alone should provide the basis for a pretty good portfolio, but by using an additional criterion you could do even better. You should select a portfolio of stocks that not only meet the P-E requirements but also are in companies with a satisfactory financial position.

Q. How do I determine that?

A. There are various tests you could apply, but I favor this simple rule: A company should own at least twice what it owes. An easy way to check on that is to look at the ratio of stockholders' equity to total assets; if the ratio is at least 50 percent, the company's financial condition can be considered sound.

Q. What's "stockholders' equity"?

A. Simply put, it's the company's net worth—the amount left over when you subtract its debts from its assets.

Q. Wouldn't I need an accountant to figure that out for me?

A. Not at all. You can easily obtain the figures for total assets and stockholders' equity from the company's annual report, or your broker can get them for you.

Q. Would you give me an example of how the rule works?

A. Say a company has stockholders' equity of $30 million and total assets of $50 million, a ratio of 60 percent. Since that's over 50, the company passes the test.

Q. Are there stocks around today that meet this requirement and have P-Es of seven or lower?

A. Oh, yes. Not nearly as many as in the market decline of 1973 and 1974, but there are still plenty; the box on page 49 [Table 9] lists some of them.

Q. Once I've gone through the screening process and settled on my "buy" candidates, how do I go about structuring a portfolio?

A. To give yourself the best odds statistically, the more stocks you have to play with, the better. A portfolio of 30 would probably be an ideal minimum. If your capital is limited, you can deal in "odd lots"—less than 100 shares of stock.

Q. How long should I hold onto these stocks?

A. First you set a profit objective for yourself. An objective of 50 percent of cost should give good results.

Q. You mean that I should aim for a 50 percent profit on every stock I buy?

A. Yes. As soon as a stock goes up that much, sell it.

Q. What if it doesn't reach that objective?

A. You have to set a limit on your holding period in advance. My research shows that two to three years works out best. So I recommend this rule: If a stock hasn't met your objective by the end of the second calendar year from the time of purchase, sell it regardless of price. For example, if you bought a stock in September 1976, you'd sell it no later than the end of 1978.

Q. What do I do with the money when I sell off a stock? Reinvest it in other issues that meet your requirements?

A. Usually, yes, with some flexibility dictated by market conditions. In times like the 1974 drop, when you find many good companies whose stocks are selling at low P-E levels, you should take advantage of the situations and put up to 75 percent of your investment capital into common stocks. Conversely, in periods when the market as a whole is overpriced you'd have trouble finding stocks to reinvest in that meet my criteria. In such periods you should have no more than 25 percent of your funds in stocks and the rest in, say, U.S. Government bonds.

Q. Using your strategy what kind of results can I expect?

A. Obviously you're not going to get a 50 percent gain on every stock you buy. If your holding-period limit on a stock expires, you'll have to sell it at a smaller profit or even take a loss. But in the long run, you should average a return of 15 percent a year or better on your total investment, plus dividends and minus commissions. Over all, dividends should amount to more than commissions.

Q. This is the return you'd have gotten over 50 years according to your research?

A. Yes, and the results have been very consistent for successive periods as short as five years. I don't think a shorter period gives the strategy a really fair chance to prove itself. In applying the approach every investor should be prepared financially and psychologically for the possibility of poor short-term results. For example, in the 1973–1974 decline the investor would have lost money on paper, but if he'd held on and stuck with the approach, he would have re-couped in 1975–1976 and gotten his 15 percent average return for the five-year period. If we get a repeat of that situation, the investor should be prepared to ride out the downturn.

Q. With the Dow around 1000 and many issues at their five-year highs, is there a danger of the kind of drop that followed the overpriced markets of the late 1960s and early 1970s?

A. I have no particular confidence in my powers—or anyone else's—to predict what will happen with the market, but I do know that if the price level is dangerously high, chances are you will get a seri-ous correction. In my own tests there were a number of periods of overvaluation, and the number of stocks available at attractive prices was very small; that proved a warning that the market as a whole was too high.

Q. Can you summarize the key to making your approach work?

A. The investor needs the patience to apply these simple criteria con-sistently over a long enough stretch so that the statistical probabili-ties will operate in his favor.

A SAMPLING OF BARGAIN STOCKS

The following stocks meet the selection criteria recommended by Ben-jamin Graham in the accompanying article—a P-E ratio of seven or less and an equity-asset ratio of 50 percent or more. All are listed on the New York Stock Exchange. [See Table 9.]

TABLE 9

A Sampling of Bargain Stocks

Company	Stockholders' Equity (millions)	Total Assets (millions)	Equity-Asset Ratio (%)	P-E Ratio (8/16/76)	Recent Price (8/16/76)
Amalgamated Sugar	$ 92	$120	77	3	36⅞
Ampco-Pittsburgh	50	65	77	7	10
Amstar	230	441	52	6	44¼
Blue Bell	164	302	54	5	39⅞
Federal Co.	81	124	65	4	25⅝
Federal Paper Board	153	291	53	5	37¾
Gordon Jewelry	82	147	55	5	10¾
Graniteville Co.	80	117	69	4	13¾
Harsco Corp.	206	358	58	6	22⅞
Houdaille Industries	126	190	66	6	16⅛
Houghton Mifflin	54	87	62	6	12
Hughes & Hatcher	26	47	54	6	7
Jantzen	40	65	62	5	18¼
Jorgensen (Earle M.)	78	122	64	5	37
Lane Bryant	76	137	55	6	11¾
Leslie Fay	31	62	50	6	8
McCord Corp.	48	68	71	6	16
Michigan Seamless Tube	42	65	65	6	20½
Murray Ohio	47	78	60	7	20¼
Norris Industries	119	196	61	6	37¾
Omark Industries	78	129	60	6	11¾
Reeves Brothers	73	108	68	6	30
Riegel Textile	82	148	56	5	16¾
Russ Togs	48	64	75	6	10⅝
Sparton Corp.	23	35	66	6	8¼
Uarco	57	87	66	6	21
Wallace-Murray	105	209	50	7	18⅜
Western Publishing	103	163	63	6	16⅜
Weyenberg Shoe Mfg.	23	40	57	7	23
Zale Corp.	292	181	61	7	17

The[se] . . . stocks meet the selection criteria recommended by Benjamin Graham in the accompanying article—a P-E ratio of seven or less and an equity-asset ratio of 50 percent or more. All are listed on the New York Stock Exchange.

An Hour with Mr. Graham

Hartman L. Butler, Jr., C.F.A.

HB: Mr. Graham, I do appreciate so much being able to come and visit with you this afternoon. When Bob Milne learned that Mrs. Butler and I would be in La Jolla, he suggested that I not only visit with you but also bring along my cassette tape recorder. We have much I would like to cover. First, could we start with a topical question—Government Employees Insurance Company—with GEICO being very much in the headlines.

GRAHAM: Yes, what happened was the team came into our office and after some negotiating, we bought half the company for $720,000. It turned out later that we were worth—the whole company—over a billion dollars in the stock market. This was a very extraordinary thing. But we were forced by the SEC to distribute the stock among our stockholders because, according to a technicality in the law, an investment fund was not allowed more than 10 percent of an insurance company. Jerry Newman and I became active in the conduct of GEICO, although we both retired a number of years ago. I am glad I am not connected with it now because of the terrific losses.

HB: Do you think GEICO will survive?

GRAHAM: Yes, I think it will survive. There is no basic reason why it won't survive, but naturally I ask myself whether the company did expand much too fast without taking into account the possibilities of these big losses. It makes me shudder to think of the amounts of money they were able to lose in one year. Incredible! It is surprising

---

how many of the large companies have managed to turn in losses of $50 million or $100 million in one year, in these last few years. Something unheard of in the old days. You have to be a genius to lose that much money.

HB: Looking back at your own life in the investment field, what are some of the key developments or key happenings, would you say? You went to Wall Street in 1914?

GRAHAM: Well, the first thing that happened was typical. As a special favor, I was paid $12 a week instead of $10 to begin. The next thing that happened was World War I broke out two months later and the stock exchange was closed. My salary was reduced to $10—that is one of the things more or less typical of any young man's beginnings. The next thing that was really important to me—outside of having made a rather continuous success for 15 years—was the market crash of 1929.

HB: Did you see that coming at all—were you scared?

GRAHAM: No. All I knew was that prices were too high. I stayed away from the speculative favorites. I felt I had good investments. But I owed money, which was a mistake, and I had to sweat through the period 1929–1932. I didn't repeat that error after that.

HB: Did anybody really see this coming—the crash of 1929?

GRAHAM: Babson did, but he started selling five years earlier.

HB: Then in 1932, you began to come back?

GRAHAM: Well, we sweated through that period. By 1937, we had restored our financial position as it was in 1929. From then on, we went along pretty smoothly.

HB: The 1937–1938 decline, were you better prepared for that?

GRAHAM: Well, that led us to make some changes in our procedures that one of our directors had suggested to us, which was sound, and we followed his advice. We gave up certain things we had been trying to do and concentrated more on others that had been more consistently successful. We went along fine. In 1948, we made our GEICO investment and from then on, we seemed to be very brilliant people.

HB: What happened in the only other interim bear market—1940–1941?

GRAHAM: Oh, that was only a typical setback period. We earned money in those years.

HB: You earned money after World War II broke out?

GRAHAM: Yes, we did. We had no real problems in running our business. That's why I kind of lost interest. We were no longer very challenged after 1950. About 1956, I decided to quit and to come out here to California to live.

I felt that I had established a way of doing business to a point where it no longer presented any basic problems to be solved. We were going along on what I thought was a satisfactory basis, and the things that presented themselves were typically repetitions of old problems which I found no special interest in solving.

About six years later, we decided to liquidate Graham-Newman Corporation—to end it primarily because the succession of management had not been satisfactorily established. We felt we had nothing special to look forward to that interested us. We could have built up an enormous business had we wanted to, but we limited ourselves to a maximum of $15 million of capital—only a drop in the bucket these days. The question of whether we could earn the maximum percentage per year was what interested us. It was not the question of total sums, but annual rates of return that we were able to accomplish.

HB: When did you decide to write your classic text, *Security Analysis?*

GRAHAM: What happened was that in about 1925, I thought that I knew enough about Wall Street after 11 years to write a book about it. But fortunately, I had the inspiration instead to learn more on the subject before I wrote the book, so I decided I would start teaching if I could. I became a lecturer at the Columbia School of Business for the extension courses. In 1928, we had a course in security analysis and finance—I think it was called investments—and I had 150 students. That was the time Wall Street was really booming.

The result was it took until 1934 before I actually wrote the book with Dave Dodd. He was a student of mine in the first year. Dave was then assistant professor at Columbia and was anxious to learn more. Naturally, he was indispensable to me in writing the book. The First Edition appeared in 1934. Actually, it came out the same time as a play of mine which was produced on Broadway and lasted only one week.

HB: You had a play on Broadway?

GRAHAM: Yes. "Baby Pompadour" or "True to the Marines." It was produced twice under two titles. It was not successful. Fortunately, *Security Analysis* was much more successful.

HB: That was *the* book, wasn't it?

GRAHAM: They called it the "Bible of Graham and Dodd." Yes, well now I have lost most of the interest I had in the details of security analysis which I devoted myself to so strenuously for many years. I feel that they are relatively unimportant, which, in a sense, has put me opposed to developments in the whole profession. I think we can do it successfully with a few techniques and simple principles. The main point is to have the right general principles and the character to stick to them.

HB: My own experience is that you have to be a student of industries to realize the great differences in managements. I think that this is one thing an analyst can bring to the solution.

GRAHAM: Well, I would not deny that. But I have a considerable amount of doubt on the question of how successful analysts can be overall when applying these selectivity approaches. The thing that I have been emphasizing in my own work for the last few years has been the group approach. To try to buy groups of stocks that meet some simple criterion for being undervalued—regardless of the industry and with very little attention to the individual company. My recent article on three simple methods applied to common stocks was published in one of your seminar proceedings.

I am just finishing a 50-year study—the application of these simple methods to groups of stocks, actually, to all the stocks in the Moody's Industrial Stock Group. I found the results were very good for 50 years. They certainly did twice as well as the Dow Jones. And so my enthusiasm has been transferred from the selective to the group approach. What I want is an earnings ratio twice as good as the broad interest ratio typically for most years. One can also apply a dividend criterion or an asset value criterion and get good results. My research indicates the best results come from simple earnings criteria.

HB: I have always thought it was too bad that we use the price-earnings ratio rather than the earnings yield measurement. It would be so much easier to realize that a stock is selling at a 2.5 percent earnings yield rather than 40 times earnings.

GRAHAM: Yes. The earnings yield would be more scientific and a more logical approach.

HB: Then with roughly a 50 percent dividend payout, you can take half of the earnings yield to estimate a sustainable dividend yield.

GRAHAM: Yes. Basically, I want to double the interest rate in terms of earnings return. However, in most years the interest rate was less than five percent on AAA bonds. Consequently, I have set two limits. A maximum multiple of 10 even when interest rates are under 5 percent, and a maximum multiple of seven times the current AAA interest rate with a maximum multiplier between 10 and 7. My research has been based on that.

I received in Chicago last year the Molodovsky Award.

HB: I understand that you have about completed this research.

GRAHAM: Imagine—there seems to be practically a foolproof way of getting good results out of common stock investment with a minimum of work. It seems too good to be true. But all I can tell you after 60 years of experience, it seems to stand up under any of the tests that I would make up. I would try to get other people to criticize it.

HB: By some coincidence as you were becoming less active as a writer, a number of professors started to work on the random walk theory. What do you think about this?

GRAHAM: Well, I am sure they are all very hardworking and serious. It's hard for me to find a good connection between what they do and practical investment results. In fact, they say that the market is efficient in the sense that there is no particular point in getting more information than people already have. That might be true, but the idea of saying that the fact that the information is so widely spread that the resulting prices are logical prices—that is all wrong. I don't see how you can say that the prices made in Wall Street are the right prices in any intelligent definition of what right prices would be.

HB: It is too bad there have not been more contributions from practicing analysts to provide some balance to the brilliant work of the academic community.

GRAHAM: Well, when we talk about buying stocks, as I do, I am talking very practically in terms of dollars and cents, profits and losses, mainly profits. I would say that if a stock with $50 working capital sells at $32, that would be an interesting stock. If you buy 30 companies of that sort, you're bound to make money. You can't lose when you do that. There are two questions about this approach. One is, am I right in saying if you buy stocks at two-thirds of the working capital value, you have a dependable indication of group undervaluation? That's what our own business experience proved to us. The second question, are there other ways of doing this?

HB: Are there any other ways?

GRAHAM: Well, naturally, the thing that I have been talking about so much this afternoon is applying a simple criterion of the value of a security. But what everybody else is trying to do pretty much is pick out the Xerox companies, the 3M's, because of their long-term futures or to decide that next year the semiconductor industry would be a good industry. These don't seem to be dependable ways to do it. There are certainly a lot of ways to keep busy.

HB: Would you have said that 30 years ago?

GRAHAM: Well, no, I would not have taken as negative an attitude 30 years ago. But my positive attitude would have been to say, rather, that you could have found sufficient examples of individual companies that were undervalued.

HB: The efficient market people have kind of muddied the waters, haven't they, in a way?

GRAHAM: Well, they would claim that if they are correct in their basic contentions about the efficient market, the thing for people to do is to try to study the behavior of stock prices and try to profit from these interpretations. To me, that is not a very encouraging conclusion because if I have noticed anything over these 60 years on Wall Street, it is that people do not succeed in forecasting what's going to happen to the stock market.

HB: That is certainly true.

GRAHAM: And all you have to do is to listen to *Wall Street Week* and you can see that none of them has any particular claim to authority or opinions as to what will happen in the stock market. They, and economists, all have opinions and they are willing to express them if you ask them. But I don't think they insist that their opinions are correct, though.

HB: What thoughts do you have on index funds?

GRAHAM: I have very definite views on that. I have a feeling that the way in which institutional funds should be managed, at least a number of them, would be to start with the index concept—the equivalent of index results, say 100 or 150 stocks out of the *Standard & Poor's 500*. Then turn over to managers the privilege of making a variation, provided they would accept personal responsibility for the success of the variation that they introduced. I assume that basically the compensation ought to be measured by the results either in terms of equaling the index, say, Standard & Poor's results, or to the extent by which you improve it. Now in the group discussions of this thing, the typical money managers don't accept the idea and the reason for non-acceptance is chiefly that they say—not that it isn't practical—but that it isn't sound because different investors have different requirements. They have never been able to convince me that's true in any significant degree—that different investors have different requirements. All investments require satisfactory results, and I think satisfactory results are pretty much the same for everybody. So I think any experience of the last 20 years, let's say, would indicate that one could have done as well with Standard & Poor's than with a great deal of work, intelligence, and talk.

HB: Mr. Graham, what advice would you give to a young man or woman coming along now who wants to be a security analyst and a Chartered Financial Analyst?

GRAHAM: I would tell them to study the past record of the stock market, study their own capabilities, and find out whether they can identify an approach to investment they feel would be satisfactory in their own case. And if they have done that, pursue that without any reference to what other people do or think or say. Stick to their own methods. That's what we did with our own business. We never followed the crowd, and I think that's favorable for the young analyst. If he or she reads *The Intelligent Investor*—which I feel would be more useful than *Security Analysis* of the two books—and selects from what we say some approach which one thinks would be profitable, then I say that one should do this and stick to it. I had a nephew who started in Wall Street a number of years ago and came to me for some advice. I said to him, "Dick, I have some practical advice to give you which is this. You can buy closed-end investment companies at 15 percent discounts on an average. Get your friends to put "x" amount of dollars a month in these closed-end companies at discounts and you will start ahead of the game and you will make out all right." Well, he did do that—he had no great difficulty in starting his business on that basis. It did work out all right and then the big bull market came along and, of course, he moved over to other fields and did an enormous amount of speculative business later. But at least he started, I think, on a sound basis. And if you start on a sound basis, you are halfway along.

HB: Do you think that Wall Street or the typical analyst or portfolio managers have learned their lessons of the "Go-Go" funds, the growth cult, the one-decision stocks, the two-tier market, and all?

GRAHAM: No. They used to say about the Bourbons that they forgot nothing and they learned nothing, and I'll say about the Wall Street people, typically, is that they learn nothing, and they forget everything. I have no confidence whatever in the future behavior of the Wall Street people. I think this business of greed—the excessive hopes and fears and so on—will be with us as long as there will be people. There is a famous passage in Bagehot, the English economist, in which he describes how panics come about. Typically, if people have money, it is available to be lost and they speculate with it and they lose it—that's how panics are done. I am very cynical about Wall Street.

HB: But there are independent thinkers on Wall Street and throughout the country who do well, aren't there?

GRAHAM: Yes. There are two requirements for success in Wall Street. One, you have to think correctly; and secondly, you have to think independently.

HB: Yes, correctly and independently. The sun is trying to come out now, literally, here in La Jolla. What do you see of the sunshine on Wall Street?

GRAHAM: Well, there has been plenty of sunshine since the middle of 1974 when the bottom of the market was reached. And my guess is that Wall Street hasn't changed at all. The present optimism is going to be overdone, and the next pessimism will be overdone, and you are back on the Ferris wheel—whatever you want to call it—seesaw, merry-go-round. You will be back on that. Right now, stocks as a whole are not overvalued, in my opinion. But nobody seems concerned with what are the possibilities that 1970 and 1973–1974 will be duplicated in the next five years or so, you can bet your Dow Jones Average on that.

HB: This has been a most pleasant and stimulative visit. We will look forward to receiving in Charlottesville your memoirs manuscript. Thank you so much, Mr. Graham!

Index

Printed in the United States
By Bookmasters